Forewarned

Forewarned

*Why the Government Is Failing to
Protect Us—and What We Must Do
to Protect Ourselves*

Michael Cherkasky
with
Alex Prud'homme

BALLANTINE BOOKS • NEW YORK

A Ballantine Book

Published by The Ballantine Publishing Group
Copyright © 2003 by Michael Cherkasky

All rights reserved under International and Pan-American Copyright
Conventions. Published in the United States by The Ballantine Publishing
Group, a division of Random House, Inc., New York, and simultaneously in
Canada by Random House of Canada Limited, Toronto.

Ballantine and colophon are registered trademarks of Random House, Inc.

www.ballantinebooks.com

Library of Congress Control Number: 2002096459

ISBN 0-345-46168-1

Book design by Joseph Rutt

Manufactured in the United States of America

First Edition: February 2003

10 9 8 7 6 5 4 3 2 1

Contents

For my wife, Betsy, who provides my security
Michael Cherkasky

For my wife, Sarah
Alex Prud'homme

Introduction

On September 11, 2001, the United States failed to protect its citizens from attack. If a similar attack were to be launched today, we would almost certainly fail again, as our system of security does not work and our efforts at homeland security have been woefully inept. In this book, I will show you how we continue to misunderstand the risks we face, and I will outline the steps needed to provide real safety to Americans without significantly impacting our fundamental freedoms.

Since September 11 we've been told repeatedly that we are at war, yet the reality of war often seems oddly distant. We've surrounded ourselves with some of the trappings of war—flag decals on SUVs, fighter jet flyovers at football games—yet we're encouraged to carry on business as usual. We've been rattled by color-coded alerts, yet we've been given no clear sense as to how we should respond. We've been told to expect a prolonged, difficult struggle against terrorism, yet no public sacrifice has been called for. From time to time, horrifying acts of violence at home and abroad punctuate the news—a bombing in Bali, a sniper attack in Maryland, a hostage situation in Moscow—yet no coordinated government response seems to be forthcoming. If this is war, it's a strange kind of war, nothing like what we remember from the Vietnam era or our fading memories of World War II.

A few cynics are wondering whether the war rhetoric is just talk, perhaps politically motivated. I'm afraid it isn't. We *are* at war: "a new type of war," in the words of President Bush. It's not a metaphorical war, like the war on poverty or the war on crime; it's a real war, being fought against determined enemies who want to kill us. Shockingly, our casualties in this war are already *greater than the total United States military casualties suffered in the last thirty years.*

Unfortunately, the true nature of this new war is still only dimly understood. The generals and politicians who want to fund lumbering howitzer systems or the multibillion-dollar Star Wars missile-defense shield are fighting yesterday's battles. Today's war is savage, nimble, and improvisational. It is being waged with homemade weapons such as plastic knives, rental trucks packed with fertilizer, and anthrax-laden envelopes. Our enemies aren't nations whose leaders can be deterred by the threat of counter-attack or who will recognize the rules established by the Geneva Convention; they are individuals organized into loose-knit, ever-shifting cells, constantly on the move and difficult to trace.

The battle is one of ideological opposites, pitting our relatively young, open, pluralistic, religiously and sexually free society against fanatics who claim to represent an ancient, conservative, patriarchal, and deeply religious culture. They believe that America is Satan, "the head of evil," an omnivorous force fueled by religious freedom, sexual promiscuity, individual rights, drugs, and rock and roll that is consuming their children and destroying their traditional way of life in a cultural genocide. "We are living in an age when the enemies of God have successfully killed the spirit of resistance and manhood in Muslims by undermining the Islamic creed," an al-Qaeda spokesman lamented in July 2002. They will do anything to stop us. The *jihadis* have been relentlessly waging this war for twenty years, but we Americans have been too self-involved to recognize that. It will be a battle to the death.

This new, twenty-first-century war is taking place in the context of the massive, epochal shift generically termed globalization, the revolution in technology, information, commerce, and transportation that is breaking down borders, dissipating the powers of church and state, and threatening traditional social structures everywhere. It is globalization that has transformed the actions of Washington, Wall Street, and Hollywood into triggers for violence from Baghdad to Kabul and brought the resentments of the Middle East to the shores of America.

Our national leaders maintain that they understand the nature of this new threat. Unfortunately, their understanding is superficial at best. Since September 11, it has become clear that our government hasn't thought through the implications of what is happening in the world. We all agree we need to fight back against terrorism, but we don't have a coherent idea of what that means or how it can be accomplished. Instead, we get a substance-free plan for homeland defense, a continuous erosion of our liberty to little or no benefit, and a string of vague warnings: We *might* be attacked on a holiday (at a sporting event, in a high-rise building); the attackers *could* come by air (land, sea). All that such rhetoric does is to sow fear and confusion in the public. In time, the government will be in the position of the boy who cried wolf: When the time comes for a true warning, the public will no longer pay attention.

I worry about such things, partly because I'm an American citizen with the same deep love of country you probably feel, and partly because I'm conditioned by my training and my career to worry about them. I am an expert on investigations, intelligence, and security. For fifteen years I prosecuted practically every crime imaginable for the New York district attorney's office: burglary, robbery, rape, murder, racketeering. I tried the notorious mobster John Gotti (he was acquitted, but later convicted for conspiring to fix the jury). I prosecuted cases of political corruption and bank fraud, including supervising the prosecution in the BCCI case, the infamous money-laundering operation that became known as the "Bank of Crooks and Criminals International." After Ramzi Yousef

and his cohorts bombed the World Trade Center in 1993, I supervised the state prosecutors assigned to the Joint Terrorist Task
Force (JTTF).

Today I am the president and CEO of Kroll, a risk management
firm with over sixty offices in eighteen countries. We have five
business segments, two of which are especially relevant to this
book. Our Investigation and Intelligence group (I&I) gathers and analyzes information to help corporations and countries make smart
decisions. For example, I&I might be asked to scrutinize the background of an Indonesian company in which a client is considering
investing, investigate the murder of a journalist in Bosnia, or discover who is behind the bombing of a factory in Uganda.

Our Security group assesses the risk to a business facility, a
company, or a system, and then helps design a system to reduce
that risk. We've performed these services for tall buildings in
Malaysia, the Sears Tower, the Canary Wharf development in
London, and buildings of the United Nations, the International
Monetary Fund, and the Federal Reserve. Kroll was the security
advisor to the Port Authority of New York at the time of the
September 11 attacks.

Our 2,300 employees are an eclectic group, ranging from former
members of the Central Intelligence Agency (CIA), the Federal
Bureau of Investigation (FBI), the U.S. armed forces, the British
MI-5 and MI-6, the French secret service, the Israeli Mossad, and
the Hong Kong police to computer specialists, architects, engineers, and accountants.

In my varied roles as prosecutor and security expert, I'd seen
plenty of evidence that Islamic terrorists were targeting America
long before September 11. I had voiced my concern and sounded
warnings on national television and at conferences around the
country. But the truth is that I had mentioned my worries only a
few times, and not very loudly. Then I returned to my busy and
comfortable life. Like so many others, I made the mistake of un-
derestimating the threat and then getting back to business as usual.
We mustn't make the same mistake again.

The horrific attacks of September 11, 2001, demonstrated vividly the new kind of security threat the United States faces. The Islamic terrorists will try hard to prevent us from fighting on a battlefield of our choosing, hoping to keep us on the defensive by targeting more high-profile people, landmarks, organizations, and facilities inside the United States. Few doubt that more terrorist attacks are coming.

Nonetheless, we are hopelessly unprepared to defend ourselves. All of the danger factors that existed before September 11 persist today. Our system of security does not work; our efforts at homeland defense have been ill-conceived and inadequate. We continue to misunderstand and underestimate the risks we face, and we've chosen the wrong ways to respond. And the ad hoc measures we are taking threaten our liberty.

As citizens, we all share the blame for these failures as well as the responsibility for improving our security. No issue could be more pressing. We know that second- and third-tier industrial powers such as Pakistan and India have nuclear warheads; that North Korea claims to possess atomic weapons; that rogue scientists and generals in a destabilized Russia have access to weapons of mass destruction as well as the materials needed to manufacture them; and that Iraq has stockpiles of chemical and biological weapons sufficient to wipe out humankind several times over. In such a world, we must assume that *all* of our enemies have or will soon have access to such deadly arms. It's a threat that demands a systematic response.

I believe we can effectively respond. We *can* create an effective national security system that preserves our open, pluralistic culture and our respect for human rights even as it minimizes the danger of a catastrophic terrorist onslaught. But we must act *now*.

In the following pages, I'll explain the security crisis America faces, and I'll present my solutions—practical, affordable steps we must take as individuals and as a nation to protect ourselves in this dangerous new world.

Some of my advice is straightforward and based on the kinds of things that the security experts at Kroll recommend to clients every day—for example, ways to protect your home, your personal safety while traveling, and the security of your company and its employees. I'll also offer broader policy recommendations, some of which will require fundamental changes in the way America approaches security.

The national security program I advocate has several interlocking components. As I'll explain in detail later in this book, security is not enhanced by creating a single heavily fortified layer of protection but rather by building concentric rings of security. Hence the need for a reasonably complex set of systems that work together to make life more difficult for anyone who would seek to harm Americans.

For easy reference purposes, I call my proposed combination of national security measures the Proteus Plan. Where does the name come from? In Greek mythology, Proteus, a son of Neptune, was a sea elder known for his wisdom and his knowledge of future events. He was also capable of changing his shape at will. The Proteus Plan is intended to help our security agencies foresee and forestall future terrorist attacks. Furthermore, it's designed for maximum flexibility, capable of being rapidly adjusted and modified in accordance with changes in the level of threat and in the specific dangers we face. Thus it seems apt to name the plan after the shape-shifting Proteus.

The Proteus Plan includes the following elements:

- *A reinvented intelligence system.* The most fundamental step we can take as a nation to defend ourselves is to become better informed. We must reenergize and reorganize our intelligence gathering and assessment capabilities, so that we have a much clearer understanding of who our enemies are, what they plan to do, and how we can thwart them. The most sensible way to do this is to create a domestic intelligence bureau that is responsible for all domestic terrorist investigations and for consolidating all information about potential terrorism, foreign and domestic. This new agency will diminish the role of the FBI and will operate along the lines of Britain's MI-5.

This will be controversial and politically difficult. The entrenched bureaucracies at the FBI have tended to focus their energy on turf wars and competition for power rather than on cooperative efforts on behalf of the American people. They've been at war with all other agencies so long that simply asking them to start working together (as Tom Ridge, the director of homeland security, did in the aftermath of September 11) is hopelessly inadequate. This is why I advocate tearing up the FBI's organizational chart and designing an entirely new agency.

Civil libertarians worry about the specter of a vast, powerful new spy agency with domestic responsibilities. I respect their concerns. Given the abuses of the past, such as the efforts of the Hoover FBI to smear and harass civil rights leaders from Martin Luther King Jr. on down, rigid safeguards to protect the privacy and freedom of Americans will have to be built into the system. But it can be done. I'll explain how.

- *A national identity card.* We need to create a national identification card that would electronically encode basic information about every citizen. Authenticating the identity of the card holder would be protected by a biometric screening device, such as a fingerprint, retinal scan, or facial recognition chip. The card could be used for basic identification, and for gaining access to commercial flights, sensitive sites such as power plants, and potentially dangerous dual-use products including firearms.

  This is another concept that is bound to be controversial. A card containing much of your vital information may raise the specter of Big Brother monitoring our intimate lives.

This issue deserves to be taken seriously. But the truth is that all of the information I would include in such a card is already widely available to government agencies and big businesses through the electronic databases that stand behind your passport, your driver's license, and your credit report. The only major change that a national ID card would bring would be to use this data to quickly and affordably solve many of the practical problems of security.

- *Rules-based screening.* An industrial civilization such as the United States is filled with potential targets for terrorist attack, from power plants and factories to shopping malls and (of course) jet airliners. Protecting these targets requires a logical system for deciding who gets in and who stays out. The current system is no system at all, but rather a crazy quilt of ad hoc measures that impose irrational restrictions in one place while leaving giant security gaps in others.

  A rules-based screening system using the national identity card would represent a practical solution. Linked to a centralized database, the card could be used to sort people as quickly as the E-ZPass in your car pays a toll. Those whose ID cards reflect routine activities would be whisked through Line A in the airport. Those whose cards show specific troubling patterns of behavior would be processed through Line B, where they would be subject to extensive search and questioning.

  For such a system to be generally accepted, the security screens must be based on clearly defined, objective rules, not on arbitrary or discriminatory criteria such as race, age, or national origin. And safeguards must be established to prevent governments at every level from using the system to harass dissidents or political opponents. But there's no reason why, for example, a fundamentalist Islamic activist, a militia leader, or a known arms trafficker should be treated the same way as a suburban grandmother or a vacationing high school teacher when seeking access to an airport or national land-mark.

Unfortunately, President Bush's homeland defense plan points in the opposite direction. Among its provisions is a reg-ulation to fingerprint and monitor all males from certain Arab countries once they enter the United States. This is a terrible mistake. Not only is it impractically time-consuming and ex-pensive, it also is wide open to abuse. Most important, it runs counter to the American tradition of equality and tolerance. The plan harkens back to the internment of Japanese Americans during the Second World War; like the intern-ment, it represents a dreadful miscalculation driven by the emotion of the moment. Rules-based screening offers an al-ternative that is more just and far more effective.

- *A national cargo ID system.* Some twenty million cargo con-tainers enter U.S. ports every year. Only 2 percent of them are ever inspected. Thus we have very little idea of what is actually in those containers and where the cargo will end up.

  The 1993 World Trade Center bombing, Timothy McVeigh's destruction of the Murrah Building in Oklahoma City, the bombing of the al-Khobar Towers in Saudi Arabia, and the dual explosions at the American embassies in Kenya and Tanzania were all made possible by trucks loaded with explosives. Even deadlier cargos could be transported in sim-ilar fashion. A dirty bomb could find its way into Los Angeles Harbor in an unchecked container aboard a tramp steamer from the Philippines. The resulting casualties, dead, injured, and exposed to radiation, might number in the hun-dreds of thousands.

  Or consider the huge bottleneck of traffic at the Mexico-U.S. border. In addition to the usual drug traffickers and ille-gal alien smugglers, the U.S. Border Patrol is now on the lookout for terrorists. Fine, but the resulting delays are al-ready hampering the U.S. economy. Auto parts manufactured in Mexican *maquiladoras* are arriving late at Big Three automobile plants in Michigan, causing a ripple of slow-downs throughout the company's production system.

It would be simple and practical to create a cargo identi-fication system tied to an international database. In the case of auto parts, the plant in Mexico would load a truck with parts, seal it, and tag it with a bar code that explains what is in it and where it is going. The bar-coded container could pass quickly across the border and arrive in Michigan on schedule. The truck itself could have a transponder mounted on the cab so that the manufacturer could track the exact whereabouts of all of its supplies. And the driver would carry a national ID card in his wallet incorporating a passport and driver's license. Those containers without the ID system would be carefully inspected, and at times of high alert they might be barred from the United States.

- *Government-mandated corporate security measures.* Much of America's critical infrastructure that is such an attractive target for terrorists is controlled by corporations. The power plants, chemical factories, oil refineries, pipelines, trans-portation hubs, and entertainment complexes are all poten-tial targets. The government needs to mandate an increase in security at these and other locations. This public-private partnership is a critical part of the system that will increase our society's security. We cannot afford to leave our safety to the discretion of corporate America.

These and other proposals that I'll detail later in this book will come at a cost. Both government and private funding will be nec-essary to make the Proteus Plan a reality. I feel certain the American people would support such spending. But it's the kind of spending that both political and business leaders prefer to delay or avoid altogether, since it is not obviously productive and offers no immediate benefits to any influential voting bloc or economic constituency. But such thinking leads to a dangerous apathy. I hope that the shock of September 11 and the ongoing anxiety Americans have felt in its aftermath will create sufficient incentive for our leaders to make the essential investments in security, and I pray another attack won't be needed to spur action.

I don't pretend that my ideas amount to a silver bullet that will solve all of our security problems. There's no such thing as perfect security—never has been, never will be. But I'm convinced that these steps will protect our citizens in a way that is both effective and consonant with the American ideals of pluralistic freedom. If my system had been in place before the September 11 attacks, those attacks probably would have been thwarted.

Furthermore, the plan attempts to address the threats we face with a pragmatism not yet evident in the responses of the White House, Congress, or the corporate community. If we are serious about combating terrorism, and we'd better be, then we need to adopt a program like the one outlined in these pages, or a better version created through a serious national debate . . . a debate that has not yet begun.

Today I see the nation as a whole, and each of us as individuals, walking a symbolic tightrope in our attempt to secure ourselves from terrorism and other risks without compromising our cherished liberties. We must keep our balance, or we will fall. We must focus on the wire, thoughtfully plan for the challenges ahead, ensure that each step is measured and careful, and ignore the distractions of fear, blind rage, and political opportunism.

If we lean too far toward security, too far toward government intrusion, too far toward accepting ethnic, racial, or religious stereotyping and away from liberty, we will fall. We will have moved away from the open, diverse, pluralistic society that makes us the envy of the world and gives us our greatest power: the moral high ground. But if we lean away from security, lean too far toward protecting the privacy of the individual, we will fail to adequately protect our families, our communities, our businesses, and our nation. In a time of crisis, keeping our heads and our sense of moral balance is especially difficult. But we can succeed if we discuss the challenges openly and honestly, learn from our past mistakes, and make informed decisions.

Why I Wrote This Book

I've been driven to write this book by two powerful emotions: a sense of obligation and a sense of outrage.

On September 11, 2001, I joined America and the Western world in crying. I cried out of grief and worry for friends, colleagues, my city, and my country; out of frustration over the impotence and incompetence of those charged with protecting our safety; and out of regret that I had not spoken out more forcefully about the dangers I'd foreseen.

I was raised to believe that I have an obligation to serve my community. I've tried to focus my life on public service, but on September 11, I realized that many Americans had not fulfilled their obligations. I was one of them. Now it's time to meet those obligations. This book is part of my personal effort to do just that. I know we are not prepared to deal with the dangers ahead. We do not have a vision or a strategy for national security. And I believe that we must have a dialogue to reach the right decisions. My obligation is to try to start that dialogue.

I also write this book out of outrage. In the aftermath of September 11, I watched as the government struggled to deal with the crisis. I understood that our leaders needed to take temporary remedial action to calm our nation. I understood why we put the National Guard in airports and searched people twice before they got on planes. I understood why we initially needed to quiet the criticism and finger-pointing. We needed to be unified in our opposition to our enemies. But that should have been the initial phase, lasting a couple of weeks or months. Instead it has lasted for over a year. Today we continue to have no coherent plan to combat terrorism. Some of the security steps we are taking are trivial, silly, and useless, an insult to America. I will talk about these failures and about how our efforts must be redirected—fast.

Another insult has been our unwillingness to truly analyze our past failures of security and intelligence. If you want to make something right, you need to figure out how it went wrong. But that has not happened. Instead, the sacred cows in Washington continue to be protected. That is an outrage we cannot allow. If the FBI, the CIA, the Department of Defense, or the president failed us, let's find out why and remedy the systemic problems that underlie the failure.

In itself, outrage is not a productive emotion. But if outrage can stimulate action, if it can shatter our complacency and move us to finally make the hard choices we must make to provide real security to our families, then I hope this book will produce in you a healthy dose of outrage.

Michael Cherkasky
New York City
November 2002

Part One

A Dangerous World

Chapter 1

Twenty Years of Terror

Did the terrorist attacks of September 11, 2001, come as a light-ning bolt out of the clear blue sky? To many Americans, the answer seems to be yes, but to those of us in the security business the answer is a resounding no.

Over the last twenty years there have been a series of increas-ingly audacious and destructive strikes against America and her al-lies by Islamic fundamentalists. America has tended to view these as discrete, unconnected blips on the radar screen, minor tragedies that usually happened in places we couldn't point to on a map. Impatient, optimistic, naive, and fast-moving, most of us didn't take the time to put together the pieces that were forming a com-plex pattern, one that, viewed carefully, showed a deadly, well-funded, highly organized, global terrorist conspiracy.

Some of us *did* see the emerging pattern and shouted out in alarm. John O'Neill, for example, who was named the head of se-curity at the World Trade Center in New York two weeks before September 11, was one. I knew and respected John; Kroll helped to place him in the job that cost him his life. He and a handful of other experts were convinced that another attack on the Twin Towers was inevitable. But like Cassandra's unheard cries, their warnings about the gathering terrorist threat were ignored.

One day John was telling Chris Isham, a senior producer at

ABC News, about his new position. Chris kidded him, saying that heading security at the World Trade Center "will be an easy job. They're not going to bomb that place again." (Chris was referring to the failed 1993 bombing of the towers, of course.) But John did not laugh. "Actually, they've always wanted to finish that job," he said. "I think they're going to try again." He was right.

When I watched the televised images of the hijacked planes slamming into the twin towers on September 11, I was filled with rage, grief, disappointment, and frustration, to the point of tears. Not only did I know people, including John O'Neill, who died that day, but I knew beforehand that such an attack was possible and indeed likely. And so did a lot of other people. This is a generally acknowledged truism today, but I am still angry about it. Even now, after the bloodiest attack on our soil since the Civil War, I am not convinced that America fully understands that we are in a state of war, and have been for close to twenty years.

Perhaps what hurts most is the knowledge that a few Americans had all of the evidence in hand—the al-Qaeda manual with instructions on how to make bombs, reams of intelligence, testimony from turncoats, even notes documenting our enemies' intentions and photographs of their targets—but didn't take it seriously enough. The threat of a catastrophic terrorist attack has been staring us in the face for a very long time, yet we chose to look away.

We no longer have that luxury. Now more than ever, I feel it is imperative that we take a hard look at the pattern formed over the last twenty years, acknowledge the mistakes we've made and the successes we've had, and try to learn from both of them. To put the material in the rest of this book in context, I will use this chapter to run through a few of the most significant attacks leading up to September 11. Most readers will be aware of at least some of these facts, but very few will have put the pieces together and studied the overall pattern. I have included this material as evidence of the ongoing terrorist threat, not as an encyclopedic retelling of every terrorist-related incident that has ever occurred. My aim is to highlight the most significant pieces of the puzzle, the worst attacks, and to connect them in order to give an understanding of who our enemies are, why they hate us, and what lengths they are willing to go to. The only way to avoid repeating our mistakes is to learn from the past; we can no longer look away, and we can no longer plead ignorance. In order to move ahead with confidence, we must first understand the threat we have been facing for over twenty years.

"I Have Killed Pharaoh!"

October 6, 1981, was a beautiful day in Cairo, Egypt, with cloudless blue skies and a light breeze. Late that morning Norb Garrett, the CIA station chief there, sat on a reviewing stand watching the annual military parade commemorating the 1973 war against Israel. About a hundred feet to his right sat Egyptian president Anwar el-Sadat.

A decade earlier, Sadat had succeeded the strongman Gamal Abdal Nasser as president, and over the next few years had opened Egypt to diplomatic, business, and cultural ties to the West. Although he had led the Egyptian war against Israel in 1973, Sadat negotiated the Camp David accords with Israeli prime minister Menachem Begin five years later, and together they were awarded the 1978 Nobel peace prize. But Sadat's diplomatic success and his opening of Egypt to foreign business and culture had infuriated Muslim fundamentalists, particularly a group called al-Gama'a al-Islamiyya (the Islamic Group) and a number of radical clerics who had been preaching a fiery vision of Islamic revolution in the streets and mosques.

One of the most outspoken of these Egyptian clerics was Sheikh Omar Abdel-Rahman, who later became notorious in America as "the Blind Sheikh," a hate-mongering fundamentalist around whom violence-prone Islamic militants gathered. These Islamists, I would later learn, were a small and tightly knit group of fanatics who claimed to represent an ancient, conservative, patriarchal, and deeply religious culture; they believed that the open, pluralistic West, America in particular, was Satan, an omnivorous devil that was consuming their children and destroying their traditional way of life in a cultural genocide.

In October 1981, Norb Garrett, who was the CIA's man in Cairo (and is now a colleague of mine at Kroll), was monitoring Middle Eastern groups that might pose a threat to U.S. interests. Garrett had been keeping a wary eye on al-Gama'a because it seemed a growing threat to Egypt's modernization and opening to the West. In the days leading up to the parade, the Egyptian Internal Service had learned that members of the group had traveled to Cairo from the provinces and had contacted local cells, for unknown reasons. This was a matter for concern but not for panic. The members of al-Gama'a were considered a bunch of wild-eyed, disorganized zealots from Upper Egypt rather than dangerous terrorists. Garrett was much more concerned about Iran's efforts to export its brand of Islamic revolution to the rest of the Arab world. Less than two years earlier, Garrett had coordinated the CIA's information collection in support of the ultimately failed operation to rescue the fifty-two American hostages held in Iran.

The parade in Cairo was a festive occasion. As the tanks rolled by, parachutists dropped from the sky and jets roared overhead trailing colored smoke; soldiers would occasionally break from their ranks, run up to Sadat, who was sitting in the front row behind a low stone wall, and salute. "It was like a big circus event," Garrett recalls. "We weren't sure what was going to happen next."

A military vehicle towing a large gun stopped in front of the reviewing stand, and about eight soldiers jumped out and began to run toward Sadat. It seemed like more of the same kind of thing they had already seen, but then the soldiers dropped to their knees and began shooting their Kalashnikovs wildly into the crowd—*pop, pop, pop* (the Russian gun makes a distinctive sound)—to cause a diversion and suppress any return fire. At first Garrett thought it was part of the show. But then a U.S. Air Force major general sitting behind him noticed a colleague had been shot in the ankle, and shouted, "That's live ammo, get down!" Women began screaming, and Garrett hit the deck. He lay there for what seemed like a very long time but was probably less than a minute. When he poked his head up, he saw a soldier, later identified as twenty-four-year-old army lieutenant Khalid Islambouli, leaning over the stone wall and firing point blank into Sadat's already lifeless body.

"I have killed Pharaoh, and I do not fear death!" Islambouli shouted. Expecting, even hoping to die as martyrs, and with no escape plan, the assassins were easily rounded up and imprisoned. Later, they revealed details of the plot, the names of the key planners, and the deep roots of their movement. The fact that Islamic extremists were among the army's rank and file came as a rude shock to the Egyptian elite. Today this may not sound very surprising, but twenty years ago the rise of extreme Islam as a revolutionary force in the Middle East was in its infancy. Very few people, even among the region's leaders, understood its widespread appeal on the Arab street.

The same applies to the meaning of Sadat's assassination. This was not a random act; it was a coolly calculated, politically motivated murder. As the winner of the Nobel peace prize, a perceived collaborator with Israel, and the man who had opened the doors of the Holy Land to what the Islamic fundamentalists referred to as Western "infidels," Sadat had been specifically targeted in order to make a statement. In the attack, al-Gama'a al-Islamiyya's fanatics also killed the Cuban ambassador, a Greek Orthodox priest, and many innocent bystanders (although they did not kill vice president Hosni Mubarak, who was sitting next to Sadat, and who has been Egypt's president ever since). Their murders, too, were part of the statement. The vast majority of Arabs are moderates, and the fundamentalists had marked them and their allies as primary targets of intimidation.

At the time I, like most Americans, had only a passing interest in the Sadat murder, viewing it a little smugly as more evidence of instability in a third world country. But in retrospect I view Sadat's murder as the first act of the new, long-term war we are engaged in today, a deadly thrust by a small group of Muslim extremists bent on cowing the Arab majority and driving the West out of Islamic countries. Sadat's killing was considered a worldwide tragedy in 1981, but it would take me years, and much bitter experience, to understand just how significant it really was.

You can pick any one of a number of dates or incidents to mark the start of the terrorists' war. Some choose November 4, 1979, when Iranian students stormed the American embassy in Teheran and took hostages. Others pick the October 23, 1983, car bombing that killed 241 U.S. marines in Beirut, Lebanon. But to me, the Iranian hostage crisis was a student revolt that an opportunistic Ayatollah Khomeini used to gain a worldwide audience, while the Beirut attack was not part of a larger conspiracy.

I point to the assassination of Anwar Sadat as the beginning of the new terror war because it was a carefully planned operation by a radical cell, al-Gama'a, that would become affiliated with a much larger organization, the Egyptian Islamic *Jihad*, a group we in the United States were only dimly aware of at the time, but which would come to play an important role in many subsequent acts of terrorism, and encouraged by radical clerics such as Sheikh Abdel-Rahman, who were bent on creating a new "caliphate," a pan-Arabic state run according to the dictates of the Quran.

Norb Garrett points to another aspect of October 6, 1981, that is an instructive as it is chilling. As in the case of the September 11 attacks in 2001, the tragedy was exacerbated by a failure of intelligence and a failure of protection. Before the assassination, the CIA and the Egyptians had good information on al-Gama'a, but it wasn't sifted and analyzed correctly. In short, we didn't take the threat seriously enough. Furthermore, Sadat's protection was haphazard: His bodyguards were not seasoned and came from three different services, each of which jealously guarded its turf, just as our CIA and FBI have not functioned in sync for decades, which led to confusion and vulnerability in the moment of crisis.

At the time, these omissions seemed like incidental details, but in light of later attacks they seem like the start of a pattern that would be repeated over and over again, with tragic results.

Not Just Another Murder

Fast-forward now to November 5, 1990, in New York City. That evening, Rabbi Meir Kahane, founder of the right-wing Jewish Defense League, was giving a rousing speech to supporters in the ballroom of the New York Marriott East Side hotel in midtown. As Kahane stepped away from the podium, a thickset man wearing a yarmulke approached, drew a .357 Magnum revolver from under his coat, shot Kahane in the chest and neck, and ran out the door.

The assassin, covered with blood and still carrying his gun, shoved his way through the midtown crowd. Years later, we would discover that he was looking for his two co-conspirators, one of whom had wandered off, while the other, the driver of the getaway car, had also disappeared. The assassin—a thirty-five-year-old Egyptian named El Sayyid Nosair, who worked as a janitor at the Manhattan Criminal Court—tried to commandeer a taxi. In the melee, he shot, and was shot by, a U.S. postal police officer and was captured. The crime was almost laughably inept, except that Kahane had been murdered.

I was head of the district attorney's Investigations Division at the time, and we were struggling with a heavy caseload. When the call about Rabbi Kahane's murder came in that night, we all knew it would be a high-profile case, splashed across front pages everywhere. Kahane was a prominent if not well-loved figure in the city. Our office scrambled to respond.

As far as the DA's office was concerned, this was a typical homicide. One man had killed another; we had apprehended the killer, and now we had to decide which division would lead the prosecution. If we decided the shooting was part of an extensive conspiracy, my Investigations Division might take the lead; if we thought it was an isolated act, which most murders are, the Trial Division would handle the case. We briefly discussed the fact that Nosair was an Arab and that Kahane was a Jewish hawk, a former member of the Israeli parliament who had demanded that all Palestinians be removed from the West Bank and Gaza to Jordan, among other things. But we quickly dismissed the idea that the murder was part of a broad-based international conspiracy. We had no evidence of that. To us it appeared that Nosair was a lone gunman: Kahane had been so inflammatory that it was entirely believable that an angry Arab had shot him, and so the case was assigned to the Trial Division.

The misclassification of the Kahane killing as the act of a lone gunman was a tragic error with long-term ramifications. Yet it was an understandable mistake. Bob Morgenthau had made the New York County district attorney's office the premier local prosecuting office in this country. Very sharp people staffed the DA's office, but in 1990 we were like the doctors who stumbled over a new disease in the 1980s, AIDS. The doctors looked at patients, shrugged, and decided, "It must be the flu," even as hundreds died. They had never seen the disease before and did not realize what they were looking at. We were the equivalent of those doctors. We had not seen a terrorist attack in our careers. In the DA's office we shrugged and proceeded as if the Kahane killing were a straightforward murder case like so many others we'd prosecuted.

In the course of the investigation, detectives learned that Nosair had attended meetings at the al-Kifah Refugee Center, a known recruiting center for the *mujahidin*'s *jihad* against the Soviets in Afghanistan, on Atlantic Avenue in Brooklyn. The al-Kifah link was interesting but appeared to be just another piece of information, a piece of the jigsaw puzzle that didn't mean much. The DA's office, being the thorough professional organization that it is, pursued the investigation and issued search warrants, discovering that Nosair's apartment in Jersey City, New Jersey, was crammed full of papers and pamphlets and notebooks, photographs, maps, and audio- and videotapes.

Our investigators dutifully collected all of this material—it filled something like fifty moving boxes—and hauled it away. A lot of the material was in Arabic, and we didn't have a translator on staff, so we put it in storage. The boxes were then sent to the FBI. The FBI was, and is, the national law enforcement agency charged with investigating terrorism. We expected them to determine if the pieces of evidence fit into a picture of a broader international conspiracy. We expected them to tell us what they found. Again, law enforcement officials simply didn't understand the significance of this evidence; it was considered supplemental material in a straightforward homicide case that was already proceeding through the courts. For over two years, the Nosair boxes sat in an obscure government storage depot, collecting dust.

In 1991, Nosair was tried for homicide and gun possession. His defense team, led by the flamboyant left-wing attorney William Kunstler, made a compelling argument: Despite the fact that there were many eyewitnesses to the murder, they claimed, the police had gotten the wrong guy. There was another shooter, Kunstler said, and a conspiracy afoot to imprison Nosair for a crime he didn't commit. The jury agreed, believing that Nosair was not the killer.

Nosair was acquitted of the murder of Kahane but convicted of shooting two others during his attempted escape and of being in possession of an illegal gun. The judge sentenced Nosair to the maximum allowable prison term, seven and a third to twenty-two years. But as we would belatedly learn, there had indeed been a broad-based international conspiracy afoot.

I was shocked by the verdict. It seemed beyond question that Nosair was guilty of the murder of Kahane. Although I didn't prosecute him, I was familiar with the evidence and couldn't believe that the case had fallen apart. But after my initial disappointment wore off, I moved on to more pressing matters, such as the city's ongoing gang wars.

Trove of Horrors

In 1993 my life changed. I had decided that after fifteen years of public service I would retire that June, to join the private sector and maybe launch a political career. I loved my work as the chief of investigations, I loved the office, but it was time to move on. My wife and I had been raising three children in a cramped two-bedroom, one-bathroom apartment with no air-conditioning. Our kids attended private school in Manhattan, which we were sacrificing everything to afford; on torrid summer days the heat would drive us out of our apartment into a local McDonald's, where we'd eat and linger in the cool air for hours. After fifteen years of this, we were ready for a different kind of life. But before I left I had some important business to finish.

By early 1993, the DA's office was in the midst of major internal changes while also pursuing a series of groundbreaking cases. A number of talented attorneys had left the office to pursue other things—people such as Eliot Spitzer, who, as head of the DA's Labor Racketeering Unit, had convicted Tommy Gambino and broken the Mafia's control of the city's garment center trucking industry. Spitzer left to work for the law firm Skadden, Arps, Slate, Meagher & Flom. Lately, he has gained fame for policing Wall Street as the attorney general of New York State.

I was involved in two cases that were the biggest, most important, highest-profile cases of my career. The first was the prosecution of Mafia boss John Gotti. In late 1989 and early 1990 he had been tried and acquitted on charges of assault and attempted murder. The second big case was the prosecution of an obscure but very powerful and corrupt Pakistani bank called BCCI, the Bank of Credit and Commerce International, which had been running a complex web of money-laundering and influence-peddling schemes around the world. (Indeed, it would later be revealed that BCCI had been the banker for al-Qaeda and other terrorist groups.) These two cases couldn't have been more different, and they represented a paradigm shift in U.S. law enforcement. While the Gotti case was the epitome of old-style, locally based organized crime, the kind of felony that the United States has been fighting since the days of bootlegging and Al Capone, BCCI represented a worrisome new form of global organized crime. Each case was absorbing. But then the future arrived.

February 26, 1993, was a cold and overcast Friday with a few snowflakes drifting out of low-lying clouds. I was in my office, which was next to Bob Morgenthau's in the Manhattan district attorney's office in lower Manhattan. My desk was piled high with papers from various ongoing investigations, including BCCI. At about 12:20 that afternoon, the phone rang: Three minutes earlier, there had been some kind of an explosion at the World Trade Center, just a few blocks from where we sat. Morgenthau called me into his office and gave me the details of what he knew. There was pandemonium around the Trade Center, he said. All communications were knocked out, as were the lights and heating. People were crowded into the narrow, smoke-choked stairwells and were slowly making their way down. Evacuation procedures at the towers had not been codified or practiced, and it took nearly five hours to evacuate the Trade Center's 110-story north tower. It was unclear what exactly had happened. At first the rumor was that a power plant substation had blown up. But within hours we had confirmed that a bomb had gone off in the B-2 level of the underground parking garage and that there were casualties.

Later we were able to say it was a miracle that the 1,500-pound bomb didn't kill more than 6 people and injure more than the 1,042 it did. Nevertheless, we were badly shaken. This was an act of aggression on American soil, in the heart of New York City, and it was completely unexpected.

A bomb in the World Trade Center? It seemed surreal or absurd. Who would do such a thing? Why?

Within a few days, we learned that a band of Muslim terrorists had rented a Ryder truck, filled its back with a bomb made from nitrate fertilizer, and exploded it in the World Trade Center's underground parking garage. Their idea had been to topple one of the towers into the other, like felling a gigantic redwood, setting off a crushing domino effect that they hoped would kill some 125,000 people.

Why did the terrorists target the World Trade Center? Whatever you thought of their architectural merits, there is no escaping the fact that those gleaming, striated towers were symbols of America's pride, vibrancy, and economic strength. But to our enemies they represented the opposite, the dark side of the same image: American arrogance and hubris. The Twin Towers epitomized what the *jihadis* (Islamic fundamentalists) called the "capitalist ed-ifices" that they believed Allah had called on them to destroy; the towers were physical representations of our intention to dominate the world. In bombing the Trade Center, the Islamic militants seemed to be saying: *Don't underestimate us. We can hit you in the very heart of your capitalist system. We will continue to attack until you leave the Islamic world. You must fear and respect us.*

Within minutes of the explosion that afternoon, law enforce-ment agencies swung into action. It was decided that this was to be a cooperative state-federal investigation under the auspices of the multiagency Joint Terrorist Task Force (JTTF).

The JTTF immediately began looking at the forensics, scroung-ing for traces of the explosives material in the underground garage so we could test it, interviewing bystanders to find out if anyone had seen the bombers, asking what details people had noticed. It was a rushed, chaotic period. But within days investigators had dis-covered the rental truck's vehicle identification number (VIN) on a piece of the blown-up rental truck; they used the VIN to trace the truck, and the terrorists, to Jersey City, New Jersey. By early March, an astonishingly short amount of time, four suspects had been arrested. But the case was not yet closed. The bombing's mas-termind had escaped.

Behind the scenes, meanwhile, friction was growing within the JTTF. While the federal prosecutors from the Southern District of New York were treating us as teammates, the FBI was acting high-handedly. They quickly cut out the New York City Police Department and eventually sidelined the DA's office from the in-vestigation, refused to share information, didn't follow up on leads, and scolded others for speaking to the press while leaking impor-tant details even before the arrests had been made.

This was a major crime with a potential impact on every citi-zen in the United States, so why was the FBI behaving this way? It could have been that the bureau was just acting as it usually does—

territorially. But then the situation grew murkier when, to our surprise, we learned that the FBI had recruited at least one informant inside the terrorists' cell. He had told agents about renting the van and mixing chemicals to make the bomb, and had provided the names of at least two of the conspirators. While the presence of an informant helped to explain why the JTTF had captured the bombers so quickly, it also raised a delicate question: If FBI agents had been monitoring their informant closely, as they claimed, then why hadn't they known about the plot to bomb the World Trade Center and stopped it?

The FBI has never provided a satisfactory answer, and I still don't know the real reason for their aggressive lack of cooperation. Perhaps one reason the FBI pushed every other agency out of the investigation was because they had failed to prevent the attack and were determined to cover their tracks.

Then came another surprise. Ramzi Yousef, a charismatic and mercurial figure, had been the brains of the operation, a true evil genius. In retracing his steps in America, we gathered information about his spiritual leader, the virulent Sheikh Abdel-Rahman, who had been blinded by diabetes as a child in Egypt and had relocated from Cairo to preach from a mosque in Jersey City. Investigators had noted that while plotting his attack, Yousef had attended Rahman's mosque and visited the al-Kifah Refugee Center in Brooklyn. That rang a bell. El Sayyid Nosair, Rabbi Kahane's killer, had also spent time at al-Kifah (the name means "the struggle" in Arabic). Then we discovered that two of the arrested bombers had been close friends of Nosair's and had visited him in prison.

We raced to retrieve the fifty-odd boxes of evidence taken from Nosair's New Jersey apartment in 1990. As the DA's investigator plowed through the material with a translator, one box at a time, he discovered a trove of horrors.

In the back of a spiral notebook filled with random personal notes and doodles, we discovered notes from a speech given by Abdel-Rahman written in Nosair's hand—it was filled with phrases like "We're going to bomb your commercial edifices"—which was the first clear line linking the conspirators. We also discovered a number of Polaroid snapshots ostensibly showing Nosair's family on a picnic on the New Jersey waterfront but which upon closer inspection proved to be surveillance pictures of the World Trade Center.

I remember being told by a DA's investigator, "Finding those things was truly bizarre."

Indeed, we were astonished to discover that Nosair's boxes were filled with the chilling details of a broad and intricate conspiracy: Led by Sheikh Abdel-Rahman, Islamic *Jihad* had planned to destroy America. There were photos of landmark buildings they had targeted—the World Trade Center, St. Patrick's Cathedral, and Rockefeller Center, among others—evidence of terrorist training camps in rural Connecticut and New York State, the chemical formula for the bomb used at the World Trade Center, and even U.S. Army special-warfare documents that had been translated into Arabic.

I'll always regret that we in law enforcement didn't expose the Islamic terror cells in America during that key period between Kahane's murder, in 1990, and the bombing of the World Trade Center, in 1993, when they were poorly organized and more vulnerable than they are today. In retrospect, it is clear that the arrival of Abdel-Rahman and Yousef in the United States was a key turning point: They were fanatical and effective leaders who quickly galvanized their disorganized colleagues in America. The question still lingers: Who sent them, and how did they get into the United States?

It's not clear how Abdel-Rahman was allowed to enter this country. He was on a terrorist watch list, yet he managed to slip across our borders without difficulty. One theory holds that the CIA helped him into the United States as payback for his help in fighting the Russians in Afghanistan. I have asked a number of people about this, and it is certainly possible. Once established in New Jersey, Abdel-Rahman didn't attempt to hide himself, but preached a dark and hate-filled anti-Americanism in the open. Unfortunately, our law enforcement agencies hardly paid attention.

In light of all that has happened since then, it seems difficult to believe that we could have allowed Abdel-Rahman to operate so brazenly, but we were naive and uninformed back then. We didn't understand, or care about, what he was saying. Yet in a 1991 speech, Abdel-Rahman made his malevolent intentions clear:

> The obligation of Allah is upon us to wage *Jihad* for the sake of Allah. It is one of the obligations which we must undoubtedly fulfill . . . and we conquer the lands of the Infidels and we spread Islam by calling the Infidels to Allah and if they stand in our way, then we wage *Jihad* for the sake of Allah.

The media caricatured Abdel-Rahman as the wacky blind cleric, as if he were just a ranting holy roller. Few of us took his hateful rhetoric seriously. Much the same was true for Ramzi Yousef, who also entered America despite being wanted, and was able to conduct his deadly business at will, albeit more surreptitiously than Abdel-Rahman, then flee.

Nosair wasn't just a lone madman, and his murder of Rabbi Kahane hadn't been such a simple affair after all. It had been part of an organized conspiracy. When we'd discovered the boxes of material in Nosair's apartment in 1990, we had advance warning of the Trade Center bombing in our hands—with motive, pictures of the target, and design of the bomb—and we had evidence linking suspicious individuals to cells of a foreign terrorist organization in America bent on mass destruction, but we had overlooked it. Upon learning all of this, I felt a bulb of cold anger in my stomach.

The evidence was revealed in a series of trials. In May 1994 four of the six Trade Center bombers were tried by a skilled team of federal prosecutors working for United States attorney Mary Jo White, and were convicted on thirty-eight counts; each received a sentence of 240 years in prison. In a second trial, El Sayyid Nosair was tried by a federal jury and convicted on various charges, including sedition. In the same trial, Sheikh Abdel-Rahman was also convicted of sedition and is currently serving a life sentence. In the course of these trials, it was revealed that the FBI had been investigating Nosair before the February 1993 bombing; why hadn't the bureau translated the fifty-odd boxes of evidence taken from Nosair's apartment *before* the bombing? I do not know. What I do know is that America had missed an opportunity to nip Ramzi Yousef's terrorist cell in the bud, and six people died as a result.

In any event, prosecutors were slowly rolling up the Trade Center bombing case. But 1993 wasn't quite finished with its lessons.

The nineties were a strange time in our nation's history. Just as the world was launching into a massive, epochal change brought on by globalization, America was turning inward. We had won the Cold War; the Soviet Union, our enemy of the past forty-five years, had dissolved, leaving the United States as the world's lone superpower. We were so dominant and so arrogant that some American academics even proclaimed "the end of history," and we somewhat smugly assumed the rest of the world felt that way too. Blind to the vast changes swirling around us, we were preoccupied with domestic policy and elected former governors of Arkansas and Texas as president, neither of whom had foreign policy experience. Even the bombing of the World Trade Center was viewed as a blip on the radar screen. But events would soon prove that assumption foolish.

"They Are All Targets"

In the summer of 1993 I left Bob Morgenthau's office and ran for district attorney of Westchester County, a New York City suburb where we had moved. Much to my wife's relief, I lost the election. I then joined Kroll as head of Monitoring Services, where I worked in a private capacity on things the government hadn't been able to do well on its own, such as overseeing the once mob-controlled garbage hauling industry on Long Island.

Over half of Kroll's consulting work is done overseas, and I was soon traveling to places I'd only read about and rubbing shoulders with highly sophisticated "citizens of the world"—Malaysians, Singaporeans, Brazilians, Russians, Qataris, and Finns, the kind of people who spoke five languages and carried thick passports and had fresh insights about America's place in the world. It was through this exposure that I witnessed firsthand the enormously powerful forces of globalization, both for good and for ill. I also came into close contact with the world's intelligence and law enforcement agencies, many of whose members were full of foreboding about terrorism.

In October of that year, eighteen American soldiers were killed in Mogadishu, Somalia, in a series of intense firefights with clansmen of Mohammed Farrah Aidid, a local warlord. Who can forget the image of the naked, lifeless body of a U.S. helicopter pilot being dragged through the streets? Some five hundred Somalis were also killed in the fighting. As Mark Bowden reported in his insightful account of the battle, *Black Hawk Down*, local militiamen used Russian-made rocket-propelled grenades to knock down three American Black Hawk helicopters by destroying their tail rotors. This was a sophisticated tactic that the Somalis had learned from Islamic Arab fighters who had perfected this technique against the Soviets in Afghanistan. It seemed, in other words, that al-Qaeda— the Islamic terrorist group that was emerging as a regional threat at the time, and which would later be led by Osama bin Laden—was supporting at least one of the Somali warlords against American troops in Mogadishu.

While this assertion has been disputed, Osama bin Laden, who was not well known at the time, would later exult to CNN: "Muslims did not believe the U.S. allegations that they came to save the Somalis. With Allah's grace, Muslims in Somalia cooperated with some Arab holy warriors. . . . Together they killed large numbers of American occupation troops."

Such talk should have set off all of our alarm bells. The network of Islamic holy warriors was growing increasingly strong, sophisticated, and interconnected, and while America may have seen it, we didn't understand it. Instead, the Mogadishu firefight hardly registered here. Most of us frankly didn't care that anarchic Somali clansmen were possibly being funded and trained by Islamic terrorists. It didn't mean anything to us.

A week after the firefight, our troops were pulled out of Somalia. A gloating bin Laden told the al-Jazeera television network that the withdrawal was typical of the "weakness, frailty and cowardice of the U.S. troops." His words inspired further action. After Mogadishu, his followers started planning an attack on the American embassy in Nairobi, Kenya—a target chosen, in part, bin Laden told al-Jazeera, because "the brutal [U.S.] invasion of Somalia kicked off from there."

By 1994, the Trade Center bomber Ramzi Yousef was the world's most wanted terrorist. After disappearing from New York, Yousef escaped to Asia, where he set off a tiny but powerful nitroglycerin bomb on a Philippines Airlines plane bound for Tokyo. The explosion ripped a hole in the fuselage and killed a young Japanese engineer. Investigators on his tail worried that this had only been a test for a much more devastating explosion.

In 1995, Yousef was allegedly planning several major attacks, including an attempt to assassinate President Clinton or the Pope in the Philippines and a planned bombing of the CIA headquarters in Virginia. But in January his most audacious plan, to simultaneously blow up eleven United States commercial airliners as they flew across the Pacific Ocean, was uncovered when his laptop computer was found in the Philippines. Once again Yousef managed to elude his pursuers. A few days later, however, he was captured in Islamabad, Pakistan, when a would-be accomplice turned him in for a reward.

As he was flown back to New York to stand trial, an FBI agent pointed to the twin towers and said, "They're still standing."

"They wouldn't be if I had enough money and explosives," Yousef replied.

He was tried and convicted in the Southern District of New

York for the 1993 World Trade Center attack and is today serving a 240-year sentence at Supermax, a high-security federal prison in Colorado.

Because of my involvement with a small part of the World Trade Center investigation, I avidly followed the subsequent arrests and trials and was asked to comment after each for television—the 1994 trial of the four bombers, and the 1995 trials of Nosair, Sheikh Abdel-Rahman, and Ramzi Yousef. I spoke with everyone I came in contact with in the intelligence community about the threat these terrorists posed. As my understanding of our terrorist enemies grew, so did my concern.

Although few American citizens were paying attention to terrorism in the mid-1990s, many law enforcement agents, including people from the CIA, FBI, JTTF, and New York DA's office, were actively pursuing the burgeoning al-Qaeda network and other terrorists. They used surveillance, wiretaps, and double agents to try to penetrate these groups, but it wasn't easy. For one thing, we weren't sure whether the terrorists were state-sponsored or independent operators. The terrorists had grown up under repressive Arab regimes and were adept at using codes, aliases, and cells. They were also very well organized and funded. And while it turned out that we had identified many of the right people as our enemies, we were unable to anticipate their next moves.

By the mid-1990s I was growing increasingly uneasy about the possibility of further Islamic terrorist activity in America. No one who read the information that the Southern District of New York attorneys had put into evidence for their series of prosecutions could fail to be very concerned.

I was so worried, in fact, that when a fertilizer-based bomb sheared the front off the Murrah Building in Oklahoma City in 1995, killing 168 and injuring 400, I went on national television and blamed Islamic militants. I was embarrassingly wrong about the perpetrator, of course. It was later discovered that the bombing had been carried out by a domestic terrorist, Timothy McVeigh. But those of us who felt this way were right in worrying that further terror was planned by Islamic militants against the United States.

If Ramzi Yousef was the terrorist kingpin of the time, a tall thin Saudi Arabian named Osama bin Laden was emerging as one of the chief masterminds and fund-raisers of al-Qaeda, the global terrorist network.

The first major al-Qaeda strike took place on November 13, 1995, when a car bomb exploded in front of the National Guard building, a Saudi-American facility in Riyadh. This explosion was a first in the kingdom, and it killed five Americans and two Indians. The alleged bombers were captured and beheaded, but not before they admitted they had been influenced by bin Laden's call for *jihad* and had been trained as holy warriors at camps in Afghanistan.

The following June 25, a far more serious attack took place in Dhahran, when a fuel truck packed with explosives was detonated outside the al-Khobar Towers complex, a residential compound for U.S. soldiers in Saudi Arabia. The explosion was so powerful that it ripped the façade off the eight-story tower, killing nineteen U.S. servicemen and injuring over five hundred others; the shock waves could be felt twenty miles away, in neighboring Bahrain. This was the first attack clearly attributable to bin Laden, and it represented a change in tactics for him: Previously reluctant to attack on Saudi soil, he had now decided to take the fight home.

Yet even with this kind of damage, bin Laden was not yet a name that I, or many others, recognized. He must have sensed that he needed to make a grand statement. In May 1998 bin Laden told ABC News that he was calling for the death of Americans, soldiers and civilians alike. "They are all targets," he said. Shortly afterward he mounted his most spectacular and devastating attack yet.

At about 10:30 on the morning of August 7, 1998, bin Laden operatives set off a huge bomb, made of TNT and aluminum nitrate packed into a truck, at the U.S. embassy in Nairobi, Kenya, injuring thousands and killing 213 (including twelve Americans). At 10:39 that day, the same kind of bomb destroyed the U.S. embassy in Dar es Salaam, Tanzania, killing eleven Tanzanians, most of whom were Muslim, and injuring many others. These two devastating, nearly simultaneous attacks were unprecedented. They had required four years of planning and training, and had been distressingly effective. It was these explosions that lit bin Laden up on everyone's radar screen.

The Kenyan embassy was attacked, bin Laden would later declare, because "it was considered to be the biggest intelligence-gathering center in East Africa. With the help of God, the hit against it was very strong against the Americans. This is so the Americans can taste something of what we Muslims have tasted."

After the attacks in East Africa, my uneasiness grew from extreme concern to absolute certainty that we would be the subject of future terrorist actions. The questions that gnawed at me were: What would it be? Where? When? Who would carry it out?

As the year 2000 approached, the celebration of the millennium seemed an obvious time for al-Qaeda's holy warriors to strike America, and so law enforcement agents nationwide were on a heightened state of alert.

On December 14, 1999, U.S. Customs inspector Diana Dean took a careful look at an Algerian man on a ferry bound from Vancouver, Canada, to Port Angeles, Washington. Dean grew suspicious when she noticed that despite the maritime chill of December, the man was sweating and shaking. When she asked him questions, he avoided making eye contact and fiddled with his car's console. When she asked for his identification, the man, Ahmed Ressam, thirty-three, bolted from the car and began to run. He was arrested trying to commandeer a car, and border authorities discovered 130 pounds of explosives in his car.

"It was a wake-up call for us at Customs," Dean told the *Wall Street Journal*. "When I look at everybody now, I leave open the possibility that they could be a terrorist."

For the next year and a half Ressam refused to divulge his intended target. At his apartment in Montreal, authorities discovered a map of California with circles around various airports. Finally, in

April 2000, after Ressam was given a 130-year sentence for terrorism, he admitted that he had intended to bomb Los Angeles
International Airport during the holiday rush. Another millennium
plot to bomb tourists in Jordan was also broken up. If either of
these attacks had succeeded, the results could have been catastrophic. But on the eve of the millennium, at least, we got lucky.

Not so the seventeen sailors killed on the morning of October
12, 2000, when a small boat packed with some six hundred pounds
of explosives punched a forty-by-sixty-foot hole in the armored
hull of the USS *Cole*, a $1 billion 505-foot destroyer, in the Yemeni
port of Aden. The *Cole* bombing had all of the earmarks of an al-
Qaeda operation: thorough training of a small sleeper cell, metic-
ulous planning beforehand, basic but enormously powerful
explosives, and a deceptively simple means of delivery. The *Cole*
survived, thanks to quick and heroic action by its sailors, but the
attack became front-page news around the world. It shocked
Washington, as never before had a couple of ragtag terrorists successfully attacked a major U.S. warship.

In 1997 I had been named chief operating officer at Kroll. I continued to comment frequently on terrorism. After the *Cole* bombing, I appeared on television and said: "Bin Laden is trying to kill
us in any way he can—be it a bomb in a boat, or an atomic or biological weapon." What I wanted to shout, but didn't, was: *Wake up,
America! We are in grave danger!* I look back with regret that I
wasn't more forceful about my worries and the deepening concern
of the U.S. government about Islamic terrorists' murderous intentions.

By 2000 the picture of our enemies was coming into focus. U.S.
law enforcement, working with our counterparts around the world,
had gathered an enormous amount of information on the reach of
al-Qaeda. It was remarkable how much America knew but how little we had learned. We knew that al-Qaeda hated the West and had
declared a *jihad* against the United States. We knew they were intent on killing as many Americans as possible. We knew that they
were capable of sophisticated operations, featuring coordinated at-

tacks by separate cells in numerous countries. Our law enforcement agencies also knew that al-Qaeda had established a terrorist
organization, compartmentalized into cells, inside the United
States a decade ago. We knew that cell members worked to fit in as
normal Americans while planning and training for attacks.

All this information was available to any of us who cared to
look.

What did the government do? It established a commission—the
United States Commission on National Security/21st Century,
chaired by former senators Gary Hart and Warren Rudman. In
January 2001 they reported:

> The combination of unconventional weapons proliferation
> with the persistence of international terrorism will end
> the relative invulnerability of the U.S. homeland to cata-
> strophic attack. A direct attack against American citizens
> *on American soil* is likely over the next quarter century.
> The risk is not only death and destruction but also a de-
> moralization that could undermine U.S. global leadership.
> In face of this threat, our nation has no coherent or inte-
> grated governmental structures.

The findings of the commission were obvious and uncontro-
versial: America faced a grave danger. What did we do in response?
Nothing.

By 2001 we could have, and should have, put the pieces of the
puzzle together. We could have drawn a line from the assassination
of President Sadat in 1981 to the ambush of U.S. troops in
Mogadishu in October 1993, the bombing of the al-Khobar Towers
in June 1996, the destruction of the U.S. embassies in Kenya and
Tanzania in August 1998, and the attack on the USS *Cole* in Yemen
in October 2000. And yet, seeing this picture clearly, we still underestimated the seriousness of the threat.

At 5:50 on the morning of September 11, 2001, I was sitting in
the early-morning dark in my Los Angeles hotel room, watching

the local news and talking on the phone to my New York office. I was on the West Coast to monitor the court-mandated overhaul of the Los Angeles Police Department. Suddenly the screen flashed to the *Today* show, live from New York, and an image of the World Trade Center on fire. They said an airplane had just hit the north tower. I was shocked, but I instantly knew that it was not an accident.

"Oh, no. They got it," I said out loud. O'Neill had been right: Al-Qaeda had finally accomplished what it set out to do in 1993.

People like to say that nothing like this attack has ever happened before, but that is not true. The fact is that al-Qaeda associates have used the same kinds of tactics over and over again. Consider the use of a hijacked airliner as a guided missile against a symbolic target, for example. In December 1994 a group of Algerian terrorists hijacked an Air France Airbus 300 in Algiers and flew it to Marseille, France, where they loaded it with twenty-five thousand gallons of high-octane jet fuel. Three passengers were murdered. The terrorists claimed to have twenty sticks of dynamite aboard and would continue to shoot passengers if any attempt was made to rescue them. Their plan was to fly the Airbus to Paris and smash it into the Eiffel Tower, killing thousands. But early on the morning of December 27, French commandos stormed the plane before it could depart Marseille, and shot the Algerians dead.

Al-Qaeda learned from this experience and refined its technique for the attacks of September 11: The hijacked planes, already loaded with enough fuel for transcontinental flights, never landed.

That morning I called my wife in New York and told her, as calmly as I could, to collect our children, buy some bottled water, and go to our home. We had plenty of friends and neighbors who worked at the Trade Center, but we left that unsaid. Within minutes the phone rang. Unexpectedly, it was CNN, which had tracked me down in my Los Angeles hotel, and wanted me to go on air to comment. But, feeling overwhelmed, I declined.

Then the second jet hit the south tower, and we learned about the Pentagon, and that United Airlines Flight 93 had disappeared into a crater in a field outside Shanksville, Pennsylvania. In my rage and grief, I began to weep. All flights were canceled out of Los Angeles, and I couldn't get back to the East Coast. Los Angeles high rises were being evacuated. I felt helpless and angry and intensely patriotic, but not surprised. I knew the destruction of the World Trade Center was only the next phase of the twenty-year-old terror war.

All the factors in place before September 11 were still in place on September 12, and they continue to be in place today. We have an implacable enemy who seeks to destroy us with every weapon available. They will not allow us to be the only ones to pick the battlefield. They will pick the battlefield and it will be inside the United States.

After U.S. and Afghani forces routed al-Qaeda and the Taliban in the spring of 2002, bin Laden disappeared from sight and stopped sending videotapes to the al-Jazeera TV network. This led to speculation that he may have died during the fighting around Tora Bora, although various intelligence agencies and Arab journalists have reported that he is alive and well, and recently an audiotape surfaced that, U.S. analysts conclude, proves him to be alive. But it doesn't matter: the threat remains. Al-Qaeda continues to carry out operations and to maintain that the *jihad* is still in effect.

"Our martyrs are ready for operations against American and Jewish targets," an al-Qaeda spokesman announced in June 2002. "America should be prepared. It should be ready. They should fasten their seatbelts. We are coming to them where they never expected. The current administration ... releases terrorist attack warnings. I say yes, yes, yes, we are going to launch attacks against America."

What's Next?

It's now obvious that terrorism is a clear, present, and growing danger to our way of life. Terrorists in the United States and around the world are making plans for monstrous attacks like those of

September 11, 2001, or worse. The West is in a real long-term war now, and we will continue to suffer real casualties.

During the few months I spent writing this book, from August through November 2002, the world saw numerous violent, random attacks that slaughtered over three hundred people in Bali, Pakistan, Israel, the Philippines, and Kenya, and aboard a French oil tanker off the coast of Yemen. For three terrible weeks in October, two American snipers went on a bizarre shooting spree in the Washington, D.C., area that killed ten people. In Moscow, Chechen terrorists invaded a popular theater and took 750 innocent men, women, and children hostage, threatening to blow them up. During a fifty-seven-hour siege, the Chechens executed at least one hostage. Finally, the Russian military pumped a fentanyl-based gas into the theater, which not only disabled the militants but killed at least 128 of the hostages.

Can it get any worse? Well, yes, it can—if one of your children is taken hostage or murdered by a fanatical suicide bomber here in America. Don't think for a minute that al-Qaeda and their ilk have not been following these stories closely and learning from them. Indeed, I believe life will get worse here before it gets better.

We will soon see terrorists using car and truck bombs in the United States in the way that the Palestinians have used them in Israel. Terrorists will take big groups of civilians hostage in the West, just as the Chechens did in Moscow. They may well send sniper teams into the American heartland to sow fear and death. And in the near future, terrorists will attempt to smuggle weapons of mass destruction—most likely chemical and/or biological weapons, or radiological "dirty" bombs—across our porous borders.

What about the other fronts in the ongoing war on terror?

Afghanistan Operation Anaconda, the United States' 2001 military campaign in Afghanistan, was brilliant in all regards. A country that had defied the world's greatest superpowers for centuries was conquered within weeks. This enormous victory shows what can be done and how to do it. But we must not believe we can accomplish the same kind of victory every time our troops set foot on foreign soil. We all know that such hubris has led to tragic mistakes in the past.

Afghanistan was, in many ways, a special case. To start with, we had hard evidence that the Taliban government had condoned and aided al-Qaeda's attacks on the United States. This was no secret, and it led most of the world's responsible Islamic countries to support our invasion of Afghanistan. Further, the Taliban was a repressive fundamentalist regime with very thin internal support, which gave way as soon as we invaded.

The results of our operations in Afghanistan have been a major disruption of and lasting damage to al-Qaeda. The organization that Osama bin Laden had built up in a protected environment over the last few years was destroyed; the cave complexes and weapons depots hidden in the mountains that many had assumed were impregnable were overrun or destroyed within weeks. The war eliminated Afghanistan as a training ground and headquarters for al-Qaeda's terror war (although the group has now dispersed and reconstituted itself).

This calm will last as long as the Western powers continue to support moderate leadership in Afghanistan. Will the West be able to maintain Hamid Karzai in power? Only if he can maintain himself. He is the world leader most targeted for assassination. Karzai is a brave man, but his close-protection detail (security-speak for bodyguards) will have to be very good, and he will have to be very lucky, to survive his presidency.

The United States must not attempt to maintain long-term control over Afghanistan. We can ensure that a friendly, anti-al-Qaeda government comes into power, and we can offer long-term support to prevent the country's slide back into anarchy. But we cannot rule Afghanistan as a distant colony. The bullet-riddled, opium-producing nation must learn to stand on its own feet.

War with Iraq The world's intelligence organizations inform us that Iraq has developed biological and chemical weapons and is attempting to build a nuclear bomb. It has the ability to deliver these weapons of mass destruction within a thousand miles of its borders using missiles, aircraft, and ships. Saddam Hussein presents the West with a grave threat: an enemy who appears ready, willing, and able to engage in warfare using weapons of mass destruction.

Looks can be deceiving, however. Saddam is a ruthless tyrant who uses every possible trick and device to increase his wealth and power and to protect his own life. But he is not a religious fanatic who believes he will be granted quick entry into heaven by martyring himself for the faith. He is calculating, not suicidal. This makes him one of our more rational, or at least predictable, enemies—someone who will do whatever is in his own best interest.

Still, Iraq represents a substantial danger to the world. In the past, Saddam has sacrificed hundreds of thousands of Iraqi lives in a meaningless war with Iran, invaded Kuwait and done massive damage there, used poison gas against Iraqi Kurds, plotted to assassinate President George H. W. Bush, and sponsored a variety of Islamic terrorist organizations that aim to harm the United States.

But I do not credit reports that Iraq's intelligence apparatus aided in the attacks on September 11. Why? Because Saddam knows that would be like writing his own death sentence. And I seriously doubt, although one can never be sure, that he would give terrorists weapons of mass destruction, for the same reason.

There is no question that the world would be a safer place without an Iraq dominated by Saddam Hussein. Is it worth going to war to get ride of him? Not if there isn't a worldwide coalition that includes leading Muslim countries such as Egypt, Jordan, and Saudi Arabia. And that will not happen. If we attack Iraq without substantial Arab support, we will likely convert the majority of the world's 1.2 billion Muslims into our enemies. We cannot afford to do that for such a meager gain.

We must stand down, await clearer evidence that Saddam Hussein has suicidal tendencies, and enhance our domestic security.

Do We Have a Handle on Terrorism?

With all that has been done, do we now have terrorism under control? My answer is a resounding no.

I don't enjoy thinking about what the world would be like today if we had not been so successful in Afghanistan. But we clearly do not have a handle on terrorism. Al-Qaeda is regrouping, and in the months and years to come we will face dangers greater than those of September 11. Yet our response has been vague and wishful at best.

Consider, for example, the following "Infrastructure Sector Notification" e-mail warning that circulated within the U.S. government's NIPC (National Infrastructure Protection Center) in October 2002:

> The U.S. intelligence community continues to maintain that al-Qaeda is planning to attack U.S. economic interests. Specifically, the terrorists have targeted America's vast railroad network. . . . The attack of the French oil tanker off the coast of Yemen, and additional information from al-Qaeda detainees, suggest plans exist to attack the global petroleum sector. . . . The U.S. intelligence community continues to receive general threat reporting on American financial institutions and other market-related facilities, the airline and maritime industries, and government facilities and installations.
>
> In view of the above, the FBI urges recipients to continue to take all prudent steps to detect, disrupt, deter, and defend against potential attacks against critical infrastructure and installations at home and abroad.
>
> Due to the lack of specificity of method, location, and timing, the Homeland Security Advisory System threat level will remain at yellow (elevated) for now.

In this banal document, the United States government is advising state and local agencies of serious potential threats, yet it provides no meaningful detail about possible targets and no concrete advice on ways to forestall these threats. I am frustrated that this appears to be the best we can do today: give vague warnings and pray.

Every poll says the American people are uneasy about the security measures we have in place. They are right. The United States *is* unprepared.

I know the government failed to protect its citizens in 1993 and 2001. I know we did not learn the lesson of 1993, and I fear we have not learned the lesson of 2001.

Why have we done so little to defend ourselves against terrorism—with that little being largely ineffectual? The chapters that follow will explain how we got into this fix and what we must do to escape it.

Understanding Our Enemies

"**T**he time of humiliation and subjugation is over. . . . It is time to kill Americans in their heartland." Those were the words of Ahmed al-Haznawi al-Ghamdi as he left Saudi Arabia en route to hijack United Airlines flight 93, the flight that ended in a smoldering pit near Shanksville, Pennsylvania, on September 11, 2001.

To fathom these hate-filled words, to comprehend the evil acts perpetrated by terrorists, and to anticipate what such people can and will do in the future, we need to understand the depth of the feelings of many, not all, Muslims. Islamic fundamentalists believe that the West, and specifically the United States, is committing a kind of cultural genocide against them, as modern Western culture increasingly attracts young people away from the traditional ways of the Quran. Under the circumstances, they feel driven to fight back, even at the cost of their lives, to stop the destruction and defeat of Islam.

This is why violent Islamic fundamentalists such as al-Haznawi al-Ghamdi are our new enemy. Relentless foes of the United States, they seek to terrorize us anywhere, in any way, at any cost. They launched the war in which we are embroiled on a timetable and a battlefield of their choosing. And so far, it must be said, *they are winning that war*. The terrorists are winning because they understand today's military, political, social, and economic landscape better than our leaders do. And the historically unique brand of warfare they wage, combining fanatical devotion to an ultraconservative interpretation of Islam with today's revolution in communications, technology, and information, is still largely mysterious to most westerners, even to those who are guiding the national and international response.

There's a general perception that our law enforcement agencies have not been paying attention to the terrorist threat over the last decade. That's wrong. I have spoken to intelligence and law enforcement leaders around the world, and they have long understood that Islamic terrorism represents a serious threat to the West, especially to the United States. What America does not understand is how lethal and determined the terrorists really are. *And even now, more than a year after September 11, we still behave as if we don't understand.*

"The threat environment we find ourselves in today is as bad as it was before September 11," George Tenet, director of the CIA, said in the fall of 2002. "It is important for the American people to know that despite the enormous successes we've had . . . al-Qaeda continues to plan and will attempt more deadly strikes against us. There will be more battles won and, sadly, more battles lost."

Tenet is right. To limit our casualties and build an effective long-term response to the terrorist threat posed by al-Qaeda and its allies, we must first understand who our enemies are, the culture they spring from, and the shifting global environment in which they operate. In this chapter, I will give a brief overview of Islam and the terror groups it has spawned, and discuss how the changes wrought by globalization over the last twenty years have provided a spawning ground for terror.

But first a couple of words on terrorism itself. The best definition I have seen comes from former Justice Department official Philip Heymann's book *Terrorism and America*. Terrorism, he writes, "is violence conducted as a political strategy by a subnational group." He explains:

> What do terrorists hope to accomplish with violence? They hope to achieve both physical and psychological results: they hope to damage and frighten Western nations so badly that they discontinue the policies that the Islamists object to; and they hope to create attention for their cause, and themselves, thereby gaining internal control and external support.

The Roots of Islam

Established by the Prophet Muhammad in the early seventh century, Islam is the youngest of the world's three great monotheistic religions, after Judaism and Christianity. Today it is the dominant religion in large portions of Africa and Asia. There are some 1.2 billion Muslims around the world, and to many of them, Islam is more than a theology—it is an all-encompassing way of life.

In Arabic, *islam* means the submission of one's will to God; a follower of Islam is called a Muslim (one who submits). Its followers consider Muhammad the last of God's prophets, who included Abraham, Moses, and Jesus. Muslims believe that Jews and Christians were given God's laws but subsequently tampered with the revelations in their scriptures. The Quran, the Muslim book of scripture, was then revealed to Muhammad through the angel Gabriel over a period of twenty-three years to correct the errors of Jews and Christians, and to bring the word of God to all unbelievers.

For Muslims, life on earth is merely a trial for the eternal hereafter, and every living moment of a person's life should be devoted to the glory of God, who is almighty, transcendent, just, merciful, and loving. Fundamentalist Muslims consider the Quran the literal word of God, superseding all of God's previous messages, including those contained in the Hebrew scriptures and the Christian Bible. It instructs them on every facet of life, including worship, morality, the relationship between God and man, and human relationships.

By following both the letter and spirit of the Quran, Muslims believe they will ascend to heaven on the Day of Judgment, when everything Muslims do, say, and think will be accounted for. On this day, the universe will be destroyed and the dead will be resurrected; God will determine who will experience everlasting bliss in paradise and who will be confined to the torturous fires of hell for eternity.

To achieve paradise, a Muslim must follow the five essential duties of Islam: faith, prayer five times daily, almsgiving, fasting during Ramadan (the most sacred month in the Muslim calendar), and undertaking a pilgrimage (*hajj*) to Mecca—Muhammad's birthplace and the holiest city in Islam.

In Islam no one stands between God and the faithful. Although there are imams who lead prayers and deliver sermons, there is no need for priests or rabbis to interpret the religion. Absolute authority belongs to God alone. After the death of the Prophet Muhammad in 632, however, the leadership of Islam was taken over by a series of caliphs, who were both temporal and spiritual leaders. A caliph's role was to defend the faith and uphold Islamic law. The caliphate was abolished in 1924 by Kemal Atatürk, the westernizing founder of modern Turkey, but one of the goals of today's fundamentalist Islamic movement is to establish a new, pan-Islamic caliphate, in which secular and religious law would be fused.

Unlike Jesus, the founder of Christianity (but like many of the Jewish patriarchs), Muhammad was a military and political leader as well as a religious teacher. In the beginning of the seventh century, Muhammad fought to establish Islam in the region around the cities of Medina and Mecca, in what is now Saudi Arabia. He later may have launched military campaigns against the Byzantines in southern Syria. A century after his death, Muslim armies led by the successors of Muhammad had extended their influence from the Indus River to the south of France, setting the stage for the religious wars between East and West that would claim millions of lives over the next five centuries.

Traditionally, Islam conquered but did not crush; it ruled over many but did not force conversions. As Islam spread during the Middle Ages, the Jewish and Christian communities it conquered came to be called "peoples of the Book," meaning that they, too, had received God's prophetic message through holy scripture. This entitled them to the status of *dhimmis*, members of protected groups who were free to practice their religion. Their civic and economic status, however, was lower than that of Muslims. Many who lived in Muslim-ruled territories embraced the faith more or less voluntarily.

One Faith, Many Forms

We in the West tend to identify Muslims with Arabs. This is a misunderstanding. It's true that most Arabs are Muslims, but fully 80 percent of the worldwide Muslim population is non-Arabic. Indonesia has the world's largest Muslim population. Other non-Arab countries with large Muslim populations are India, Iran, Turkey, China, and Russia. And North America, Europe, and sub-Saharan Africa are all home to large and growing numbers of Muslims.

We also think of Islam as a monolithic faith. This too is inaccurate. There are two major branches of Islam. Most Muslims are members of Sunni Islam. Smaller groups are adherents of Shi'ism, which is dominant in Iran and southern Iraq, and which is subdivided in turn into a number of branches. Various other movements have sprung up within Islam, each with its own variations in belief and practice.

It's natural for non-Muslims to have an oversimplified image of Islam. Particularly today, when the war on terror seems to place the West in a life-and-death struggle against Islam, it's easy to stereotype Muslims as violent, hateful, and destructive. Of course, no religion with over a billion adherents can be so easily pigeon-holed.

A prime example of the complexity of Islam is the various meanings of the word *jihad*. Scholar Matthew S. Gordon comments, "In the Quran, and in the tradition, *jihad* is understood as 'struggling in the name of, or in the defense of, the faith.' " In today's context, *jihad* has come to mean violent battle on behalf of Islam, including the targeting of innocent civilians by bombs and other weapons. Yet, as Gordon explains, this interpretation ignores at least half of the meaning of the word *jihad:*

> The greater, internal, struggle is striving to resisting wrong-doing ("sin"), heedlessness, and immorality—this is carried out by performing the ritual duties of Islam and by otherwise serving as an example of piety and righteousness to others (Muslims and non-Muslims alike). The second, external, struggle . . . calls upon Muslims to act with force, indeed to wage war, when Islam, or the Islamic community (*Umma*) is perceived to be under threat—for example, by invasion, oppressive foreign rule, or forced conversion.

Thus *jihad* is far from a synonym for terrorism, or even for war. Physical struggle is supposed to take a backseat to spiritual struggle within the individual believer. In fact, Muhammad himself is quoted as saying, on returning from a military campaign, "We have returned from the lesser *jihad* to the greater *jihad*."

Thus is it fair to call Islam a "martial faith," as many have done? That phrase is probably a little too pat, a little simplistic. But as we'll see, in combination with complicated and largely tragic political, economic, and social conditions in the modern Arab world, fundamentalist Islam has provided fertile ground for the growth of violent anti-Western sentiment.

Islam and the West

Since the Crusades of the eleventh and twelfth centuries, many in the Islamic world have felt besieged by the West. Today, many Arab and Asian Muslims blame Western imperialism and its by-products, colonialism and modern nationalism, for the currently heightened tensions in their regions.

The modern European occupation of the Middle East began in 1798, when Napoleon's troops invaded Egypt. The French were expelled in 1801 by the Ottoman Turks and the British. Following World War I and the dissolution of the Ottoman Empire, the British and French carved up the region into spheres of influence. By 1920 they controlled Algeria, Tunisia, Egypt, Morocco, Iraq, Lebanon, Palestine, and Syria. This resulted in the creation of artificial nation-states that disregarded existing tribal, cultural, religious, and linguistic boundaries. The French carved out a portion of Syria to make modern-day Lebanon, while the British created the borders for present-day Saudi Arabia, Iraq, and Kuwait. The arbitrary nature of these borders has been the root cause of some of the region's most violent conflicts, including the Lebanese civil war and Syria's subsequent intervention, as well as Saddam Hussein's invasion of Kuwait.

The colonial powers instituted British-style constitutional monarchies and French-style republics. But after World War II, the European nations were weakened and Arab countries regained their independence—Syria, Lebanon, and Jordan by 1946, Egypt in 1954, Tunisia and Morocco in 1956, Iraq in 1958, and Algeria in 1962. With independence, almost all of the Western-style Arabian governments were overthrown and replaced by autocratic Arab regimes.

Religious movements within Islam echoed the growing tensions between "modernism" (i.e., Westernization) and traditional culture. One of the most influential of these movements was Wahhabism, founded in the eighteenth century by Muhammad bin Abd al-Wahhab, who launched a campaign to renew and "purify"

Islam. Think of Wahhabism as roughly parallel to the various fundamentalist movements that have arisen within Christianity in reaction to the pressures of modern life. Its values are puritanical, its
interpretation of the Quran is literal, and its attitude toward other
faiths is hostile, even aggressive. Wahhabism has been a major social and political factor in the history of the Middle East, especially
in Saudi Arabia, and today it attracts millions of followers who
share the desire to rid the Islamic world of the effects of secularization and modernization.

The creation of Israel in 1948, and its continued support by the
West, gave Muslims a new, common enemy. The Palestinians who
had formerly occupied lands now controlled by Israel feared having
to choose between displacement and life under Israeli rule. Arab
leaders had their own reasons for taking up the Palestinian cause;
for example, both Syria and Jordan hoped to annex parts of
Palestine. In any case, many Arab leaders elected to focus on the
external enemies, Israel and the West, rather than focus on internal
problems such as poverty and lack of education.

The Arabs took up arms in support of their anti-Israeli cause. In
1948, 1956, 1967, and 1973, full-scale war erupted between Israel
and its neighbors. Today, tensions between the two sides continue
to fester, exacerbated by the unresolved issue of a Palestinian
homeland.

The so-called Arab nationalist leaders rallied their people
around the Arab-Israel conflict and the effort to rid the region of
imperialist (Western) forces. But the defeat of Egypt, Syria, and
Jordan in the 1967 Arab-Israeli War helped shatter the illusion of
Arab unity and made way for the rise of Islamic opposition groups.
Fundamentalist Muslims gained popularity as the result of weak
economies, failed social reforms, political corruption, and military
defeats.

Scholar John L. Esposito identifies the year 1967 as the turning
point for those Muslims who blamed the West for their moral and
spiritual decline:

Disillusionment with the West and in particular with the United States, its pro-Israel policy, and its support for authoritarian rulers like Iran's Shah fed anti-Western feelings. Muslim religious leaders and activists believed their message had been vindicated, maintaining that the failures and troubles of Muslims were a result of turning away from God's revealed path and relying on the West. From the 1970s onward, religious revivalism and the role of Islamic movements became a major force in Muslim politics.

Today, as journalist Thomas Friedman points out in his book *From Beirut to Jerusalem,* Middle Eastern politics remains an amalgamation of ancient tribalism, ruthless autocracy, and fitful attempts at modern, Western-style governing. While the Arab people seem to understand this amalgamation of old and new intuitively, it can be confusing to the outsider—especially to Americans. As a result, westerners have repeatedly misinterpreted political and social forces in the Middle East. Friedman quotes the Lebanese historian Kemal Salibi:

> The liberal tradition in the West tries to impute to the behavior of the native or the underdog an idealist position which is not really there. They want to think of the peoples of this region as "noble savages," as Jean-Jacques Rousseau put it. Instead of saying, what we have here is an outmoded form of thinking clashing with an attempt to construct modern states. . . . When it comes to thinking about Middle East politics, the American liberal mind is often chasing rainbows. They are living in a world of delusion.

It seems clear that the dream of turning the Arab world into a peaceful, unified, pro-Western empire is one example of such a delusion. That dream, which dates back to T. E. Lawrence (Lawrence of Arabia), resurfaces every few years; its latest form is the wishful opti-

mism with which some spokesmen for the Bush administration
speak about quickly transforming Iraq, after Saddam Hussein, into a
pro-American democracy. But anti-Western sentiment simply runs
too deep in the Middle East for this to be a likely scenario.

Again, however, it's important to avoid the temptation of as-
suming that the entire Muslim world is monolithic. Many
Muslims are not eager to live in a theocratic state ruled by fundamentalist interpretations of Islamic law. Some would like to see
the founding of Western-style democratic institutions in their
nations. And even those who admire Islamic tradition do not necessarily support its most extreme forms. When the ultrafundamen-
talist Taliban movement rose to power in Afghanistan in 1998,
imposing harsh laws in the name of Islam, most Muslim governments reacted with condemnation. Only three nations in the
world, Saudi Arabia, Pakistan, and the United Arab Emirates, recognized the Taliban government. And on the evening of September
11, 2001, six thousand young Iranians gathered in the streets of
Teheran with commemorative candles, shouting "Death to terror"
and proclaiming their solidarity with the suffering people of America. Facts like these belie any notion that the Muslim world is uni-
formly intolerant and hateful.

Nonetheless, we have to recognize that widespread approval or
at least tolerance of anti-Western hatred is fueled by economic and
political conditions in much of the Islamic world. Many Muslims
today seethe with anger and despair, believing that neither the
Arab despots who rule them nor the meddlesome Western powers
give them the respect and material advantages they would like. In
reaction, many have retreated into their faith as a kind of sanctu-
ary. But others have reacted by lashing out. Their targets are moderate Muslims and the West.

The Birth of Islamic Terrorism

The Muslim Brotherhood was the precursor to modern terror
groups such as al-Qaeda. Formed in Egypt in 1928, the Brotherhood

maintained that religion and politics were inseparable and that any nominally Muslim society that failed to live by the Quran was impious and thus an enemy. Its goal was to create a pan-Arab Islamic republic. Standing in its way was the region's authoritarian governments. To achieve its goal, the Brotherhood combined a fierce devotion to Islam with bombings, assassinations, and other terrorist tactics, which raised its profile and influence on the Arab street. Operating in nations dominated by corrupt and repressive regimes, the Brotherhood's leaders developed such survival tactics as dividing their followers into small independent groups, or "cells," to protect against intelligence failures, for example. These same tactics form the basis of how terrorist organizations operate today.

As the Muslim Brotherhood gained influence and waged guerrilla warfare across the Middle East, the ruling governments often retaliated with tremendous brutality. Syria, for example, declared it a capital crime to join the Muslim Brotherhood. Nonetheless, the group continued to gain support and even turned a number of cities into strongholds of conservative Muslim belief. In the late 1970s and early 1980s, the Brotherhood began agitating more openly, essentially calling for a revolution against the government of Hafez al-Assad.

In 1982, Assad decided to take action. In the course of a long and vicious battle that lasted the entire month of February, his troops obliterated the city of Hama, once renowned as one of Syria's largest and most beautiful centers of trade and culture, to set an example. Although exact numbers have never been agreed upon, it has been said that Assad's troops slaughtered between ten thousand and twenty-five thousand men, women, and children, flattened virtually every building, and left many thousands more destitute in Hama. According to Patrick Seale's biography, *Assad*, Assad's hotheaded brother Rifaat exhorted his troops by noting that Stalin had sacrificed ten million people to preserve the Bolshevik revolution, and that Syria should be willing to do the same. Thomas Friedman reports that Rifaat personally oversaw the bulldozing of Hama's buildings and the barbaric torture of many of the city's survivors to make an unmistakable point about the consequences of rebellion. Yet even these harsh steps did not stamp out the spread of the Brotherhood's message throughout the region. Indeed, the malicious tactics of Assad and other Arabian strongmen may have actually strengthened the fundamentalist Muslim movement over the long run.

The Goals of the Fundamentalists

The common goal of fundamentalist Muslim groups is the establishment of a pan-Islamic state, or caliphate. Achieving this objective, they believe, requires ridding the region of Western influences, as well as of any Muslims who sympathize with the West or who have supported secularization. This may seem a far-fetched goal to most Americans. Our traditional separation of church and state makes the idea of a theocratic government appear impossibly dated. Yet three pivotal events in recent history have convinced Islamic militants that it is attainable.

The first was the Iranian revolution of 1979, the establishment of an Islamic republic by Ayatollah Ruhollah Khomeini, and the reversal of Iran's westernization. During the 1960s and 1970s Iranians had been growing increasingly disaffected with the shah and his Western-style reforms. People in every segment of Iranian society were alienated by the shah's "White Revolution" land reform program, his use of brutal police and intelligence agencies, and his relatively cozy relationship with the United States during the Cold War. Khomeini, a religious leader who had lived in exile since 1964, used Iran's mounting discontent to create an Islamic republic. This demonstrated to Muslims everywhere that it was possible to overthrow a repressive regime backed by the West and establish a modern Islamic state.

The second pivotal event, which also took place in 1979, was the Soviet Union's invasion of Afghanistan. This incursion created an enormous backlash among Muslims, thousands of whom flocked from around the world to join the Afghani *mujahidin*'s anti-Soviet Islamic *jihad*. The Muslim warriors—including Osama bin Laden—received a tremendous amount of training, weaponry, and support from the United States. These skills and tools would later be turned against us, by these same Muslim militants, in a classic case of blowback. The Soviet occupation ended in defeat and a humiliating withdrawal from Afghanistan in 1989. This war demonstrated to Muslims that they could defeat Western forces on the battlefield, even those backed by a global superpower.

The third pivotal event was the assassination of Egyptian president Anwar el-Sadat in October 1981. As we've seen, Sadat was viewed by Islamists as a traitor because of his diplomatic overtures to the West and his signing of the Camp David accords with Israel. The murder of this Nobel peace prize winner caught the world off guard. Only a few people realized that it signaled the deadly intentions of Muslim terrorists. Sadat was replaced by his vice president, Hosni Mubarak, who remains in power today, and the Egyptian-Israeli accords are still in force. But Sadat's assassination garnered tremendous attention and established the possibility of eliminating moderate Arab leaders who strayed from the path of what the fundamentalists considered righteousness.

Taken together, these three key events reinforced the belief among Muslim extremists that the establishment of a large Islamic republic was indeed within their reach.

The Theology of Terror

Islamic terrorists come from many countries, disparate socioeconomic backgrounds, and varied levels of education. What they have in common is a strong, even fanatical devotion to Islam.

Those who volunteer to become suicide bombers believe that God will reward them for their martyrdom with direct ascendance to heaven. While the average Muslim must wait in purgatory before achieving paradise, martyrs to Islam may bypass the intermediate state between one's death and the Day of Judgment and go directly to the seventh heaven, the highest realm, where the prophets reside. It is this Quranic promise to martyrs that terrorist leaders exploit when recruiting potential suicide bombers:

> If you are killed in the cause of God or you die, the forgiveness and mercy of God are better than all that you amass. And if you die or are killed, even so it is to God that you will return. (3:157–58)

Militant fundamentalists have repeatedly used martyrdom as a terror tactic. By narrowly interpreting this and other Quranic passages, the leaders of groups such as al-Qaeda are able to convince the foot soldiers of their movement that suicide is a legitimate weapon in a holy war.

As we've seen, it's clear that the history of Islam does include a strong military tradition. Muhammad himself was a warrior, and some martial element is included in the concept of *jihad*. If warfare in defense of Islam is permissible or even a religious requirement, what rules does Islamic teaching set forth under which such warfare should be conducted? Do the terror attacks we see carried out in the name of Islam fit the definition of "just warfare" in Muslim theology?

There is no single answer to this question on which all Muslims would agree, any more than all Christian theologians would agree on the morality of, for example, the bombing of Hiroshima or the American war in Vietnam. However, most Islamic scholars condemn terrorism and the targeting of innocent civilians as barbaric acts unjustified by the Quran and the teachings of the Prophet. Islamic doctrine contains multiple admonitions against any form of suicide. Furthermore, Islam has clear rules of engagement for soldiers, and attacking civilians is not allowed. According to the Quran, women, children, and the elderly are to be spared in war, as are homes, synagogues, and churches. The violence perpetrated by suicide bombers against such targets stands in direct contradiction to these elements of the faith they claim to follow.

Most important, a holy war must be conducted either in defense of one's faith or in retaliation for an aggressive act. Can the events of September 11, 2001, be justified as acts of holy war? Can the violent attacks by Islamic militants be regarded as a defense of Islam? Few serious scholars of Islam believe this. They agree that Osama bin Laden and his defenders have perverted the teachings of Muhammad to defend violence that is driven by their own political and even personal agendas.

In his book *When Religion Becomes Evil,* Charles Kimball refers to this kind of abuse of sacred text as an "absolute truth" claim:

> When zealous and devout adherents elevate the teachings and beliefs of their tradition to the level of absolute truth claims, they open a door to the possibility that their religion will become evil . . . people armed with absolute truth claims are closely linked to violent extremism, charismatic leaders, and various justifications for acts otherwise understood to be unacceptable.

While the number of Muslims who would commit atrocities such as those perpetrated on September 11 are few, it's clear that many Muslims, even moderates, deeply resent the West and its influence on their lands. Our history of meddling in the Middle East, especially since the discovery of vast oil reserves in the region, has left the Arabs feeling eclipsed and taken advantage of, and has provided fodder for extremist movements bent on exacting revenge.

Target: America

American foreign policy during the last thirty years has been largely insensitive to the unique cultural and religious sensibilities of the Arab and Asian world. And while the average American may be only dimly aware of the often inconsistent stands and politically expedient policies of our government, the people who are affected by them can't help but notice. For example, while the United States was supplying arms and money to bin Laden and the Islamic *mujahidin* during the Soviet-Afghan war, we were simultaneously denouncing Iran's Ayatollah Khomeini as an Islamic fanatic. Many viewed this as inconsistent and hypocritical.

The United States supported Iraqi dictator Saddam Hussein in his decade-long struggle with Iran while overlooking the fact that he was killing his own people. Again, this hypocrisy did not escape the Arab world.

Further angering Arabs has been the United States' unfaltering support of Israel. In the spring of 2001 a survey was conducted of five Arab states, Egypt, Saudi Arabia, the United Arab Emirates, Kuwait, and Lebanon, which concluded that the "majority in all five countries said that the Palestinian issue was the single most important issue to them personally."

Such policies have served to inflame Muslim extremists and convince them that there is a Western conspiracy against them. In a letter excerpted by the *New York Times*, Kamel Daoudi, an alleged Algerian terrorist currently serving time in a French prison, wrote tellingly of his motivations:

> The West hated us because we were Arabs and Muslims. France did everything possible to ensure that Algeria would not be an Islamic state. It backed an illegitimate and profoundly one-sided regime by sending weapons, helicopters and even the Foreign Legion (not many people know about that). The massacres committed by the Algerian army were the last straw for me. . . . The Algerian war, the Bosnian war, the Gulf War, Kosovo, Afghanistan, Palestine, Lebanon—all of these events strengthen my conviction that the Judeo-Christian community influenced by atheism has a visceral hatred of the community of Muhammad.

Islamist militants have astutely used such grievances, the promise of special status for martyrs, and the West's moral ambiguity to recruit legions of followers. Our inconsistent, sometimes hypocritical, and often ham-fisted diplomatic maneuverings in the Middle East haven't helped matters. When President George W. Bush referred to our war against terror as a "crusade," carelessly reigniting a thousand years of Arab resentment of the West, he was playing into the hands of those who hate us.

The Face of Terror: Osama bin Laden

Osama bin Laden was born in 1957 in Riyadh, Saudi Arabia, the seventeenth of fifty-two children born to Muhammad bin Laden. Originally from Yemen, the elder bin Laden had moved to the kingdom around 1930 and established a small construction company. As a result of successful relationships he forged with the royal family, Muhammad's company was awarded many exclusive government contracts. Over time, the Binladen Brothers for Contracting and Industry grew into an industrial empire.

When Osama was just thirteen, his father died. Four years later, Osama married a young Syrian woman who was a relative. He received a degree in public administration in 1981 from King Abdul-Aziz University in Jeddah.

In 1982, Osama bin Laden traveled from Saudi Arabia to assist the Afghani *jihad* against the Soviet Union. Under the auspices of Maktab al-Khidmat lil Mujahidin al-Arab (MAK), a services organization, bin Laden helped to house, train, and finance the Afghan *mujahidin* resistance. MAK, which had recruitment centers around the world—including at the al-Kifah Refugee Center, in Brooklyn, New York (where El Sayyid Nosair, Rabbi Meir Kahane's killer, was indoctrinated)—was supported by the United States as part of our effort to contain the Soviet Union.

As the war in Afghanistan wound down in the late 1980s, bin Laden established a new organization called al-Qaeda ("the base," in Arabic), which inherited much of MAK's infrastructure and resources. Loosely organized from the start, al-Qaeda grew into an organization that used Afghanistan as its base, running training camps in the desert and operating cells of terrorists around the globe. The cells went into action when signaled from the top, or sometimes on their own initiative.

After the Soviets withdrew from Afghanistan, bin Laden returned to Saudi Arabia, where he was initially received as a hero. But he quickly grew disillusioned with the House of Saud and his inability to effect change in his homeland. Bin Laden's opposition to Saudi policies grew increasingly vocal, especially about Saudi Arabia's alliance with the United States.

When Iraq invaded Kuwait in August 1990, he offered to bring his *mujahidin* comrades to Saudi Arabia to defend the kingdom. But King Fahd replied that American forces were en route to do the job. To bin Laden, this was a shattering betrayal. He would later say that the decision to allow non-Muslim troops onto holy Islamic soil, and their ongoing deployment there after the Gulf War, changed his life and led to his call to arms against the West.

In response, the al-Saud family stripped bin Laden of his citizenship and froze his assets there. Bin Laden's own family also renounced him. Yet his wealth remained largely intact, and he was able to move around the Islamic world easily.

Like many of history's tyrants—Genghis Khan, Stalin, Saddam Hussein—bin Laden is a megalomaniac who brooks no dissent in his ranks or from his peers. In November 1989, for instance, he publicly praised Abdullah Azzam, a co-founder of al Qaeda and his mentor, while facilitating Azzam's assassination in Pakistan after a power struggle. For bin Laden the ends always justify the means.

In 1991, bin Laden moved to Pakistan and then to Sudan, where he cemented alliances with other Islamic militant groups from around the world. Al-Qaeda began to train, finance, and provide logistical support to radical Islamists, thereby advancing its objectives while staying out of the limelight. It wasn't until 1996, three years after the first World Trade Center bombing, that the U.S. State Department put bin Laden on a list of sponsors of terrorism.

That year, bowing to international pressure, Sudan asked bin Laden to leave. He found refuge in Afghanistan, where he continued to train and arm radical Islamists from around the world until the American incursion in October 2001. Bin Laden disappeared during the fighting, but as of this writing, it is clear he survived and continues to threaten the West. But whatever the long-term fate of bin Laden, al-Qaeda is very much alive.

Bin Laden's top deputy, Ayman al-Zawahiri, the former leader of Egyptian Islamic *Jihad*, recently threatened America and its "deputies," France and Germany, with further violence. An attack in April 2002 killed sixteen people, including eleven German tourists, at a synagogue in Tunisia. In May 2002 a bus attack in Pakistan killed eleven French engineers. In October 2002 a car bomb in Bali, Indonesia, killed some two hundred people, most of them visiting Australians. In the same month, another bomb in Zamboanga, Philippines, killed six and injured hundreds.

While it remains unclear how directly involved al-Qaeda was in these attacks, it is clear that a network of Islamists trained by al-Qaeda or inspired by its ideology are continuing to fight the international *jihad* on a local level.

How al-Qaeda Works

There is an enormous amount of open-file information available about al-Qaeda, both from the group's public statements and from evidence revealed in various courts about investigations and prosecutions of the terrorists. As CEO of Kroll, I have had the opportunity to learn about radical Muslim groups from law enforcement and intelligence officers from many nations.

Al-Qaeda is more than just a terrorist group like the IRA or Red Brigades. It is an ideology as much as it is a collection of operatives, a multinational Islamist movement, and the leading terrorist organization of the twenty-first century. In the process of redefining what such an organization is, notes al-Qaeda expert Rohan Gunaratna, "al-Qaeda has moved terrorism beyond the status of a

technique of protest and resistance and turned it into a global instrument with which to compete with and challenge Western influence in the Muslim world." Indeed, al-Qaeda has managed to
unite many Muslims behind a single objective: the preservation of
Islam through the destruction of the West.

Through strategic alliances with like-minded Islamic groups,
al-Qaeda is thought to have agents from some forty nations operating in ninety-four countries. Its loose command structure, with
vertical leadership that provides direction to a horizontal network
of cells and affiliated organizations, is very effective for a terrorist
group and is largely responsible for al-Qaeda's ability to maintain
secrecy, regenerate itself, and continue to operate globally. Al-
Qaeda cells are usually made up of anywhere from two to fifteen
operatives, and each cell appears to have a high degree of auton-
omy. Their only connection to the group's upper echelon is through
their "agent handlers." As in the Muslim Brotherhood, these cells
operate independently of one another, which protects their operations from exposure.

Although the leadership of al-Qaeda was clearly disrupted by
American operations in Afghanistan, it has since managed to regroup
throughout the world. Further, it has long-standing ties to other terrorist groups, including Jemaah Islamiyah in Indonesia, Abu Sayyaf
in the Philippines, and Kumpulan Mujahideen Malaysia, which may
have been involved in the terrorist acts of 2002.

While America works to climb a steep learning curve about
this complex, multinational group, al-Qaeda has demonstrated that
it understands how our nation works and how to take advantage of
it. Its members understand our laws, our immigration system, our
extradition policies, and how to use our high technology. Indeed,
terrorists hiding in the United States have used some of our most
cherished rights—freedom of association, freedom of speech, freedom of religion—as a cover to raise funds, recruit members, train
with weapons, and plot our demise. We have consistently underestimated their resourcefulness.

For example, when Ramzi Yousef first entered the United States, on September 1, 1992, he was arrested at Kennedy Airport for entering the country without a visa. After claiming political asylum and lying to officials of the Immigration and Naturalization Service (INS), Yousef was released on his own recognizance. He was free to roam the country.

His partner Ahmad Ajaj wasn't quite so lucky. After arriving from Karachi, Pakistan, on the same flight as Yousef, Ajaj was arrested for passport fraud. Authorities also confiscated a bag filled with bomb-making manuals. But even while in federal custody, Ajaj stayed in touch with his co-conspirator. He never contacted Yousef directly; he would call a friend and have him patch in Yousef, thereby making law enforcement's efforts to trace his calls more difficult.

These terrorists understood our legal and technical weaknesses and exploited them at every opportunity. In February 1993 Yousef led the bombing of the World Trade Center, then escaped the country.

Al-Qaeda's ability to recruit is bolstered by its capacity to infiltrate local Muslim communities around the world. It has used local mosques, Muslim student organizations, and Islamic charities to indoctrinate believers. Steven Emerson, a specialist on the subject of fundamentalist Muslim activities in the United States, has identified immigrants or second-generation American Muslims as the group that disproportionately fills the fundamentalist ranks. In June 1997 he told the *Middle East Quarterly:*

> It is both ironic and tragic that many immigrants who come here to flee the violence of Islamic fundamentalism in their homelands are subsequently converted to that very cause. Take the case of El-Sayyid Nosair, the Egyptian who assassinated Rabbi Meir Kahane in November 1990. He arrived in the United States as a Westernized, secularized middle-class immigrant and became radicalized in Pittsburgh.

Al-Qaeda relies on financial support from around the world. We know that Osama bin Laden has devoted much of his personal wealth—estimated to be anywhere from $30 million to $250 million—to al-Qaeda, and that he persuaded wealthy individuals, and several nations, including Sudan, Afghanistan, and Iran, to aid his cause. But tracking this financial network has proven tricky because of its complexity, its compartmentalized structure, and the sheer number of revenue streams. The organization relies on profits from ostensibly legitimate business endeavors, such as investments and the trade in honey, as well as illegal activities such as credit card fraud and heroin trafficking.

We are only now beginning to understand how deeply al-Qaeda has infiltrated unwitting Islamic nongovernmental organizations (NGOs) and rerouted philanthropic monies to fund mass terror. In October 2002 the head of one of the largest Islamic charities in the United States, the Benevolence International Foundation, was indicted on conspiracy and racketeering charges: Enaam M. Amaout, a father of four from suburban Chicago and a graduate of the *mujahidin* camps in Afghanistan, allegedly helped to launder the charity's proceeds to pay for terrorism. While the United States continues to crack down on this type of operation, al-Qaeda uses *hawala*, an informal banking system common to the Middle East that relies on trust, family relationship, and regional affiliations, to move money around the world. This further complicates the job of tracking the terrorists' resources.

In sum, American intelligence officials estimate that before September 11, at least ten thousand men were trained at al-Qaeda camps in Afghanistan, although only about three hundred were made full members. There is no question that some of these agents are planning further attacks on America and her allies.

Islam, the West, and Globalization

The emergence of fundamentalist Islam as a political, social, and religious force has occurred against a backdrop of dramatic global changes. These changes have both intensified the conflict between Islam and the West and multiplied the dangers posed to the world by any armed, militant force.

America is now the most powerful country in the world, and arguably the most powerful country in human history. We spend more on our military forces than Russia, China, and the European Union combined. The U.S. economy represents almost one-quarter of the world's gross national product; the state of California alone would be the world's sixth largest economy. And we are culturally dominant. In his book *The Paradox of American Power,* Harvard professor Joseph S. Nye Jr. has coined the phrase "soft power" to describe a nation's ability to influence the rest of the world through its culture. America's soft power is overwhelming—we export our culture in every way, from our movies and music and books to our science and sports and our espousal of a pluralistic democracy.

By contrast, the Islamic fundamentalists and the terror organizations they have spawned have very limited power. They have no tanks, no submarines, no ballistic missiles. They have limited economic resources; while al-Qaeda's total economic wealth is measured in the tens of millions, America's economic resources are measured in the trillions. And outside the Muslim world, it has no soft power to speak of. It doesn't even have a nation to call its own. Given this vast disparity in power, how is it possible that al-Qaeda and its allies have succeeded in holding America hostage to terror?

The answer is that the world has changed. Power isn't what it used to be.

One of the first harbingers of change was the collapse of the Soviet Union in 1989. There were many reasons for that collapse, but the salient point here is that the Soviets discovered the hard way that military might and fortified borders could not prevent the flow of information. As questions about the quality of life built, and spending on the wrong things hobbled the giant nation, the Soviet Union finally collapsed under its own rusty weight.

Welcome to the globalized world, where walls and fences no

longer afford security. How did we get here? Through the combined effects of three interlinked revolutions—in information, technology, and transportation.

The Information Revolution In the early 1980s, information was accessed primarily in physical form, through documents such as books, newspapers, and government reports. In Western societies, you could gain access to information by visiting a library or a government archive. In a country such as Afghanistan, Syria, or Iraq, only the elite could gain such access.

By the end of the 1990s, with the advent of the Internet, hundreds of millions of people around the world had increasing access to broad and deep information of every kind. Nearly all human knowledge is available on the Web. Most of this information is benign: the works of Shakespeare, the collection of the Museum of Modern Art, tips on planting a vegetable garden. Much of the information has dual uses, both benign and sinister: Maps of watershed areas are important to environmental groups that are eager to monitor pollution hazards and protect our drinking water, but they can also be used by terrorists to suggest possible targets for attack. And some of the information is purely toxic. There are sites containing instructions on how to build a nuclear bomb, sites spewing anti-American hate propaganda, and sites encouraging violence against government agents.

The Technology Revolution E-mail, fax, digital imaging, fiber-optic networks, cell phones, pagers, satellite communications, and all the other technological breakthroughs of the last few years have made communication simple, instantaneous, global, and cheap.

This increase in speed and flexibility has had profound societal effects. In the West, NGOs from Greenpeace and Planned Parenthood to the National Rifle Association and the Christian Coalition have been able to use the new technologies to rapidly inform, influence, and mobilize their members, sometimes affecting the outcomes of elections and votes in Congress. Now third world groups that once would have been virtually powerless are able to use the same technologies to multiply their influence and to spread their views around the world.

The Transportation Revolution The advent of the eighteen-wheeler, the jumbo jet, and the supertanker has allowed people and goods to move around the world more efficiently and cost-effectively than ever before. These advances allow corporations to plan and execute coordinated actions on a worldwide basis, making possible such business strategies as global outsourcing and lean, fast, just-in-time manufacturing. Fish from Argentina, textiles from Africa, oil from the North Sea, and appliances from Korea flow to the United States in bulk. We send back Pentium computer chips, Donna Karan dresses, KFC chicken, and *Spiderman* DVDs.

Today, every market is open to every product. American sit-coms play on television in Kiev. Operators in India make telemarketing calls to the American Midwest. Kids in Australia play video games on the Sony PlayStation or the Microsoft Xbox. Movie audiences in Senegal watch musical romances produced in Bombay. And teenagers in Vancouver download world music tracks recorded by artists in Ecuador and Indonesia.

Globalization is great for the creative growth of business. But it also facilitates the worldwide spread of Islamic terrorism from its sources in the Middle East. In the globalized world, any individual or group can organize, proselytize, and carry out violent actions wherever they like. Terrorists have access to information that allows them to design and build powerful weapons; they have access to trucks, planes, and boats that allow them to move themselves and their weapons with near impunity. In short, we live in a world that makes it easy to organize and execute plans of mass destruction. The same forces of globalization that make it possible for terrorists to strike at Americans anywhere, anytime have contributed enormously to the friction between Islam and the West. And there is a rich irony in the way Islamist leaders have turned the West's modern technology against its inventors to build a caliphate based on feudal, seventh-century theology.

We've already seen that Osama bin Laden's hatred for America was triggered in part by the U.S.-led Gulf War and the subsequent stationing of American troops in Saudi Arabia. In bin Laden's mind, this amounts to a desecration of holy ground. Thus it is largely the projection of U.S. force into Muslim territory that provokes the fundamentalists' rage.

But the globalization of information, technology, and transportation means that the projection of U.S. might around the world isn't only a matter of airfields, battleships, or armored divisions. It's also a matter of American corporations, American movies and music, and American values that rankle our foes and some of our friends.

Allies including France and Canada have clashed with the United States over the ubiquity and intrusiveness of American popular culture. Even red-white-and-blue Americans such as Pat Robertson and Tipper Gore are horrified by some aspects of our culture. Now imagine the feelings of Islamic fundamentalists who see a world increasingly dominated by an American culture that represents everything they fear and loathe: sexual license, materialism, lack of respect for authority, breakdown of gender roles, mockery of traditional religion, open political debate. No wonder they feel threatened by the unchallenged global power of the United States and are determined to strike back by any means available.

Our Other Foes

Today, the primary focus of our antiterror efforts is al-Qaeda and the groups that it supports. But there are many other organizations that we in the West need to be secure against tomorrow.

The most obvious are the other Islamic terrorist groups, including Hamas, Hezbollah, and Palestinian Islamic *Jihad*. These groups share the grievances of other extreme Muslim groups against Western-style democracies, particularly the United States. Members of these groups have already attacked and killed Americans. At the moment, they are focusing their anger on adversaries in the Middle East, particularly Israel. But that could change at any time. These groups are made up of well-trained, well-funded suicidal extremists who could pose a real danger to the West.

Another source of potential danger are the so-called rogue states: nations ruled by regimes that either refuse to recognize international law or have a history of repeatedly flouting that law in secret. These countries endanger the world through their ability to produce weapons of mass destruction and deliver them either through conventional military means, such as missiles, or nonconventional means, such as container ships or airliners. I have no doubt that within the next fifteen years the United States will be faced with the open hostility of a third world country armed with nuclear weapons. We must prepare to deal with that threat today.

The list of rogue states changes from time to time. I place Iraq, North Korea, and Sudan near the top of today's roster. Iran and Libya could join the list at any time. And intelligence analysts have told me that Pakistan and Indonesia represent the two countries most likely to be taken over by Muslim radicals. Pakistan, our putative ally in the terror war, is an enormous potential threat—I have nightmares about waking up one morning to the news that General Musharraf has been overthrown and that Muslim extremists now control Pakistan's arsenal of nuclear weapons.

I believe that the list of rogue states will invariably expand as the economic and cultural gap between the world's have and have-not peoples increases. What happens if Indonesia becomes destabilized? More Muslims live in Indonesia than in any other nation, and the extremist wing of Islam is waiting for an opportunity to seize power there.

The rogue states are working to develop the capability of threatening the United States directly. But I believe the indirect threat they pose through their backing of terrorist forces is even greater.

The United States and its Western allies can deal with the military threat from any sovereign state, as illustrated most recently by our quick and historic victory over the Taliban in Afghanistan. But the threat posed when a country covertly sponsors terrorism is much harder to deal with. When terrorists are given safe harbors in which to plan, train, and arm themselves, the risk to the world grows exponentially. Syria and Iran have aided terrorists; Libya formerly did so.

Non-Islamic political and economic groups sometimes cross over into fomenting violence as well. Today there is a large, loosely organized collection of international groups that might be labeled anarchist in tendency. They represent the extreme fringes of world politics, often focused on single hot-button issues: abortion, international corporate power, economic globalization, environmentalism, global warming, animal rights. A few extremists in these movements threaten the use of violence to advance their positions. I believe that some of these modern-day anarchists will become the Symbionese Liberation Armies and the Red Brigades of the future.

Finally, there are the ultranationalists. These groups, which exist in almost every country, from the breakaway Soviet republic of Chechnya to the Basque region of Spain, represent a very real danger that will increase along with their access to weapons of mass destruction. The United States is not immune to this danger. Our ultranationalists are a loose collection of white supremacists and militia organizations that have already used violence to publicize their paranoid message. Timothy McVeigh, who believed America was becoming a totalitarian state, did not hesitate to kill hundreds of innocent men, women, and children when he attacked the United States government as represented by the Federal Building in Oklahoma City. If he'd somehow gotten access to a nuclear weapon, would he have hesitated to use it? I'm afraid not.

In recent months, rumors have circulated about possible connections between some of these non-Islamic terror groups and the Muslim fundamentalists. These rumors have at least a tinge of plausibility. After all, although groups such as al-Qaeda and Aryan Nation have widely differing worldviews, they do have a handful of similarities; for example, both are deeply anti-Semitic. However, I can tell you that, based on all the current information I've seen, there is no evidence of any cooperative link between the Islamic terrorists and any non-Islamic terror organizations. So far that particular nightmare does not seem to have materialized.

Nonetheless, the world we live in is a dangerous one and far more complex than the one we grew up in. The monolithic threat posed by the Soviet arsenal during the Cold War has been superseded by the dangers from a shadowy assortment of new foes around the world. The one thing they have in common is an abiding hatred of America and the rest of the West, and a willingness to attack our people by any means available. In the next chapter, we'll consider some of the terrible new tools of violence that are now finding their ways into the hands of these implacable enemies.

The Threats We Face

Now that we know the nature of the enemies we face, what about the threats they pose? How is it possible that people from thousands of miles away can endanger the health and safety of our citizens here at home? The answer lies in the kinds of explosives and weaponry created over the past century, which modern manufacturing, communication, and transportation methods can put into the hands of almost anyone anywhere, even those with modest means and limited technological expertise.

In this chapter, we'll consider the kinds of weapons that terrorists can now deploy and discuss the dangers they pose to America.

Low-Tech Attacks

There has been a lot of attention paid to the potential for terrorists to obtain or manufacture weapons of mass destruction and deliver them to a target inside our borders. There are good reasons for those concerns, as we will see later in this chapter, but the most immediate danger we face is from conventional weapons.

In the hundreds of attacks by terrorists in the past decade, only a couple have involved high-tech methods, such as the sarin nerve gas attack on the Tokyo subway system by members of a cult, and none of those has been traced back to Islamic extremists. All the rest have been low-tech, if deadly, assaults that employed guns, explosives, hostage taking, and so on. Furthermore, people who have been in the field in Israel and Afghanistan and have seen al-Qaeda training manuals tell me that Islamic terrorist groups have focused on training their operatives to do maximum damage with limited funds, facilities, and logistical support.

Bombings are perhaps the most common form of terrorist attack, as bombs are relatively cheap to build and easy to hide and transport. During the last two years, Israel's public transportation system has been attacked 114 times, resulting in the deaths of 171 people. The vast majority of these attacks took place on buses and were perpetrated by suicide bombers.

The West has also been the victim of random terrorist bombings. Until recently, London averaged seven bombings a year, mostly the work of the Irish Republican Army (IRA). The United States suffered two serious terrorist bombings in the last decade: the 1993 truck bombing at the World Trade Center by Islamic terrorists and the 1995 truck bombing in Oklahoma City by Timothy McVeigh. Recently we have seen devastating car bombings in Bali, the Philippines, Pakistan, and Kenya, all apparently in retaliation for the West's war on terrorism.

We have seen in the Middle East just how difficult it is to stop a determined bomber. Over the last sixty years, since the time of the British occupation of Palestine and the 1946 bombing of the King David Hotel by Jewish partisans, terrorist bombings have been part of the landscape. Yet in all that time no one has devised a method for stopping such attacks. In response to attacks by the IRA, Britain enacted legislation that allowed for preventive detention and the use of coerced confessions. The Israelis have the world's most vigilant civilian population; a system of guards, searches, and intelligence that is second to none; and an aggressive response system aimed at stopping the bombers at their bases. Still, the bombings continue. Add to this the recent willingness of bombers to die in their own attacks, and the difficulties are multiplied. Indeed, we can expect this tactic to be used as long as it continues to be successful.

A spate of car and truck bombings like those endemic to the Middle East is likely to come to our shores, and, unfortunately, soon. We Americans have a better opportunity to thwart such attacks than any other nation. We have unique benefits of geography and technology. But we must understand the problem before we can develop a system for stopping it.

The same goes for other low-tech terrorist techniques. In October 2002 residents of the Washington, D.C., area were shocked by how effectively a team of two snipers could paralyze a community of several million people. During that same period, we saw a group of heavily armed Chechen rebels take over a theater in central Moscow; after a siege and commando raid at dawn by Russian forces, most of the Chechens and many hostages were killed. Incidents like these can be expected to continue and to multiply in the years to come.

Our transportation system, America's economic lifeline, lacks sufficient security to protect against the range of attacks that al-Qaeda has threatened. We know from various failed attempts that Islamic extremists have focused on interrupting our transportation infrastructure—as in the thwarted plot to bomb New York City's Holland Tunnel in 1993. What is worrisome, though, is that al-Qaeda has proven to be a patient and determined enemy, one that learns from its mistakes and improvises new methods of attack.

While there has been much debate about securing our airports, the November 2002 terror attacks in Kenya—in which two shoulder-fired missiles barely missed an Israeli passenger jet carrying 270 people (and an Israeli-owned hotel was bombed)—highlighted a little-discussed, but worrisome threat to commercial aviation: small, portable, shoulder-fired missiles, like the American-made Stinger missiles used by the *mujahidin* against the Soviets in Afghanistan. These weapons, technically known as MANPADs (man-portable air defense systems), are distressingly cheap, widely available, easy to smuggle, and effective. Typically five feet long and weighing less than 35 pounds, a shoulder-fired missile travels at 1,500 miles an hour and can destroy an aircraft up to four miles away. Airliners—which fly on a set schedule, and travel slowly and in a straight line at take-off and landing—are extremely vulnerable to such missiles. At the moment there is no viable way to protect commercial jets from shoulder-launched missiles, nor is there much debate about how to do so. Yet twice—in 1997 and 2001—smugglers have been arrested in Florida attempting to bring MANPADs into America. I fear we will be hearing more about these weapons in the near future.

Every day large fleets of trucks travel from city to city on our nation's highways: they are easy to take for granted, until you think of them as fuel-laden weapons ripe for stealing. Many carry hazardous materials; in fact eight hundred thousand loads of hazardous cargo travel our highways each day, while fuel trucks, each carrying as much fuel as a Boeing 757, make another fifty thousand trips on our roads. These trucks can often be found sitting unattended in unguarded lots for hours at a time.

In the last year, terrorists have used trucks as bombs in three separate incidents. On April 11, 2002, on the Tunisian island of Djerba, a truck carrying liquefied natural gas was ignited in front of Africa's oldest synagogue, killing nineteen people (mostly European tourists). And in May and August 2002 remotely triggered bombs were attached to fuel tanker trucks and detonated in Israel. There's no reason similar attacks cannot occur in the United States. But so far our response to this danger has been paltry. Congress has earmarked a mere $500,000 a year for classes intended to raise truckers' awareness of unusual behaviors.

The vulnerability of our transportation system is compounded by the absence of policing at our land and sea borders. Containers arriving in the United States from overseas ports don't even go through an inspection process until they reach their final destination. For example, a container arriving in New York from Germany with a final destination of Chicago will be hoisted off a cargo ship and fastened onto either a truck or train and permitted to travel across and through our country without being inspected until it arrives in Chicago.

These containers could hold just about anything. Shortly after

September 11, a cargo ship destined for Toronto from Italy was found to be housing an al-Qaeda operative. He had equipped the container with a bed and makeshift bathroom, and he had in his possession an airline mechanic's certificate and security passes for three airports in Canada, Thailand, and Egypt.

Just think of the damage a container filled with weapons detonated remotely by cell phone could do. As Stephen Flynn, former U.S. Coast Guard commander, aptly states:

> If a missile was fired at a U.S. city and it could not be intercepted, it could cause horrible destruction and mass casualties. But if a weapon of mass destruction were loaded on a boat, truck, train, or maritime container and set off in a congested seaport, on a bridge during rush hour, or downtown in a major urban center, the results would be even worse. In addition to the local destruction and casualties, such an attack would expose the lack of credible security within the country's transportation networks and bring them to a complete standstill. The first scenario would involve damage caused by the adversary; the second would include both the damage caused by the adversary and the costs associated with a self-applied tourniquet to our global transport lifelines.

Maritime terrorism is another concern. Attacks on ships in our harbors and at sea could disrupt global commerce and the peaceful use of the oceans. In the past, terrorists have reportedly used submersibles, minisubs, and high-speed boats rigged with explosives and rocket-propelled grenades to attack targets in Latin America, Europe, the Middle East, and Asia. Imaginative terrorists can come up with a dozen scary scenarios of seagoing terrorism. For example, maritime security consultant Robert Bevelacqua warns that terrorists could sink a ship in a narrow commercial channel, thereby blocking vital imports from our shores. And cruise ships are not well protected.

Even our naval ships are vulnerable, as evidenced by al-Qaeda's attack on the USS *Cole* (and an earlier, failed attack on the USS *The Sullivans*). Largely unnoticed by the media, such maritime incidents are increasing. The International Maritime Bureau reported a total of 469 attacks on ships in 2000, resulting in seventy-two seafarers being killed and ninty-nine injured—a startling increase from three killed and twenty-four injured in 1999.

America's energy infrastructure is equally vulnerable to attack. The implications of an attack on our nation's power plants, power lines, gas pipelines, and power facilities would go far beyond economic disruption. It would cause widespread panic and anxiety about America's future. In 2002 former senators Gary Hart and Warren B. Rudman, in their report "America Still Unprepared—America Still in Danger," noted that our electric power systems are vulnerable to both physical and cyber attacks. According to their report, "a coordinated attack on a selected set of key points in the electrical power system could result in multi-state blackouts." Certain congested power lines are particularly critical to the operation of the power grid and its security.

Electricity isn't our only concern. The penetration of a nuclear power plant or a dam by terrorist operatives could be devastating to the surrounding areas. Sixteen years after the Chernobyl meltdown, the area within a six-mile radius surrounding the Chernobyl nuclear reactor is still uninhabitable. Imagine the horror that could be caused by a deliberate attack on a facility such as the Indian Point reactor in the northern suburbs of New York City. Our nuclear facilities were constructed with the threat of an attack in mind, but new methods of sabotage have made the security built into these facilities obsolete. For example, they were not built to withstand the force of an impact from a commercial jet.

The oil and gas pipelines that crisscross North America are far too extensive to patrol. Hence they too remain exposed to potential terror attacks. Two acts of sabotage on the trans-Alaska pipeline system highlight our vulnerabilities. In 1987 vandals blew up a small section of the line with conventional explosives, causing a seven-hundred-thousand-barrel spill. In October 2001 a gunman fired a bullet through the pipeline. It took thirty-six hours for technicians to stop the leak.

I have described only a handful of the kinds of low-tech terror assaults that our enemies could launch. Further possibilities are limited only by the imagination of the terrorists. The examples I have given, however, may suffice to suggest the breadth and complexity of the security challenges we face, even when only conventional weapons are considered. Once weapons of mass destruction enter the equation, the picture becomes even more grim.

Chemical and Biological Weapons

While chemical and biological agents are both considered weapons of mass destruction (WMD) and require some of the same kind of responses, they are in fact quite different from one another. *Chemical agents* can kill or injure within minutes, and require an immediate lights-and-sirens response that includes antidotes and a system of decontamination. *Biological agents* can take days or weeks to harm. Smallpox, for example, can take seven to seventeen days to develop; glanders can take ten to fourteen days, and brucella can take five to sixty days. But all can cause potentially major public health emergencies that require response from a strong public health system.

Fears about both kinds of attack have increased lately, in part because of the stalled investigation into 2001's anthrax-laden letters, in part because of documents and intelligence gathered from captured Taliban and al-Qaeda members. This information provides clear and convincing evidence of the development of chemical and biological weapons, and efforts to learn how to deliver them effectively. Add to the mix the occasionally sensationalistic media speculation about such possibilities as chemical attacks using crop-dusting planes or the poisoning of city water supplies, and it's understandable that millions of Americans are nervous about these technological weapons, even though most people know very little about them.

Unfortunately, the anxieties are well-founded. Government officials have long worried about the potential use of WMDs by al-Qaeda. In the 1990s, both the CIA and the FBI had hard evidence that al-Qaeda was attempting to develop WMDs. President Clinton was briefed by experts as to the possible consequences of an attack on American cities using such weapons. Other WMD programs are known to exist, such as the Iraqi bioweapons program directed by Dr. Rihab Taha—the forty-seven-year-old woman widely feared as "Dr. Germ." In a 1998 speech at the National Press Club, Secretary of Defense William Cohen specifically warned about a bioterrorist attack, saying:

> Our American military superiority presents a paradox . . . because our potential adversaries know they can't win in a conventional challenge to the U.S. forces, they're more likely to try unconventional or asymmetrical methods, such as biological or chemical weapons.

In the event of a chemical or biological attack, local governments must be prepared to handle the initial crisis. During each type of attack, a window of opportunity exists in which first responders can take action to reduce the incidence of death and severe illness. For a chemical attack, the window is very short, only minutes to three hours; for a biological attack, the window is one day to weeks.

The federal response will focus on postincident support, long-term patient care, decontamination of the affected areas, management of the deceased, investigation of the attack, and funding of disaster assistance.

Chemical Agents As the name suggests, chemical warfare is the use of toxic chemicals, such as pesticides, nerve gas, choking agents, blister agents, and pulmonary agents, to damage or kill humans, animals, and plants. Various chemical agents differ in their operation. Cyanide and other nerve agents can cause death within minutes and require immediate medical attention, whereas sulfur mustard and other pulmonary agents take hours to show their effects.

Chemical warfare is extraordinarily efficient. Small amounts of readily available chemicals—such as chlorine or cyanide—could, if delivered effectively, kill tens of thousands of Americans in a matter of hours. It's frighteningly easy to create chemical weapons. Many of the solids, liquids, and gases used in various combinations to sicken or kill are commonly available dual-use products.

The first chemical warfare agent to be used in battle was based on the common chemical chlorine. Chlorine gas was used at the 1915 Battle of Ypres, in Belgium, by German troops against the British, to devastating effect. Later in the war, both sides used mustard gas, a blister agent, which also inflicted heavy casualties. Chlorine still has terrifying potential as a weapon. The derailment of a large chlorine tanker car (by a small bomb, for example) could virtually wipe out the population of a town or a small city.

Cyanide, which is frequently used in the manufacturing of jewelry and as an agricultural poison, is another deadly chemical. So are common insecticides such as malathion.

While armies around the world have created a wide variety of munitions to disseminate weaponized chemicals, including bombs, artillery shells, missiles, grenades, and mines, there are many more mundane ways to spread these agents. Crop-dusting planes, suitcase-sized generators, and even hand pumps or underarm-deodorant spray cans could serve as effective aerosol generators.

A terrorist using one of these low-tech methods is likely to spray a chemical agent upwind of a city or business area for maximum effect. A malathion spray could kill hundreds of people if spread by, say, an ordinary pesticide disperser mounted on the back of a pickup truck. In fact, on a number of occasions, terrorists have reportedly attempted to contaminate office workers by using jerry-built pumps to mist chemical agents into the ventilation systems of individual buildings. Thankfully, they have been unsuccessful so far.

Biological Agents According to the 1972 biological weapons convention, biological warfare is the "use for hostile purposes of living organisms . . . or infective material derived from them, which are intended to cause disease or death in man, animals, or plants."

Biological agents are less commonly available than chemical agents, but far more deadly. Compare, for example, the biological agent anthrax with the nerve gas sarin. Ten grams of anthrax may produce as many casualties as 100,000 grams (1 metric ton) of sarin. Similarly, botulinum toxin is fifteen thousand times more toxic than VX (a viscous chemical) and a hundred thousand times more toxic than sarin.

Biological warfare dates back at least as far as 1346, when Tatar invaders laid siege to the city of Kaffa in what is now Ukraine. When Tatars began dying of bubonic plague, which is transmitted by fleas, they catapulted bodies of the victims over the city walls hoping to spread plague inside the city. The defenders included Genoese merchants who fled Kaffa and took the disease back to Italy, thereby helping to spread the Black Death throughout continental Europe.

America has a long history with biological warfare. In 1763 Sir Jeffrey Amherst, commander of British forces in North America, allegedly presented his enemies, the local Indians, with smallpox-laden blankets and other gifts. Subsequently, smallpox nearly wiped out the tribes.

Although biological warfare was officially prohibited by the 1925 Geneva Convention, the practice has continued sporadically. Japan's notorious Unit 731 conducted extensive, grisly biological experiments on Manchurian civilians and Western prisoners of war in the 1930s and 1940s. This research was later co-opted by the United States, which had established its own program at Camp Detrick, Maryland. Despite another agreement, signed in 1972, prohibiting biological warfare, the United States and Soviet Union continued to test and stockpile these highly controversial weapons.

Experts that I have spoken to believe that biological weapons are attractive to terrorists for four main reasons. First, they are relatively easy to obtain; some of them can be culled from the soil, others from beans or dead animals. Second, they are relatively inexpensive to produce. Third, a biological attack is hard to detect, as most biological agents are odorless, colorless, and tasteless, and the technology to detect them is still under development. Finally, the sheer potency of biological weapons makes them ideal for spreading terror throughout a society. After a major biological attack, the hundreds of thousands of potential casualties could quickly overwhelm the resources of treatment centers, possibly leading to riots, mass flight, and others forms of civic collapse.

For all these reasons, the United States acknowledges that biological weapons demand a greater degree of preventive scrutiny than conventional or chemical weapons.

While it's hard to predict which biological agents a terrorist might attempt to use, government and civilian experts have identified the most dangerous agents, including anthrax, smallpox, botulism, plague, tularemia, and viral hemorrhagic fevers, and have begun to build a knowledge base for diagnosing and treating the diseases they cause. Below is a chart of some of the most likely pathogens that might be used against us and the time between exposure and onset of the disease (incubation):

Threat Agent	Incubation Time
Bacillus anthracis (anthrax)	1–6 days
Yersinia pestis (plague)	2–3 days
Brucella spp.	5–60 days
Burkholderia spp. (glanders)	10–14 days
Francisella tularensis	1–21 days
Botulinum toxin	1–2 hrs
Ricin	1–2 hrs
Staph enterotoxin B	1–2 hrs
Variola virus (smallpox)	7–17 days
Venezuelan equine virus	1–5 days

CHART: Sceptor Industries

In defending against a biological attack, the first challenge is to recognize that a release has occurred and to do so quickly enough to provide time for an effective response. Because incubation times are commonly measured in days, until recently the only way to detect a possible biological attack was to monitor broad public health trends. Such "syndromic surveillance" detects spikes in disease or death and identifies the communities affected. However, it may not be able to identify the specific cause of such a spike. People in the target area could be falling ill or dying because of a heat wave, a flu epidemic, or an intentional spraying of anthrax spores. Syndromic surveillance couldn't tell the difference.

Now a number of automated biological detection systems that collect and identify airborne pathogens are under development. The U.S. Postal Service, for example, is testing a high-speed system that collects and detects biological threats in near real time (i.e., in as little as fifteen to twenty minutes after exposure). Most monitoring systems, however, will take longer to produce accurate results. Biological detection stations could be put into an office tower's heating, ventilation, and air-conditioning (HVAC) system, for example, or placed in strategic locations around a building. On-site analysis would give preliminary results in an hour or two, while lab analysis would yield more detailed results within one or two days. This is fast enough to make timely treatment possible. These technologies are still being tested but should be commercially available soon.

The United States is blessed with one of the world's most effective public health systems. However, our response to the potential threat of biological warfare has been spotty at best. The controversy over the government's official smallpox vaccination plan typifies the problem. Critics worry that current vaccines are crude and potentially dangerous, while others argue that the vaccines are safe and should be given to every American. As the debate rages, no clear plan has been developed to forestall panic and minimize the damage from a smallpox attack.

Nuclear Weapons

One of the most frightening potential threats that terrorism currently poses is the danger of a so-called dirty bomb. A dirty bomb is a conventional explosive that is laced with low-grade radioactive materials. When the bomb is detonated, the radioactive debris scatters. As with any conventional explosion, the blast itself would likely kill or injure people in the immediate vicinity. The scattered radioactive material would also expose people over several city blocks. How many people would be injured and how large an expanse would be contaminated would depend on the bomb's sophistication, how windy it was on that particular day, and how efficiently the area was evacuated. If all these conditions worked in our favor, the damage might be no greater than that of a conventional bomb blast.

Dirty bombs can range in size from as small as a few sticks of dynamite to as large as a truck bomb. Perhaps the most significant difference between a dirty bomb and a conventional one is the psychological and economic impact of an attack. Panic, terror, and confusion—three primary objectives of terrorism—would likely grip the public in the wake of a dirty bomb attack. Mass evacuations could wreak havoc on our roads. And the cleanup of ground zero could take months or even years, rendering the area virtually uninhabitable and costing billions of dollars.

While it is no more difficult to build a dirty bomb than a conventional bomb, obtaining the radioactive material makes it a challenge. Fortunately, the most destructive radioactive materials, such as plutonium and uranium, are the hardest to acquire and, of course, the most difficult to handle. A bomb maker could easily kill himself and his partners just fastening the materials together.

Nevertheless, there exists a significant black market in nuclear materials. According to the International Atomic Energy Agency, there is evidence of at least 175 nuclear smuggling incidents since 1993, 18 of which involved highly enriched uranium. Al-Qaeda leader Osama bin Laden and his operatives made repeated attempts to purchase these materials in the 1990s.

Another potent source of materials for dirty bombs is the spent fuel rods from the more than 550 reactors and nuclear research centers around the world. While some of these reactors are no longer operating, most of them continue to store spent nuclear fuel. Security at these aging facilities is a major concern, especially in the economically struggling countries of the former Soviet bloc. Even security at the United States' 104 commercial nuclear reactors isn't above criticism.

An even greater source for radioactive materials is the medical, industrial, and research facilities around the world. The materials we employ to irradiate our food and sterilize our medical equipment could easily be used by terrorists in the assembly of a dirty bomb. However, while the detonation of a crude dirty bomb would cause considerable havoc, exposure to such low levels of radiation would likely sicken those contaminated, not kill them.

While dirty bombs are deadly, nuclear weapons can be thousands of times more devastating. How likely is it that al-Qaeda or other terrorists could build their own nuclear weapons? At the moment, not very. Building a nuclear weapon requires money, technological infrastructure, and a highly skilled team of physicists, metallurgists, chemists, engineers, explosives experts, and machinists. Even with all of these factors in place, the would-be bomb maker would still need enough highly enriched uranium or plutonium to sustain a complex nuclear-fission reaction.

For two decades Iraq has attempted to build a nuclear weapon. In 1981 Israel bombed and destroyed Saddam Hussein's Osiraq nuclear reactor, derailing Iraq's nuclear efforts. After the 1991 Gulf War, Iraq's weapons program was again dismantled, this time by United Nations inspectors. It is widely believed that Iraq was within a couple of years of obtaining enough uranium to build a weapon when the inspectors arrived. If a relatively advanced, powerful state such as Iraq, with money, expertise, and infrastructure, can't pull off the creation of a nuclear weapon, the chances are good that al-Qaeda won't be able to either.

The question then becomes, if the terrorists can't build a nuclear weapon, can they buy or steal one?

After the breakup of the Soviet Union, the threat of "loose nukes" falling into the wrong hands became very real. The term refers both to poorly guarded nuclear weapons and to the nuclear materials and expertise necessary to build them. In its heyday, the Soviet Union had approximately twenty-seven thousand nuclear weapons and enough nuclear materials to triple that number. Where are these nuclear materials today? Mostly sitting in storage sites and power plants, being watched by demoralized guards, who are lucky if they get paid. Even basic security precautions at these locations, such as fences, doors, and padlocks, are often defective.

Russia's own internal security agencies claim to have broken up hundreds of nuclear-material smuggling deals and seized technology documents that had fallen into the wrong hands. In October 2001 Russian authorities reported thwarting two separate incidents during the previous eight months, in which a secret weapons storage site was being staked out by terrorists. Another equally worrisome threat is the potential for unemployed former Soviet nuclear scientists to sell their skills to the highest bidder.

There has been much speculation in the press about Soviet "suitcase bombs" and the possibility that bin Laden has acquired one or more of these weapons. A suitcase bomb is a transportable nuclear weapon about the size of a large suitcase (measuring roughly 60 by 40 by 20 centimeters). If detonated, a suitcase bomb could wipe out an area approximately half a mile in radius. In a densely populated city, such an area might include a hundred thousand people or more. Radioactive fallout would kill many more beyond this area. Most frightening of all, suitcase bombs, originally designed for use in sabotage missions, can be detonated in approximately half an hour from a remote location.

Several Soviet suitcase bombs were reported missing by Russian general Alexander Lebed in 1997. His statement was bolstered by the arrest of two Russians in Miami in 1997 for offering to sell an undercover U.S. Customs agent a suitcase nuke. Reports are now circulating that bin Laden's operatives received an untold number of these bombs from the Chechen mafia in exchange for $30 million and two tons of Afghan heroin. However, we have seen no hard evidence to support these claims, and none of the experts I have consulted believes al-Qaeda has access to such weapons.

The United States has found evidence that al-Qaeda has been accumulating information on the subject of nuclear weapons. A twenty-five-page document was discovered in an abandoned house in Afghanistan that included a design for a nuclear weapon. Bin Laden has declared that acquiring nuclear weapons is a "religious duty." "If I have indeed acquired [nuclear] weapons," he once said, "then I thank God for enabling me to do so."

The Motive, the Weapon . . . the Opportunity?

We've seen, then, that the United States and other Western nations are today confronted by a collection of ruthless, determined adversaries with long-standing grievances against America and its allies. We've also seen that modern technology has placed weapons of unprecedented power in the hands of those adversaries. The next question is, what have we done so far to protect our land, our cities, and our citizens? We'll address that issue in the next chapter.

Chapter 4

National Security: The Missing System

As we've seen, the United States is at enormous risk for further attacks by Islamic extremists. Despite the danger, America has no true system of national security. What we have is a hodge-podge of programs that lack focus, coordination, detail, and leadership. The terrorists are nimble, terribly creative, and so deeply committed to their backward-looking version of Islam that they are willing to martyr themselves to kill our citizens and destroy the symbols of our power. And they have at their disposal frightful weapons capable of doing terrible damage to millions of Americans.

Washington's jumbled efforts are epitomized by a report issued by the Office of Homeland Security in July 2002 entitled *National Strategy for Homeland Security*. It condenses into a single document an overview of the terrorist threat to America, a strategy to meet the threat, and the tactics for implementing that strategy. The report was a worthwhile idea, and Tom Ridge and the various agency personnel who contributed to it faced an immensely difficult task. Nonetheless, the report must be considered a failure.

The *National Strategy* document makes many valuable suggestions. In the area of airline security, it calls for screening all bags (both carry-ons and checked bags) for explosives and for the matching of bags to individual passengers. It urges better training for first responders (police, fire, and ambulance crews) in how to deal with biological, chemical, and other forms of terrorism. It calls for an expansion of the proactive analytical capabilities of our intelligence agencies. All of these are sensible ideas.

However, the report fails to articulate a *detailed* and *integrated* approach to the terrorist threat. The individual ideas remain just that: Individual ideas that don't work together to make life more difficult for terrorists. And there is no plan for a flexible, graduated response as terror threats grow in seriousness. It's a one-size-fits-all-circumstances approach, which experience shows is rarely of lasting value.

The same is true of America's other responses to the attacks of September 11, 2001. Posting National Guard soldiers in airports or sending FBI agents door-to-door in search of terrorist cells may look good on the evening news, but in reality such steps are empty theatrical gestures. The effect is to give the nation a false sense of security and to protect Washington's sacred cows—the very people and agencies that have been so ineffective against terrorism for the last twenty years—rather than American citizens.

If we continue on this path, we risk our lives and, potentially, our way of life. If America suffers another terrorist attack, especially one that surpasses the attacks of September 11 in destructive power, our leaders may overreact and sweep aside the civil liberties we often take for granted. In fact, we seem to be incrementally losing some important rights without increased security. This would be a victory for the terrorists, for they will have succeeded in fundamentally changing America for the worse.

In the following chapters, I will lay out my plan for just such a framework. It includes a host of basic, cost-effective measures to build a meaningful system of national security. First, however, a brief overview of some of the measures already in place, necessary background to understanding the kinds of changes I propose.

Today's Security Efforts

The Office of Homeland Security For months after September 11, the Bush administration rejected the idea that a cabinet-level office was needed to coordinate domestic security efforts. Instead, Pennsylvania governor Tom Ridge was appointed to serve as a presidential advisor on security and a liaison to the various existing agencies involved in security: the FBI, the CIA, the State Department, the National Transportation Safety Board, local police departments, the Department of Energy, and a host of others. Given the history of mutual distrust among many of these organizations and the sheer complexity of coordinating so many sets of activities without a clear mandate, congressional authorization, or budgetary clout, it's no wonder that Ridge was able to accomplish relatively little.

In June 2002 the Bush administration reversed itself and endorsed the notion of creating a cabinet-level security agency. They dubbed it the Department of Homeland Security (DHS), although I think a more accurate name would be "Department of *National* Security," since the reach of such a department must extend beyond our borders. As mapped by the administration, the DHS will combine the tasks of twenty-two federal agencies into one department, which represents the largest reorganization of the federal government since World War II. Over 170,000 employees will be affected, and the departmental budget will exceed $37 billion.

I agree with the creation of a DHS. But the one proposed is a dauntingly complex plan that has drawn criticism as a Rube Goldberg contraption, so complicated that it may take years to thoroughly sort out and get into efficient working shape. Moreover, there are some critical omissions that ensure a dysfunctional security effort. For example, why is the Secret Service included within DHS while the FBI remains in the Department of Justice? Why is the Coast Guard part of the DHS while the CIA's antiterrorist intelligence effort is not?

The White House plan creates a new bureaucracy without giving it the muscle needed to carry out its job. DHS has a wide range of broadly defined duties, but these do *not* include the responsibility for fighting terrorism inside the United States, which remains with the FBI. Furthermore, it will not collect and coordinate the flow of intelligence about terrorism generated by the CIA, the FBI, and the Department of Defense. By excluding DHS from those critical duties, the White House has rendered the department peripheral and betrayed its own lack of willingness to respond seriously to the terrorist threat.

As I write, Congress has just approved the DHS blueprint, after more than five months of political squabbling over civil service protections. This delay was outrageous! In the midst of a war on terrorism, in which days can make the difference between life and death, our leaders dickered over turf and procedural minutiae. This speaks volumes about Washington's true priorities. Instead of a meaningful debate about the role of the FBI or the impact domestic surveillance might have on our civil liberties, politicians were deadlocked over such things as who gets to control the hiring, firing, and promotion of workers at the DHS. What conclusion could anyone outside the Beltway draw but that the politicians in Washington do not have a clue?

Frankly, I see no connection between the department's mission and the president's desire for "flexibility" in making personnel decisions. The administration's stance on this issue seems to reflect its conservative approach to labor-management relations rather than any true concern about national security. It seems that both the president's team and the Democratic opposition would rather score ideological points than get the DHS up and running quickly—yet another reflection of our loss of focus on terrorism. What I saw in this mess was business as usual, which gave us 9/11 in the first place.

DHS, as currently conceived, does little more than shuffle bureaucratic boxes around with no gain in national security; it will take years, and billions of dollars, to get this humongous operation up and running. As Senator Robert C. Byrd, Democrat of West Virginia, recently put it: "we have talked a lot about homeland security, but we have done very, very little . . . [DHS is] a bureaucratic behemoth, complete with fancy, top-heavy directorates, officious new titles and noble sounding missions instead of real tools to help protect [the people] from death and destruction. How utterly irresponsible."

Threat Alerts The security advisory office headed by Tom Ridge has created a system of color-coded terrorist threat levels (the Homeland Security Advisory System), which it has been using since March 2002 in public communications. The system ranks terror threats according to five color levels: green, blue, yellow, orange, and red. The approach is analogous to the military Defcon ("Defensive Condition") system, which ranks the current national security risk according to numerical levels, from one through five. But there's a major difference between Defcon and the homeland security system. Each Defcon level is associated with a list of specific actions to be taken by the military. As the United States moves from a lower to a higher level of Defcon alert, extra planes carrying missiles are launched, leaves by military personnel are canceled, reserve troops are activated, and so on.

In contrast, a meaningful list of required responses has been created for the homeland security system. During the late summer of 2002, when Tom Ridge announced that the terrorist threat level was being increased from yellow to orange, mayors and police chiefs around the country complained that they had been given no instructions as to what this meant or how they ought to react. As a result of this vagueness, the system has been largely ignored and subjected to ridicule.

The government's continual stream of warnings about terrorists, presented without any qualifying detail about the threats or specific advice about how the public ought to modify its behavior in response, has either scared people unnecessarily or anesthetized them to future warnings. Communicating with the public about the dangers we face is crucial. But the way it is being done now is doing more harm than good, sowing confusion and undermining Americans' sense of confidence in the national leadership.

Airport Security The Bush administration's current airport security program is a mess. Many of the steps that have been taken are largely irrelevant to the real terrorist threat. And because they divert attention and resources from other, more worthwhile approaches, these steps are worse than useless; they are actually harmful.

We now have National Guard soldiers armed with M-16s in many airports. This makes me feel *less* rather than more secure, because these earnest young sentries are not given close-weapons training or antiterrorist combat techniques; if they start shooting their big guns inside an airport, the chances are good that innocent people will be hurt. This opinion has been echoed by every weapons training expert I have spoken to.

After September 11, much ink and oratory were devoted to debating how airline passengers ought to be screened. Unfortunately, most of the debate centered on relatively unimportant issues. For example, the qualifications, training, and supervision of the personnel charged with screening airport passengers are only part of the problem. It doesn't take a college degree to screen bags. And everyone in the security industry understands that such guard jobs are inherently mind-numbing. So it doesn't matter whether the checkpoints are staffed by government personnel, private employees, or union members. What does matter is the protocols and systems they follow. If the protocols and system are not right, the billions spent on improving quality of staff and training are a waste. That is exactly the position we are in today.

The way those protocols have been changed in the last year is also counterproductive. The attempt to ban all sharp instruments from carry-on luggage is a waste of time and billions of dollars. Trying to ban any and all objects that can be transformed into makeshift weapons, including nail files, golf clubs, and letter openers, is probably impossible. Therefore, we should allow most low-level sharp instruments back into carry-on bags.

Is this lunacy? No, it's common sense based on years of experience.

As a prosecutor working on the streets and in the jails of New York City, I have seen a nearly endless variety of commonplace items, from a ballpoint pen to a simple corkscrew to a high-heeled shoe, used as deadly weapons. Those weapons and countless others—shims made from pieces of bed frame, toothbrushes turned into stilettos—have been discovered inside our maximum-security prisons. Similarly, a psychiatric nurse I know who works in a hospital for deeply disturbed teenagers tells me that the most dangerous of these troubled kids manage to injure themselves and others using everything from shards of shattered CDs to pajama tie strings, the latter turned into makeshift garrotes or nooses. If we can't keep such items out of prisons or hospitals, where we have every security advantage, then we certainly can't keep them off commercial airplanes.

Yet the White House has devoted enormous quantities of time, money, and attention in an attempt to do precisely that. Instead, we need to concentrate on weapons that could destroy a plane, such as bombs, or weapons that could overcome our current defenses, such as guns. This simple policy change would free up literally billions of dollars that could be better spent on identifying and stopping the real dangers.

Another seemingly small but important change must be made in screening. Today, passengers and their luggage are screened at the security desk and then are often checked again at the gate, sometimes more than once. This is bad policy and a waste of precious time and money. Soon passengers will tire of repetitive screenings, and we will slip back into pre-9/11 apathy. Whatever screening we do should be done effectively and done once.

The current security plan, which calls for airports to X ray *every* checked bag and to ensure that every bag is tied to an identifiable passenger on the same flight, is scheduled to be in effect by January 1, 2003. Implementation of this program has already been delayed by a confused government bureaucracy, the high cost of providing the screening machinery to airports, and a host of questions about logistics and privacy. The best bag-screening machines available today sell for $1 million each; yet even with their advanced X-ray technology, it is estimated that nearly a quarter of screened bags will contain objects that are so dense they will fail the test and will have to be inspected by hand.

Imagine opening and searching one-quarter of all checked baggage! It would create a logistical nightmare and open a Pandora's box of questions about privacy, theft, and damage. How and where will we open all those bags? What happens if something is broken or stolen while they are open? What if the bags are locked? Will the search cause bags to miss the plane? Like almost everything we are doing to improve security now, it seems that we have no plan that anticipates these obvious questions.

Do all bags need to be screened? Maybe not if we had the national identification card system I propose in Chapter 7. This is a critical issue, one that's far more deserving of attention, and money, than the cover-your-rear screening procedures now in place.

Border Security Today, there is really no system in place for securing American borders against those who would do us harm. Every year, some four hundred and ninety million people cross U.S. borders, along with some twenty million cargo containers. Virtually none of these people or containers is stopped and searched. In order for a forty-foot container or an eighteen-wheel truck to be thoroughly inspected, it takes about three hours of work by five inspectors. In reality, inspectors at the Ambassador Bridge between Detroit, Michigan, and Windsor, Ontario—the world's biggest land border crossing—spend on average two minutes per truck. When we try to impose more serious security regimes, it causes enormous backups at the Canadian and Mexican borders. The U.S. Customs Service instituted more thorough screening after

September 11, for instance, but the resulting protests quickly forced Customs to back down and return to business as usual.

Our borders are not locked tight. This is a security hole we need to address. The best way to create a border security system that works is not to add more guards, but rather to invest in the technologies that track and block people's movements into the United States.

Port and Maritime Security Ninety-five percent of all non–North American trade arrives in the United States through 361 major ports, and very few of them are well protected. Seaports play a vital economic and military role for the United States, yet vulnerability studies of the nation's fifty largest ports will not be completed until sometime in 2007. Many of these ports stretch over thousands of acres of land, are used by millions of people every day, and can be reached by land, sea, or air. And they are wide open to attack.

In recent years, ship-borne energy and cargo imports have been consolidated in just a few superports, making these sites especially choice targets. The Port of Los Angeles, for example, is one of the ten busiest ports in the world. Approximately 43 percent of all containers arriving in the United States in 2001 came through Los Angeles and neighboring Long Beach. Some three thousand vessels flow in and out of Los Angeles Harbor every year. It has twenty-nine cargo terminals, handling everything from automobiles and dry bulk to oil and natural gas; six container terminals, handling eighty million metric tons of cargo every year; and three passenger terminals, handling some one million cruise ship passengers every year. There are military and petroleum facilities in the harbor, and major recreational, educational, and residential areas nearby.

The port's—and the nation's—vulnerability was demonstrated in the fall of 2002 by the port closures caused by a labor dispute. The result was a huge backup in shipments and a cost of some $1 billion per day to the U.S. economy. A terrorist attack could result in far worse losses. A simple maritime attack (like the one launched in Yemen against the USS *Cole*) against an oil tanker in the harbor could cripple southern California and shut down much of the nation's trade.

As the October 2002 Hart-Rudman report, *America Still Unprepared—America Still in Danger*, notes:

> If an explosive device was loaded in a container and set off in a port, it would almost automatically raise concern about the integrity of the 21,000 containers that arrive in U.S. ports each day and the many thousands more that arrive by truck and rail across U.S. land borders. A three-to-four week closure of U.S. ports would bring the global container industry to its knees. Mega-ports like Rotterdam and Singapore would have to close their gates to prevent boxes from piling up . . . trucks, trains, and barges would be stranded . . . boxes bound for the United States would have to be unloaded from their outbound ships. Service contracts would need to be renegotiated. As this system becomes gridlocked, so would much of global commerce.

A busy harbor such as Los Angeles provides terrorists with three main opportunities:

- *Threats to people.* An attack on a cruise ship passenger terminal or a large container facility could cause widespread mayhem and allow terrorists to access strategic facilities such as fuel depots.

- *Threat to structures.* The sinking of a vessel in a channel, the destruction of a nearby bridge, or the detonation of a bomb in a fuel storage or cruise ship facility would cause widespread destruction and death.

- *Threat of transshipment.* Every year twenty million containers enter our ports, only 2 percent of which are inspected. Terrorists could ship bombs to America and explode a biological or chemical weapon in one of our ports, many of which are symbolically important, have large populations, and are militarily significant.

The American Association of Port Authorities estimates the cost of adequate port security to be some $2 billion. So far, only $92.3 million in federal grants for this purpose has been authorized, and that money has not been doled out on the basis of ports' significance to the nation. The ports of Los Angeles and Long Beach, for example, requested $70 million in grants for security but have been given only $6.2 million. This is simply an inadequate response to a large gap in our national security system.

Nor are ships at sea necessarily safe. In October 1985 members of the Palestine Liberation Front, one of the groups that made up the PLO, hijacked the Italian luxury liner *Achille Lauro* in the Mediterranean, planted bombs around the ship, and held 413 crew and passengers hostage for two days. Demanding the release of fifty Palestinian prisoners held in various countries, the terrorists shot Leon Klinghoffer, a sixty-nine-year-old wheelchair-bound tourist from New York City, and dumped his body, in his wheelchair, into the Mediterranean. And in October 2002, the French tanker *Limburg* was rammed by a speedboat laden with explosives off the coast of al-Mukalla, Yemen, killing one Bulgarian crew member and leaking some ninety thousand barrels of crude oil into the Gulf of Aden. Given our lack of a comprehensive maritime security program, it is very possible that such attacks will occur with greater frequency, will involve large numbers of hostages and casualties, and could well take place in U.S. waters.

The U.S. Coast Guard provides the front line of maritime defense, but the service has been long treated as an ugly stepchild to the other services. Before September 11, the Coast Guard had suffered major funding reductions. Consequently, during fiscal years 2000 and 2001, it was forced to reduce operations by 30 percent. New funds have since been approved, but the Coast Guard remains stretched thin. Since September 11, the service has launched the largest homeland defense operation since World War II, using its cutters, aircraft, and small boats to protect navy vessels, cruise ships, nuclear power plants, and major ports such as New York, Boston, Seattle, and Long Beach. But with the Coast Guard's traditional missions still demanding attention, it seems clear that the service is ill-equipped to carry out its new antiterror functions.

Financial Tracking Lately, commentators have urged the global community to use financial regulations to track and halt terrorist activities. If the money supporting groups such as al-Qaeda can be frozen, the reasoning goes, so will the terrorists' attacks. The USA Patriot Act of 2002 included a series of financial provisions, one of which requires U.S. banks to know where all of their foreign correspondent banks get their cash from. Unfortunately, this is simply not realistic. How can Citibank, for example, be expected to monitor all of the transactions carried out by foreign banks with which it does business? It can't, and regulators have not tried very hard to enforce this requirement.

As a prosecutor in the BCCI case and through my work at Kroll, I have had extensive experience in tracking money and trying to discover its source. It is very difficult.

Trying to stem terrorist attacks by tracking the money behind them is likely to prove impossible. For one thing, terrorism doesn't cost very much, and the amounts transferred are generally negligible. It is estimated that the September 11 hijackings, the most ambitious and effective terrorist attacks to date, were financed for something in the high six figures, which is not much money by most business standards. Further, terrorists generally use low-tech methods, including simple exchanges of cash, to transfer money, which makes their finances almost impossible to monitor and control.

Citizen Informants In June 2002 Attorney General John Ashcroft proposed the Terrorist Information and Prevention (TIPS) program, which encouraged Americans to spy on one another. Under this program, civilians who had occasion to enter the houses and apartments of other citizens—package delivery workers and readers of utility meters, for example—would be asked to report on any suspicious activities they observed. The idea was a silly and dangerous one, reminiscent of the tactics used by totalitarian organizations like the Stasi (the former East German secret police) or the Soviet KGB. In every country where such tale-telling is socially and legally encouraged, the results have been pernicious. Neighbors report one another based on misunderstandings; a few use the program to act out grudges against others. Most of our citizens rightly scoffed at such a plan as antisocial and un-American. The TIPS program's minimal benefits were vastly outweighed by its high cost to our liberty and to the cohesiveness of our society. Not surprisingly, TIPS drew heavy criticism from both the political left and right, and became an embarrassment to the White House. The Homeland Security bill signed into law by President Bush in November 2002 included language that explicitly prohibited the program's implementation.

Racial and Ethnic Profiling Profiling is the use of group characteristics by law enforcement officials to identify potential targets to be investigated, detained, questioned, or searched. Over the past decade, profiling has generally been denounced as unfair and ineffective. In a few places, such as New Jersey in 1998, politicians who countenanced profiling by police departments have suffered at the polls as a result. Yet today this technique has come into vogue among politicians and law enforcement officers. Why? Because at first blush it seems to make perfect sense.

The Islamic terrorists who attacked the World Trade Center in 1993 and 2001 were all young men originally from the Middle East (fifteen of the nineteen hijackers were from Saudi Arabia alone). So, the argument goes, it makes sense to identify "them"—young Middle Eastern men—as a suspicious class, one that we should spy on, investigate, search, and detain. The cost to American liberty appears low.

But despite its simplistic appeal, such profiling is ineffective and destructive. During World War II, we identified people of Japanese descent who lived in America as a suspect ethnic group; our citizens harassed them, and the government placed over 110,000 of them in internment camps, as if they were prisoners of war. In truth, however, not a single Japanese American was ever convicted of treason during the war. The vast majority were loyal and patriotic Americans, and the famous 442nd Regimental Combat Team, made up of Japanese American soldiers, became one of the most highly decorated American combat units in the war. The internment of the Japanese Americans is a shameful blot in our national history.

Any policy that allows the state to categorize people as enemies simply because of their ethnic, religious, or racial background is unconstitutional and undermines American civil liberties. Furthermore, racial profiling is fool's gold. It's based on assumptions that are often invalid rather than on real information about individuals, and it casts too broad a net and is therefore inefficient. I know this from personal experience.

I am currently working as the court-appointed monitor of the Los Angeles Police Department (LAPD), a famously troubled organization. As such, I report to a federal judge about the LAPD's compliance with a consent decree between the Department of Justice and the City of Los Angeles. Among other things, the decree is meant to ensure that the LAPD does not engage in racial profiling, something it has been accused of in such notorious cases as the videotaped beating of Rodney King.

My up-close experience with the LAPD has made me all the more fervently opposed to racial profiling because of the justifiable, virulent backlash by the branded group and its ineffectiveness. Yet in September 2002 the State Department announced a new plan that makes racial profiling federal policy. For several years, nationals of Iraq, Iran, Libya, and Syria have been subject to fingerprinting and photographing upon entry to the United States because their governments have been designated as sponsors of terrorism by the State Department. In 2001, Sudan was added to the list. Under the new plan, the list will be expanded further to include what the Justice Department has vaguely termed, "certain nationals of other countries whom officials determine to be an elevated national security risk." Once they arrive here, these people will be subjected to government monitoring—whether or not they have any ties to terrorist organizations. The new information collected on foreign visitors will be loaded into the world's largest biometric database, the Integrated Automated Fingerprint Identification System, operated by the FBI.

I'm a strong proponent of having the government trace the whereabouts and activities of individuals who are personally linked to terrorism. And I favor using information technology to capture and analyze data about the movements of individuals into and around the United States. But singling out citizens of particular foreign countries for this treatment is a huge mistake. The effect will be to encourage the 1.2 billion Muslims around the world, the vast majority of whom are politically moderate and potential American allies, to distrust the United States as a bigoted and heavy-handed bully. Such tactics can only work against us. As Philip Heymann notes in his book *Terrorism and America*,

> by discriminating against an identifiable group of citizens of which the terrorists represent a radical fringe, it can reduce the reserve of loyalty and patriotism within this group and build a fund of hostility and fear, leading others to join the terrorist cause.

America should end all of its racial and ethnic profiling policies immediately, including the fingerprint policy mentioned above. The program's limited value weighs far too heavily on our constitutional rights, our image abroad, and what Joseph S. Nye Jr. calls America's "soft power." We are already seeing the world's almost unified abhorrence of this policy. And the world is right.

Does this mean we should never use any form of profiling? No. Profiling can be quite useful. But it means we should not employ profiles based on ethnicity, religion, or race. Profiling that uses rules-based criteria, such as suspicious acquaintances, travel patterns, or other terrorist-related behavior, can be very useful and should be pursued aggressively. Unfortunately, the existing databases that are supposed to link individuals to terrorist activities are inadequate, as are the systems to disseminate that information. Therefore, there is much work to be done before rules-based screening can be implemented. I will explain how such a program can and should be created in Chapter 7.

Electronic Surveillance and Wiretapping Electronic surveillance is the interception of private communications or images. It includes wiretapping, which is listening to a phone conversation; bugging, which is eavesdropping on conversations in a room or car; and videotaped surveillance, which is the recording of images of private actions. For simplicity's sake, I will refer to all of this activity as wiretapping, because that is the term I used as a prosecutor, when I oversaw dozens of surveillance operations.

Wiretapping is governed by a federal law, known as Title III, which allows the government to monitor a suspect under strictly defined rules and procedures. One set of rules governs wiretapping in criminal investigations; another, less stringent set governs wiretapping for the purposes of gathering national security intelligence. A court order is always needed before wiretapping can be done. To obtain such an order in a criminal case, the law-enforcement professionals must show that there is probable cause that certain designated felonies, such as murder and racketeering, will be discussed, and that they have exhausted all other law enforcement techniques.

Once the order is issued, wiretapping can be carried out within narrowly defined parameters. Privileged conversations, such as lawyer-client conferences, can't be taped. Neither can conversations that have nothing to do with criminal activity. Thus, if a mobster starts discussing his sex life, the detective who has tapped his line is required to stop listening. He or she can tap back in a few moments later. And after a specified period of time, usually thirty days, the court order expires and must be renewed if the surveillance is to continue.

Are these rules really followed by police departments and investigators? Actually, they are, much more so today than in the

past. One reason is technology. Today's sophisticated taping techniques make it very easy for the behavior of detectives to be checked
and analyzed after the fact. Any violations of the rules may result in
evidence being thrown out and a possible acquittal for the defen-
dant. The police understand this, and they generally are very serious
about sticking to the letter of the law on wiretapping.

Wiretapping can play a critical role in antiterrorist activity. To
plan an attack, the terrorists need to communicate with each other,
which gives law enforcement and intelligence operatives an opportunity to monitor them. Of course, they know about our ability to
intercept their e-mails and cell phone calls, and so our attempts to
do so involve an elaborate game of cat and mouse. The terrorists try
to communicate crucial information in code, by word of mouth in
secure locations, or through encrypted computer files, and we try
to penetrate these and other ruses.

The terrorists are smart, with a sophisticated understanding of
both our technical methods and of the rules restricting their use,
but my experience gives me hope that we can trip them up. As a
prosecutor, I supervised over one hundred investigations that involved wiretapping, and I learned that it is a powerful technique for
penetrating the most secretive groups, including the Mafia and
drug cartels. Criminals and terrorists are human, after all, and even
the most paranoid, vigilant conspirators make mistakes, especially
when they are under pressure from law enforcement. If we're patient and keep the pressure on, the terrorists *will* make mistakes
and reveal secrets in electronic or nonsecure conversations that are
bugged.

In one case that I remember vividly, the New York Police
Department was listening to two mafiosi speaking on the phone
about a meeting to transfer a shipment of heroin. One of the two
gangsters warned the other, "I think this line is tapped. Let's meet
tomorrow to make the deal." And he explained when and where,
using a code to prevent detection. He was right; we *had* wiretapped
his phone. But he didn't realize that we had also bugged his room.

He hung up the phone and told a buddy, "I'm meeting Sam tomorrow at Forty-seventh Street and Madison at three-thirty." We staked out the meeting place and watched the deal go down. Eventually both gangsters went to jail for a long, long time.

Civil libertarians dislike wiretapping. They rightly fear the chilling effect it can have on private and public discourse. A government that wiretapped its political enemies and used the secrets it uncovered for blackmail or to silence opposition through threats of public embarrassment would be a terrible threat to freedom. Thus wiretapping must be restricted to the narrowest technical means possible under the circumstances, and the uses of the information obtained must be strictly limited.

Wiretapping is a hot-button issue today. In November 2002 a special federal appeals court granted the Justice Department broad new authority to tap phone calls, monitor Internet use, intercept mail, and search the homes of ordinary Americans without probable cause of criminal activity. The ruling—which allows the government to remove the separation between officials investigating foreign agents and those investigating common criminals—has been controversial. Attorney General Ashcroft declared this shift "a giant step forward," while critics denounced it as an assault on the Fourth Amendment. The *New York Times* editorial page wrote: "The Supreme Court and Congress should reverse this misguided ruling."

This is a complex issue and I have a somewhat complex response.

In battling terrorists or other foreign agents, American law enforcement is currently allowed to use wiretaps for intelligence gathering, under the Foreign Intelligence Surveillance Act. This makes good sense. During the summer of 2001 FBI agents in Minnesota tracking alleged terrorist Zacarias Moussaoui were denied broader use of wiretaps because agency supervisors decided there was insufficient evidence for a warrant; we shouldn't lose such opportunities in the future. At the same time, any changes to the restrictions on wiretapping should be made with extreme deliberation and as part of a larger security effort. The new ruling does not fit these criteria.

I advocate giving a wide scope to the use of wiretapping for intelligence purposes, though always under systematic rules that require high-level executive approvals, congressional advice and consent, and oversight by the courts. With appropriate protections against abuse in place, wiretapping is a valuable tool for national security.

Military Force "We are at war with al-Qaeda. If we find an enemy combatant, then we should be able to use military forces to take military action against them," a Pentagon official said in 2002.

America has the world's biggest and most effective military, but history has taught us to pick and choose our battles with extreme caution. In routing the Taliban and al-Qaeda troops from Afghanistan during Operation Anaconda, the U.S. military waged an extremely quick and effective campaign. But as I mentioned earlier, there is a danger in believing that we will achieve the same kind of results in every conflict. There is more to war than battle, after all.

If we invade Iraq, for example, I am confident that American troops will prevail and that we can topple Saddam Hussein. But what will such a victory cost over the long run? If we act unilaterally and invade Iraq without Arab support, will we turn the world's Muslims into our enemies? Would such a war incite a new wave of Islamic terrorist attacks against civilian targets inside the United States? The answer to these questions, I fear, is yes. The danger we face is of winning the battle but losing the war.

Even if we soundly defeat Iraq, what happens to the Iraqi people? Are we prepared to rule Iraq for a long period of time, rebuild the nation's shattered infrastructure, and help the impoverished Iraqis create a new nation out of tattered cloth? Will we provide them with the tremendous amount of resources they will need for years to come? What are the repercussions of such a policy in the Arab world and at home? It's not clear to me that the White House has thought about Iraq beyond the short-term goal of dethroning Saddam Hussein and rooting out his weapons of mass destruction. We must be patient, not impulsive, and learn to carefully choose how and where to apply our awesome military powers. If we simply lash out, the results, as we have seen before, can be tragic and far-reaching.

On August 20, 1998, President Clinton ordered simultaneous cruise-missile strikes against an alleged chemical weapons plant in Khartoum, Sudan, and terrorist training camps in Afghanistan. The strikes were called in retaliation for Osama bin Laden's bombings of the American embassies in Kenya and Tanzania; the White House asserted they were necessary because of an imminent threat to national security. Some seventy-five Tomahawk missiles were launched from warships in the Arabian and Red Seas, timed to explode simultaneously on two continents. The operation was lauded as the largest attack ever against a private terror group. Indeed, the missiles hit their targets precisely, which boosted American morale. Unfortunately, the strikes were later revealed to be expensive failures.

The four targeted al-Qaeda camps had already been largely abandoned by the time the cruise missiles—which have the explosive punch of a five-hundred-pound bomb, and cost $1 million apiece—hit the arid ground near Kabul, Afghanistan. (About twenty militants were killed in the attack, some of whom were Kashmiri terrorists.)

The attack on the al-Shifa pharmaceutical complex in Sudan, meanwhile, resulted in at least one death and the destruction of a legitimate business. Al-Shifa was targeted after U.S. agents had allegedly collected soil samples from outside the plant; the National Security Council (NSC) maintained that the soil showed traces of elements used to make EMPTA, a precursor to the deadly nerve gas VX. Further, an NSC spokesman said that Osama bin Laden had links to the company that owned the plant. On the day of the attack, a U.S. warship in the Indian Ocean launched twenty cruise missiles at al-Shifa; within half an hour, the large factory was completely flattened.

Not long after the attack, Kroll was hired by a law firm representing Salah Idris, the Sudanese owner of the plant, to establish the facts about al-Shifa. (Kroll conditioned its acceptance of this assignment on being able to do an independent investigation with full access to people and documents, and being paid in advance of the release of its report.) The investigation revealed that al-Shifa was a legitimate business that did *not* produce any chemical warfare precursors. Indeed, it could not have done so, as it was equipped only to mix and package human and veterinary pharmaceuticals. Kroll had another soil sample taken from the most logical site at the plant, and had it tested by three different laboratories in Britain and the Netherlands; it showed no traces of VX precursor chemicals. Nor had Salah Idris ever met Osama bin Laden or any other Islamic terrorist. In other words, the American cruise-missile strike destroyed a thriving business, killed an innocent person, and no doubt turned many Sudanese against the United States. When questioned about its choice of targets, the NSC cited no evidence other than the disputed soil sample. Indeed, the al-Shifa incident has largely been forgotten, except that Idris has filed a $40 million suit against the American government for damages.

The war on terror recently took on a new military aspect when the United States brought its technical edge to bear on terrorists in Yemen. Yemen—Osama bin Laden's ancestral home, a largely lawless region where many al-Qaeda fighters have regrouped, and the site of the USS *Cole* bombing and the recent attack on a French oil tanker—has become a major focus of U.S. counterterrorism operations.

On November 4, 2002, a CIA Predator drone, a small remote-controlled aircraft, tracked a car filled with six alleged terrorists and bomb-making equipment in a remote northwestern Yemeni province. According to local spies working with the CIA, one of those in the car was Abu Ali, a senior al-Qaeda leader who was suspected of playing a role in the bombing of the USS *Cole*. As a task force of lawyers, intelligence experts, and Pentagon officials monitored the operation in a Florida command center, the drone's operator pushed a button and fired a Hellfire missile that incinerated the car and its occupants halfway around the world.

Was this a legitimate military action against an enemy combatant?

President Bush had no qualms about assassinating terrorists. After the strike, he said: "The only way to treat them is [for] what they are—international killers. And the only way to find them is to be patient and steadfast, and hunt them down." In a similar strike in 2001, a missile-firing Predator reportedly killed Muhammed Atef, al-Qaeda's chief of military operations, near Kabul, Afghanistan; there may have been other such robotic killings. But the assassination of Abu Ali in Yemen signaled a new direction in the war on terror: It was the first time military action against al-Qaeda had been extended beyond Afghanistan, and it was a departure from the U.S. practice of working with other nations to capture suspected terrorists.

Although such a killing might give us a short-term thrill, I have serious qualms about such tactics. Would the world be better off if Osama bin Laden were dead? Yes, of course. But we cannot adopt a policy of flying our drones across borders and assassinating those we don't like in an ad hoc way. That will breed widespread resentment and mistrust of the U.S. government, both abroad and at home; any short-term gains from such a policy will result in long-term losses.

Instead, we must create a well-thought-out process, with layers of approval and oversight, by which we conduct such operations. What was the process to authorize the Predator strike? What was the standard of proof required to justify taking those people's lives? The answers to these questions must be clearly stated in the future.

I fear that with the advent of armed Predators we are yet again looking for a quick, painless fix to a dark and difficult problem. But we have seen in the past how a reliance on such high-tech gadgets can end badly—as in the mistaken bombing of the al-Shifa pharmaceutical complex in Sudan. What would the consequences have been if there had been a child in the Yemeni car, or if we had targeted the wrong car and killed innocent people? I have no doubt that such mistakes *will* occur. For proof, look no further than the killings of civilians by Israeli troops hunting Palestinian terrorists, and the damage to Israel's worldwide reputation as a result.

Yes, we are at war. But we must use our powerful weapons selectively and very carefully, and never forget that the world is watching our every step. The use of robotic attacks and the U.S. government's approval policy for them must be carefully thought out and explained.

The Price of Failure

As we've seen, the federal government has not ignored the terrorist threat since September 11. It has stepped up its use of some traditional weapons against terrorism, introduced some new weapons, and proposed still others. The creation of a Department of Homeland Security, the system of color-coded threat alerts, the rejiggering of airport security systems, the proposed use of citizen informants, and increased reliance on wiretapping and other forms of electronic surveillance are all part of this attempt to enhance our arsenal of antiterrorism weapons.

Unfortunately, few of the moves made so far are likely to improve our national security. Many of the changes have been more cosmetic than real. Others will probably prove to be counterproductive. Worst of all, there is no overall plan behind the changes. They amount to a collection of unrelated, one-off moves that do not reinforce each other.

In short, we have no national security system—just fragments of one.

It's disheartening to observe this colossal failure of understanding, will, and nerve. And it's frightening to contemplate the possible consequences if we don't act quickly to remedy it. Those consequences could include both another horrific terrorist assault and a backlash that would drive Americans to embrace truly extreme measures: unlimited search and seizure, preventive and unrestricted detention, internment camps, coerced confessions, and assassinations.

Such unregulated measures would erode our civil liberties and would have few lasting benefits in terms of real security. But we are in a long, brutal war. In certain circumstances, the nation may deem such methods necessary and acceptable.

Imagine, for example, the chaos, fear, and hysteria that could follow a terrorist attack on an American city using a weapon of mass destruction—a dirty bomb, say, or a chemical agent. Imagine hospitals overwhelmed by thousands of casualties, rumors sweeping through the media, roads clogged by millions fleeing the site of the attack. Then imagine, in such a crisis, a terrorist leader—Osama bin Laden, or his successor—releasing a videotape promising a series of such attacks to follow. Many Americans would demand that the president do anything necessary to stop him. Some might take matters into their own hands. It's not hard to imagine riots, mosque burnings, and lynchings of Muslim Americans.

Striking the right balance between security and liberty is profoundly difficult and crucially important. If we lack the nerve to make the right choices today, tomorrow we may face a nightmare scenario like the one I've just described.

The Barriers We Must Overcome

Any objective analysis of our security measures to date paints a discouraging picture. Where did we go wrong? Why is America falling so far short in its efforts to safeguard its citizens? Are our elected leaders in the administration and in Congress stupid, uninformed, or simply not trying hard enough?

None of these is the case. But America's efforts to create an effective security shield faces three difficult barriers.

First, we still don't seem to fully understand our enemies, their hatred of us, or the nature of the war they are waging against us. Although the war on terrorism involves a new kind of enemy us-

ing innovative tactics in pursuit of nontraditional goals, our response has remained grounded in traditional military doctrine. We
must completely rethink our definition of war and develop new
strategic doctrines better suited to this twenty-first century battle.

Second, the same institutions that have mismanaged this conflict for at least twenty years remain in power. It's now clear that
almost everyone in Washington—from the White House and
Congress to the CIA and the FBI, from the leaders of the U.S. military to the administrators at the INS and the Federal Aviation
Administration (FAA)—underestimated the terrorist threat before
September 11. It was a mistake that cost three thousand lives. Yet
no one has been fired or even reprimanded as a result, no serious
investigation has been launched, and the essential reform effort has
not even begun. The point is not to identify scapegoats but to
change the institutions and their underlying problems. We must
acknowledge our mistakes, demand accountability, and take cor-
rective steps—and fast!

Third, the politics of security preparedness is perhaps our most
substantial barrier. Who is in favor of security? Everyone. But who
is willing to advocate a tax increase to pay for security we may
never use? Who is willing to set up a system to potentially restrict
personal privacy *before* the mob howls for revenge after another
September 11–like attack? Who are the lobbyists pushing to reform
our entrenched bureaucracies? The politics of balancing security
and liberty poses a tremendous challenge to a Washington that has
become ever more intensely politicized and partisan in recent
years. As the power of narrow interest groups, wealthy contribu-
tors, and single-issue lobbies has grown, it has become harder and
harder for even well-meaning members of Congress to focus on the
long-term national interest. Hence the seeming impossibility of
achieving crucial reforms in so many vital areas, including social
security, health care, education, tax policy, military preparedness,
and the environment. In each of these fields, what some have
called "the politics of personal destruction" hampers meaningful
discussion and appropriate action.

I'm afraid that the security issue is becoming another of these politicized arenas, an ideological third rail that no politician with an instinct for self-preservation will dare to touch. Specifically, America is saddled with an odd-bedfellows coalition of the right and left that opposes security-enhancing steps that could potentially impinge on the "core constitutional right to privacy." Their reasons vary widely, and they are not purely self-serving or worthy of immediate dismissal. But the knee-jerk rejection of any enhancement of federal power in the pursuit of security is naive and self-defeating. If we acquiesce to this rejection or enhanced security, our nation will be left unacceptably vulnerable. Even worse, we could see, as we are seeing today, a slow, pernicious loss of liberty *without* commensurate gain in protection.

Since the attacks, many have urged Americans to unite, avoid criticism and finger-pointing, and concentrate on defeating our enemies. The sentiment is admirable. But when our leaders lack the political courage to act, and their inaction threatens to bring on new preventable disasters, then it is time to speak up and demand accountability.

Will it be easy to break away from politics as usual? Of course not. But we have no other choice. In the chapters that follow, I'll lay out my security plan for America, in hopes that it will at least trigger the national conversation we ought to be having.

Part Two

Keys to Security: The Proteus Plan

Chapter 5

A Security System That Works

Today, the confluence of many factors has produced an exceed-
ingly dangerous moment in world history: a moment of cross-
civilizational conflict, when one of the parties to the conflict,
fundamentalist Islam, has both the motive and the means to
launch repeated terrorist attacks against millions of innocent civilians on the other side. To combat this danger, we in the West have
three potential solutions to consider.

First, America can continue to respond as it always has—react-
ing to crises as they arise, belatedly rushing our military forces here
and there in response to terrorist attacks around the world. But this
has not proven to be an effective deterrent, and it is likely to further antagonize the global community over the long term. A policy
of *pax Americana* is inconsistent with our oft-stated belief in the
freedom of choice and respect for the individual. If America continually imposes its will militarily, the world will tire of us playing
global cop and may coalesce against us. Thus we risk squandering
the benefits of America's "soft power"—our widespread cultural
influence—which allows us to lead by example.

Second, we can attempt to seal our borders so as to make the
movement of terrorists, their philosophies, or their weaponry into
our country difficult, if not impossible. This isolationist approach
is also unlikely to succeed. Our economy is dependent on almost

unfettered commerce. After September 11 we slowed the truck traffic across the Mexican and Canadian borders; within a week, we had parts shortages in the automobile industry that threatened to cause plant shutdowns. We cannot afford to go backward. Likewise, restricting the flow of information is also unlikely to succeed. The genie is already out of the bottle and cannot be put back in. Furthermore, restricting information is not consonant with America's belief in freedom of expression, and would surely backfire on us if we tried it.

Third, we can establish a new, technology-driven system of security for the twenty-first century. This is the answer. A system that recognizes and incorporates the changes that globalization has wrought is our only hope of building meaningful security.

The rest of this book will be devoted to explaining and justifying such a system.

Good Security Versus Bad Security

Human beings have studied and experimented with the principles of security for centuries, and by now the fundamentals are well understood.

Poorly constructed security consists of a single layer, a rigid, static line of defense, like a castle wall. One violent thrust can penetrate that wall and allow an enemy into the vital inner space—of your house, your corporation, your nation—and cause tremendous damage. The classic example of a poorly conceived defense is the Maginot Line, the chain of fortifications built by France on its eastern border with Germany during the period between the First and Second World Wars. Built with massive bunkers and enormous gun emplacements, it was considered impregnable: The Maginot Line reflected the overconfidence of the French and their reliance on heavy technology in place of a flexible, redundant system of defense. In 1940 Hitler's light, fast blitzkrieg attacks easily outflanked the Maginot Line and opened France to the Nazi invasion.

Good security, by contrast, has three characteristics. First, a well-conceived security plan has layers and depth. This means that if the enemy penetrates the first line of your defense, the effect will be limited and not catastrophic because there will be other defensive layers to compensate. Compare this to a well-coached defense in football. The defense doesn't line up in one single straight line of defense; there are several lines—the defensive linemen, the linebackers, the defensive backs, the safety—so that if an opponent punches through the first line it will be met by another. This provides a deep, layered, redundant defense, at least in theory. As anyone who has watched the game knows, during sixty minutes of competition and the running of over a hundred separate plays, the offensive team usually manages to find a way through the defense to score at least a couple of times. But a single-line defense would allow far more points to be scored and virtually guarantee a lost game.

Second, good security must be designed to react quickly and adapt to changing circumstances. In movies or on TV, attacks by criminals or terrorists are often portrayed as methodical and predictable. But the real world is chaotic. There is nothing stopping a terrorist from changing the objective, strategy, or theater of operation while in the midst of an attack. The best protection against such an opportunistic attack—whether on the gridiron, in the Afghan desert, or in your own hometown—is a layered, redundant defense that can react quickly and intelligently.

Third, and perhaps most important, good security needs to be informed and proactive. It's never enough to just sit back and wait to see what your opponent will do. It is far more effective to figure out what the enemy's plans are, or might be, and to use a variety of defensive methods to keep it mentally off balance, disrupt its plans, reduce its capabilities, and restrict its options. This requires information and intelligence gathering.

As the Department of Defense says in one of its manuals, the purpose of layered security is based on the threefold philosophy of *delay, determine, respond:*

- Delay the attackers to evaluate their methodology

- Determine the nature of the threat

- Respond to the committed attack

What Needs to Be Done: An Overview of the Proteus Plan

My proposed system of national security, which I've dubbed the Proteus Plan, has two central elements: the hardening of our physical defenses against attack, and the gathering of information and intelligence. The first step is defensive, the second step is offensive.

In military jargon, hardening a position means fortifying it with troops, weapons, or armor. Hardening targets inside America will impede the terrorists' efforts to attack us, force them to spend more time and money on their plots, raise their profile, and prod them to take greater risks—all of which will make them more vulnerable to detection and more likely to fail. Gaining access to reliable intelligence and information, and analyzing it in a timely manner, is a proactive step that allows us to anticipate our enemies' movements, disrupt their plans, and thwart their attacks. Working in tandem, these two steps will vastly increase our national security.

First, target hardening. The Proteus Plan requires cooperation by all elements of society—the individual, the corporation, the government, and the international community—to fortify the nation, and indeed the world, against terrorist attacks. Here is a brief discussion of the role each element must play.

As individuals, Americans must understand that we are in a war and behave accordingly. Individuals won't usually have the kind of specific information needed to break up a terrorist cell, but we can all keep our eyes and ears open for suspicious activity, we can have personal emergency plans in place, and we can pressure Washington to build an effective response to terrorism and engage in multilateral efforts to reduce the threat.

Corporations should be legally required to help secure the key infrastructure elements they control: power plants, pipelines, munitions, food distribution systems, roadways, ports, and airlines. Businesses should be required to participate in the system of security as full partners of the government, for their own good and for the nation's.

Local and state governments should have local oversight of security while also participating in the national security effort. They must harden local and state-owned facilities and infrastructure components according to federally mandated guidelines, and they should police corporate compliance with the new security regulations.

The federal government must lead and coordinate the overall security system. It must harden government facilities and public infrastructure, set and enforce standards for local, state, and corporate security efforts, engage in diplomacy and intelligence gathering, and keep the public informed about the status of the threats to our security and of our response.

The international community is an important element as well. Because terrorism is a global problem, America can't tackle the challenge alone. We need to engage in a vigorous and ongoing dialogue with other states—even some we've traditionally considered our enemies—about security issues of mutual interest, such as control of weapons materials and technology. We must also work to share intelligence and take coordinated military and law enforcement actions with other nations.

So much for defensive actions. The second, and equally important, element in any true security program is collecting intelligence about our enemies.

America has the most advanced intelligence-gathering operation in the world. Used well, it could give us insight into who and where the terrorists are, what they plan to do, and how we can stop them.

Since the calamities of September 11, our national intelligence operations have received a new surge of interest and support. This alone will make us at least marginally safer. Yet I worry that we are squandering the opportunity to truly reform and improve our intelligence capabilities. Many of our politicians and military leaders have not adapted to the new era. They remain committed to intelligence-gathering systems that were designed for the Cold War. We need to retool our formidable intelligence capabilities to defeat the new enemy.

To that end, we should create a new domestic spy agency, which I call the Domestic Intelligence Bureau (DIB). The DIB would be given a single mission: to uncover terrorist activity against the United States or its allies. It would be a small but powerful agency, subject to clear guidelines about what it can and cannot do. It would operate under the aegis of the Department of Homeland Security, and would be sent into action only at the discretion of the president and the Congress.

Would the Proteus Plan work? Yes. Would it be costly? Again, yes. But the attacks of September 11 cost us three thousand lives and cost New York City alone an estimated $95 billion. I for one would be willing to contribute, both in higher taxes and in higher costs for some goods and services, to prevent similar tragedies in the future. I think nearly all Americans would feel the same way.

Local and State Governments

Today, local and state governments are a woefully undervalued, and potentially wonderful, security resource for the nation. Their obligation should be threefold: first, to harden locally controlled infrastructure and high-value targets; second, to be the first responders to an attack; third, to oversee the mandated hardening of corporate sites under their jurisdiction.

Intergovernmental cooperation and communications are critical in any system of security. For counterterrorism investigations, state and local law enforcement authorities need to be incorporated as full partners in my proposed Domestic Intelligence Bureau's (DIB) efforts to spy on and gather information about terrorists operating inside America. This could be modeled on the FBI's Joint

Terrorist Task Force, which has been a moderately successful program. I believe the JTTF could become a highly effective operation if it was run by the DIB.

For response to crises, local authorities must be trained as first responders—the first group on the scene of a disaster, who will make the critical early decisions that will save or cost lives. For them to be effective, the local authorities must be given the proper equipment, manpower, and training. Dollars spent here will pay real dividends in the long run.

Finally, state and local governments are the backbone of my proposed national identification system, as I will discuss later at greater length.

The Federal Government

The tone is always set at the top of an organization, and the role played by the federal government is key to the success, or failure, of any national security plan. In the war on terror, the federal government oversees policy, physical security, investigation intelligence, screening, and response—both at home and abroad.

The federal government's policy responsibilities includes setting the standards for hardening by corporations, states, and localities. It includes developing standards and practices for domestic intelligence investigations. It also includes creating policy for the use of the national identification card in determining access to air travel, sensitive locations such as power plants, and purchase of dual-use products.

In terms of physical security, the federal government must move promptly to harden the critical infrastructure elements it controls, and set standards for such hardening by the private sector.

The federal government will oversee the nation's information, intelligence, and investigative efforts, both foreign and domestic, mostly through the CIA and my proposed DIB.

First, domestic intelligence. As I've indicated, we must create a new, autonomous Domestic Intelligence Bureau (DIB). This agency will be in charge of domestic spying and other domestic countert-errorism measures, restricted by careful oversight and clear laws.

As for foreign intelligence, the CIA should shift its focus away from military intelligence and toward the war on terror. This means devoting more resources to human intelligence, including the recruiting and use of informants, and retooling its clandestine eavesdropping apparatus. The agency should also be allowed wider latitude in its "black" operations than it has now. For this we must construct rigid protocols about what the agency is able to do, based on an ascending ladder of danger. Extreme actions, such as assassinations, should *not* be ruled out—provided that a condition of significant danger has been established and certified by senior officials.

The federal government must be the source of funds for upgraded local and state first-responder programs. It must also set standards for their training and activities, and provide communications and logistical support for first responders.

An Immediate Challenge: Airport and Airplane Security

Securing airplanes from hijacking and destruction is one of America's greatest short-term security challenges. Thus, airplanes and airports are a good first place to take a fresh look at ways to bolster our defenses.

For over forty years—ever since the first of the Cuban airline hijackings in 1958—airplanes have been a target for extremists attempting to make a political point or spread terror. During the 1990s, they became potential weapons of mass destruction, as in 1994, when an Air France Airbus was hijacked by Algerian terrorists intent on destroying the Eiffel Tower, or in 1995, when Ramzi Yousef plotted to blow up eleven airliners over the Pacific Ocean. Luckily, both plots were stopped. But the terrorists learned from their mistakes, refined their techniques, and kept scheming. On September 11, 2001, the nineteen al-Qaeda agents led by Mohammed Atta finally succeeded in turning four jetliners loaded with fuel into guided missiles.

It's clear that airplanes provide terrorists with an opportunity to accomplish a number of their goals at once. The destruction of an airliner is a publicity-grabbing event that shows the power of the terrorist and the impotence of the West. It also creates a ripple effect of fear in the general populace and a protracted reaction that can wreak havoc with the American economy.

From the terrorists' perspective, then, destroying an airliner is a worthwhile operation. And it is relatively simple to accomplish. It can be done via hijacking, as on September 11; through a bomb placed on board the plane, as in the 1998 destruction of Pan Am flight 103 over Lockerbie, Scotland, by Libyan agents; or by means of a missile fired from the ground, as was recently attempted in Kenya.

These risks must be eliminated as quickly and completely as possible. But how? Through a series of policy changes and actions.

The best way of protecting an airplane is to know the background of those boarding it, then deciding which passengers and their baggage to search, and how thoroughly. The alternatives are profiling passengers, which is unfair and ineffective, or screening everyone and everything, which is too expensive and time-consuming when attempted on a massive scale.

Thus far, the single most effective measure against terrorists gaining control of a plane has been a change in response. When a plane was hijacked before September 11, it was standard operating procedure for the pilot and crew to cooperate with the hijackers and attempt to land the plane in order to limit the threat to passengers. Today, I've been told, that approach has shifted 180 degrees, and pilots will use every trick and resource available to maintain control of the plane and bar hijackers from the cockpit. The security of the airplane now comes before the security of its passengers. To put it bluntly, if a pilot must crash a plane, killing all on board, to prevent greater destruction, it's his or her job to do so.

This new policy is an example of a hard-nosed but appropriate response: It weighs the threat to society posed by terrorists who gain control of a commercial jet against the relatively small risk the terrorists pose to the passengers on that jet, and judges the former to be more significant. As difficult as such a triagelike response might be to accept, we must think and act this way for the greater good. Indeed, the same kind of thinking should be extended to other aspects of airline security, and to national security in general.

As a result of the shift in protocol, many airlines have now fortified their planes' cockpit doors to make it harder for terrorists to enter the pilots' inner sanctum and take control. Furthermore, pilots are now allowed to arm themselves with guns. This has been controversial, with both pilots and airline executives divided over whether arming the crew will enhance or weaken safety. Critics fear that having guns in the cockpit will offer terrorists further inducement to storm the cockpit (to seize the weapons), and they question the wisdom of pilots firing pistols inside a crowded plane at high altitude.

I used to be on the fence about guns in the cockpit, but no longer. I'm a strong believer in gun control and in most circumstances feel that the fewer guns available, the greater the public's safety. But I now believe that arming pilots creates a worthwhile measure of last resort, provided the pilots are thoroughly trained in how and when to use their weapons. I also believe pilots should be trained in aggressive flying maneuvers that will help them to disable hijackers who have taken over an airliner's cabin.

Since September 11, we've rushed to expand the air marshals program. Some have gone so far as to suggest that an armed air marshal in plain clothes should be present on every flight. The sheer cost of this idea probably makes it impractical. There are over *seven million* scheduled airline flights every year, and putting an air marshal on every one would cost billions. The airlines, already cash-strapped, can't afford to foot the bill. Besides, such a drastic step is not needed today. The most practical alternative is to allocate marshals according to the level of threat—the higher the threat, the more marshals should be assigned to flights. How do we assess threat levels? Through an effective system of gathering and analyzing intelligence.

Training air marshals, and updating that training, is crucial. I have been told that in the first few months after 9/11, we were putting dangerously untrained men and women on airplanes as marshals because of the urgent need; the results could have been tragic. The training program is beginning to show results, but it will take more time and money to create an adequate force of well-trained marshals.

Now, how do we stop bombs and guns from getting on airplanes?

If we do not have a national identification system, then all baggage—not just carry-on bags, but also checked suitcases—must be subject to screening for explosives and guns. We have the technology to automatically screen passengers and their carry-on bags, but we don't yet have a system that uses electronic bar codes to match each piece of baggage to an actual, checked-in passenger on the same flight. This basic measure would prevent a terrorist from checking in a piece of explosives-laden luggage and walking away— as the Libyan agents responsible for the Lockerbie bombing did.

The biggest problem at check-in is volume. We are not yet capable of screening *all* checked baggage in a timely, effective, and affordable way. Again, the only real solution is to know the background of those boarding a plane and to search the bags belonging to those who represent the greatest threat and others randomly. This requires good intelligence and the development of a national identification system, which I will discuss in Chapter 7.

Airport workers represent another security challenge. These people—mechanics, custodians, food vendors, monorail drivers, and the like—have access to most parts of a typical airport, even restricted areas. In September 2002 three suspected members of an al-Qaeda sleeper cell were arrested in Detroit; two of the men reportedly worked as dishwashers for Sky Chef, the airline food vendor. Whether or not these individuals are guilty of terrorism, their job seems like good cover for terrorists wishing to plant a bomb in a food cart that is bound for a commercial jet. Airport service staff should be required to undergo extensive background checks and continuous security monitoring.

The steps described so far, while costly, would be reasonably easy to carry out. My next recommendation will be more difficult. If we are truly serious about airport and airline security, we need to redesign airports so that all passengers and their baggage enter through a single, centralized check-in portal. Channeling all travelers through such a central hub would allow for the most efficient use of screening machines and security personnel.

Clearly, this kind of major rethinking of airport design will take years to become reality and will be hugely expensive. But it's such an important safety step that the job must be undertaken despite the cost. As a practical matter, the financial burden should be shared by the airlines and the local and federal government. And while the airport makeovers are in process, we must streamline and centralize screening at existing facilities as much as is practical.

The steps above will help to secure domestic aircraft and airports. But what about airplanes coming into the United States from abroad? This is another huge weakness in the overall security system, and one that is of the moment.

U.S. law enforcement officials suspect that on September 11, al-Qaeda had planned another set of hijackings in Europe. According to intelligence gathered since then, the plan was to hijack aircraft originating in foreign airports and crash them into targets in London, England. For reasons yet unknown, the plot failed. But its existence highlights the problem. We need to be sure that aircraft entering American airspace are as secure as those originating in our own country.

How do we accomplish this? First, we need to build a cooperative security effort with other nations, one that guarantees the same level of screening and identification on foreign aircraft as we demand for our domestic carriers. Furthermore, we must be allowed to put U.S. air marshals on their flights into the United States. Conversely, other nations should also be allowed to put their version of air marshals on international flights that originate in the United States.

A program like this requires real international cooperation. We cannot fight the war on terror alone. Unfortunately, the Bush administration has shown little interest in truly cooperative international efforts. Whether for ideological reasons or because of sheer arrogance and ignorance, the White House apparently believes that the United States can achieve security with or without help from its allies around the world, and that international treaties and organizations are at best fig leaves in which to cloak American unilateralism.

It's another illustration of the shockingly shortsighted, business-as-usual mentality that still pervades our government more than a year after September 11. It may take more painful lessons in our own vulnerability before our national leadership wakes up to the seriousness of the danger we face and the absolute necessity for global cooperation to combat it.

Chapter 6

Intelligence in the Age of Terror

O n September 11, 2001, every one of America's intelligence agencies failed. The results were catastrophic. Now we must acknowledge where our intelligence system is broken, understand why, and carefully restructure our approach to collecting and analyzing information about our enemies.

Before the 9/11 attacks, both the FBI and CIA missed clear indications of danger and failed to communicate effectively with each other. I do not want to oversimplify the difficulty of predicting terrorists' intentions, but these missteps continue to haunt us.

The FBI ignored warnings from one of its own agents in Phoenix, Arizona, who in July 2001 warned Washington that followers of Osama bin Laden might be studying at U.S. flight schools in preparation for terrorist attacks. The bureau also blocked its Minneapolis office from investigating one of those trainees, Zacarias Moussaoui, who had told instructors he wanted to learn only how to take off and fly a plane, not how to land it. On September 11, 2001, the FBI had only one full-time analyst assigned to follow al-Qaeda.

In 1998 the CIA learned that Muslim terrorists were planning to fly a bomb-laden jet into the World Trade Center, but the FBI and FAA dismissed the agency's report as unlikely. New York and Washington were repeatedly identified as likely targets for attack, yet American intelligence failed to follow through. By early 2001 the CIA had learned that two Arab men—Khalid al-Midhar and Nawaf al-Hazmi—were al-Qaeda operatives who had made repeated visits to the United States and had attended flight schools here. But the agency didn't put them on an immigration watch list until August 2001; as a result, they were able to enter the country, disappear, and ultimately carry out their hijackings on 9/11. While the CIA had received warnings from one or more friendly nations with spies planted inside al-Qaeda, the agency failed to penetrate the terrorist network itself and had no high-level sources inside al-Qaeda—probably the only way for it to gain credible advance notice of an attack as momentous as those of September 11.

Frustrated former agents from both agencies have complained that the post–Cold War FBI and CIA have become rigid, politicized, and risk-averse. Yet, despite such harsh criticism and a congressional investigation, the agencies have changed in only minor ways.

Terrorist groups, on the other hand, have scattered around the world since the war in Afghanistan, and have continued to evolve and adapt to new conditions. Enemies like al-Qaeda, Southeast Asia's Jemaah Islamiah, and the Palestinian group Hezbollah are cunning and sophisticated, and they have been adept at gathering intelligence about us. They do months and sometimes years of research and planning before striking at Western targets, such as the American embassies in Africa. They avoid speaking on phones that we can intercept, use the latest computer technology to encrypt sensitive information, and entrust the most sensitive information only to family members. They move their people around at night or in bad weather, when our spy satellites can't detect them.

Planning for the September 11 suicide hijackings began at least two years before they took place. The al-Qaeda members involved paid close attention to the tradecraft preached in their training manuals, which U.S. intelligence has copies of: They lived in the United States legally, shaved their beards and avoided other

Muslims, and paid their parking tickets on time (to avoid un-
wanted attention from law enforcement). They visited and photographed the World Trade Center, bought handheld global
positioning equipment to identify the exact coordinates of the
buildings, took numerous test flights, and studied videotapes of the
instrument panels of the jets they were planning to hijack. In short,
these men were not amateurs.

If America hopes to thwart and destroy this new breed of hard-
core, professional terrorist, we must first learn as much about them
as they know about us. This is the vital role to be played by our
intelligence agencies. To understand how to fix our intelligence
agencies, we must first understand what they do, and why they
sometimes fail.

Lessons from History

Of course, September 11 wasn't the first serious intelligence failure
in history. From 1940 to 1942, for example, the Allies suffered a series of surprise attacks by the Axis powers. Each represents a lesson for the war on terrorism. In 1940 the Germans surprised the
French and British in the Ardennes Forest. Local intelligence had
accurately predicted the route of the attack, but the Allies dis-
counted the information because it did not fit into their precon-
ception of what a "reasonable" enemy would do. On December 7,
1941, much of the U.S. Pacific fleet was destroyed by the Japanese
surprise attack on Pearl Harbor—despite the fact that the United
States had broken the Japanese navy's "Purple" code. In 1942 Hitler
surprised Stalin with his invasion of the Soviet Union, despite the
fact that Stalin had been forewarned by the United States and
Britain. Stalin had refused to listen to the Allies because he mis-
trusted them and had already invested so much effort in diplomacy
with Germany.

How could these mistakes have happened? In the Ardennes and
Soviet cases, a misguided, closed-minded worldview was to blame.
Allied leaders in both cases ignored warning signs in favor of what

their instincts told them *must* be true. In the same way, before September 11 U.S. security agencies never considered that terrorists might use jetliners as guided missiles against symbolic targets in heavily populated urban areas—this despite the fact that Algerian terrorists had attempted much the same kind of attack with an Air France jet against the Eiffel Tower in 1994.

In the case of Pearl Harbor, information overload was partly to blame. In an article in *Foreign Affairs,* Richard Betts points to a problem that is exponentially worse today than it was fifty years ago: "the problem of signals (information hinting at the possibility of enemy attack) getting lost in a crescendo of 'noise' (the voluminous clutter of irrelevant information that floods in, or other matter competing for attention)." The terabytes of information gathered by our intelligence services today dwarf the clutter produced in World War II. As indicated by the intercepted but untranslated messages from September 10, 2001, managing information overload may be the key to winning the war on terror.

Another crucial factor at Pearl Harbor was the failure of U.S. intelligence services to share information. Because of the broken codes, America knew that a Japanese attack was imminent long before December 7, 1941. But if our intelligence "failed to produce an accurate image of Japanese intentions and capabilities, it was not for want of the relevant materials," wrote Roberta Wohlstetter in her important 1962 study of the attack. "Never before have we had so complete an intelligence picture of the enemy." The broken code was deemed too secret to share with field commanders, and interservice rivalries led to intelligence about Japanese movements being hoarded and split up among many competing fiefdoms in the U.S. government. As a result, no one saw the whole picture, and the Japanese were able to unleash a devastating surprise attack.

The lessons of this mistake are clear, if tragically ironic.

The CIA was created after the Second World War largely to prevent another surprise attack like Pearl Harbor. The idea was to create a single clearinghouse for all foreign intelligence, and to streamline information sharing. But after the Cold War the CIA began to drift, and the U.S. intelligence community became nearly as splintered and rivalrous as it had been before Pearl Harbor. Indeed, as Tim Weiner has reported in the *New York Times*, the heads of American intelligence warned the president that if "sweeping changes in the way the nation collects, analyzes and produces intelligence" were not made, the result would be "a catastrophic, systemic intelligence failure." That statement was made on September 11, 1998.

It's important to acknowledge that we have had some intelligence successes in the war on terror. These, too, have lessons to teach.

One of the most effective intelligence organizations in the United States is the New York Joint Terrorist Task Force, which links representatives of the New York Police Department, the FBI, the Bureau of Alcohol, Tobacco and Firearms (ATF), the Port Authority of New York and New Jersey, and other local, state, and federal organizations. Among other successes, the task force helped to prevent a planned 1993 attack on the city's Holland Tunnel. The lesson: If we pool our resources and work together, it can be done.

In 1995 the CIA used information provided by Philippines intelligence to thwart a planned attack on eleven airliners over the Pacific Ocean. After September 11 U.S. intelligence helped to rout al-Qaeda and the Taliban from Afghanistan, and in 2002 our agents worked with those from other nations to trap leading al-Qaeda operatives, including Omar al-Faruq in Indonesia and Ramzi Binalshibh in Pakistan.

More difficult to appreciate are the unacknowledged successes. Sources in Washington have told me that "hundreds" of planned terrorist attacks have been uncovered and disrupted, and I believe that is true. But in order to protect our agents and methods we cannot yet give credit where credit is due.

Once again, history has lessons to teach. Notice that each of the antiterror successes described above involved a *cooperative* effort among several intelligence organizations, and sometimes more than one country. This is exactly the approach we'll need to win further intelligence-based victories. Unfortunately, as you'll see, it's also one of the major weaknesses of our current intelligence system.

Make no mistake, intelligence is a difficult business, and we must be realistic about what kind of performance we can reasonably expect from our spy agencies. They should be able to tell us who and where our enemies are, and give us an indication of what the terrorists plan to do. But we cannot expect a fully detailed biography of every Islamic *jihadi* and a complete blueprint for every future attack. We live in a somewhat chaotic world, where even past events are in dispute, never mind present or future events. Nonetheless, the power of intelligence to contribute to our ultimate victory in the war on terror is enormous. Thus the failures we've tolerated so far have been doubly tragic.

Why Our Current Intelligence System Has Failed

Technical Intelligence: Its Use and Abuse The United States does everything in a big way, and intelligence gathering is no exception. We have thirteen main spy agencies that provide intelligence under the National Foreign Intelligence Program. The list of spy agencies grows to more than fifty when it includes tactical military intelligence and security organizations, as well as those responsible for security responses to transnational threats, including terrorism, cyber warfare and computer security, covert development and spread of weapons of mass destruction, narcotics trafficking, and international racketeering. Exactly how much the federal government spends on these spy agencies is classified, but it has been estimated at some $30 billion per year.

This enormous sum buys us the most sophisticated information-gathering system in the world, especially on the technical side. With a fleet of sophisticated spy satellites, we are the nation best equipped to intercept and decipher electronic data and voice communications, and we have the world's most advanced satellite photography systems. This technical prowess has given us enormous advantages in military preparedness, helped us to emerge victorious from the Cold War, and has played an important role in every humanitarian aid effort and international police action that we have participated in since.

Our spy satellites keep us well informed about Iraqi troop strengths, and well prepared for the highly unlikely event of a Russian invasion of Western Europe. They have also played an important role in the war on terrorism. In January 2001, when Osama bin Laden was a wanted man for his terrorist efforts, our intelligence network captured images from space of the caravan of automobiles in which bin Laden traveled to his son's wedding. It probably would have been possible to kill him then, if the Clinton administration had been willing to accept the diplomatic, political, and military costs of such a preemptive strike. A year later, the same network of satellites helped us detect al-Qaeda formations in Afghanistan, making it easier for our ground troops to attack them.

So technical intelligence has much to offer. But spy satellites alone can't win the war on terrorism—especially given the fact that the ways we analyze, use, and share the information the satellites create are woefully inadequate. We must rethink and retool the way we use technical intelligence for the fight against unconventional enemies such as al-Qaeda, adapting to the new, post–Cold War world and the new type of war we now find ourselves fighting. Today's intelligence challenge is to determine which terror group or U.S.-based cell will next threaten our citizens with attack. When and where will this attack take place? Who will carry it out? We must quickly build expertise and reallocate resources to meet this challenge.

Will this change happen quickly? Not likely. The need to refocus our intelligence efforts is widely acknowledged, but making it happen will require a tough bureaucratic fight. Too many special-interest groups oppose change. Spy satellites, other technical intelligence devices, and the personnel who build, support, and maintain them are phenomenally powerful—and phenomenally expensive. This means there is a huge constituency of technical specialists with a built-in desire to maintain the status quo.

The Need for Cooperation Another change we *must* demand from our intelligence agencies is that they develop the ability to work together for common goals. Lately, the CIA and FBI have come under heavy, legitimate criticism because prior to September 11 they failed to share intelligence about terrorist activities with each other in an effective and timely fashion. Two of the terrorists who hijacked the flight from Boston on that date were actively being tracked by the CIA, which had seen them meeting with al-Qaeda operatives overseas. If the FBI had been involved in the manhunt, it's likely the two men would have been seized before the plane left the ground. But the CIA hadn't informed the FBI about the men until just two weeks before September 11—not nearly enough time for the bureau to get the word out to its far-flung offices.

There is currently no system to ensure that once the intelligence is analyzed it gets shared among federal, state, and local agencies. This is nonsensical. It is the responsibility of the federal government not only to drive the gathering of information but to ensure that it is disseminated in a detailed, timely way among agencies at every level of government and, when appropriate, to the private sector. Some agency leaders balk at the idea of sharing high-level intelligence. But with terrorist cells having apparently been planted in small-town America, local authorities may well be on the front lines of the war against terror. It only makes sense, then, that they should be included in the information-sharing chain.

I understand the instinctive desire on the part of the intelligence agencies to protect their secrets—after all, I lived in that world for years. People *never* want to share intelligence. Every time you disclose any piece of information, you are, directly or indirectly, revealing a source, and thereby compromising that source. So there are built-in conflicts between intelligence and action and between any two groups developing intelligence. But this natural tension isn't a legitimate excuse for the communications breakdowns we've seen in the United States intelligence community. Yes, if you share information, it could be compromised. But if you *don't* share it, the information is useless. We must pool resources to fight our enemies, not one another.

Too Much Data, Too Little Analysis A third serious issue is the volume of information our spy agencies must contend with. Once we have gathered the information, what do we do with it? All too often, the answer is nothing. With the flood of information being transmitted today by e-mail, pagers, cell phones, fax machines, and the Internet, the big-ear spy satellites of the U.S. National Security Agency (NSA) are intercepting far more data than agency analysts can process. Even with sophisticated computer programs sorting the data, the NSA can analyze only about 3 percent of the relevant information. Our eye-in-the-sky satellites take a lot of photographs, but the NSA and CIA look at only about 10 percent of them.

The overwhelming volume of information we gather and our lack of timely analysis have hobbled us. We now know that on September 10, 2001, the NSA collected two Arabic-language messages warning of a "major event," but the messages weren't translated until September 12.

Our intelligence agencies employ smart, dedicated analysts who are trying their best to decipher data and relate it to world events. It's a difficult job. Even with all of their high-tech spy gear, analysts are equipped with imperfect knowledge and come up with imperfect conclusions. In general, they are overworked, underappreciated, and underpaid.

The end of the Cold War brought an era of budget tightening in every defense-related operation. Our spy agencies had to trim their spending. Unfortunately, they tended to maintain spending on hardware while cutting costs on personnel. As a result, today, more than a decade later, our analytical staff members are not as well trained or focused as they used to be. This makes a real difference in the effectiveness and productivity of their work. To take a simple example: Suppose you are a CIA analyst charged with monitoring developments in Saudi Arabia. If you have a deep, historically based understanding of the economics, politics, and culture of Saudi Arabia, you can sort through newspapers, radio and TV transcripts, government documents, and other sources very quickly. If not, you have to read them all in search of what's truly important— and even then, it's likely that you'll miss a key insight or two. No wonder the rule of thumb is that it takes ten years to make an intelligence analyst. And only seasoned analysts can really conquer the information overload that plagues intelligence operations.

The leaders of the U.S. intelligence community are smart people. By the mid-1990s they were aware of problems such as our overreliance on technical data and our neglect of human intelligence. Even before September 11, both the CIA and the National Security Agency were spending billions in an effort to upgrade their human intelligence capabilities—by recruiting experts in Arabic languages and culture, for example. But it's hard and time-consuming to repair a deficit that was almost a decade in the making.

And we still make needless mistakes—such as when American intelligence agencies appointed a woman to a leadership position in a country where Muslims were an important political force. Don't misunderstand: I'm all for equal rights. But in this case we were naively trying to impose our values on another society, a situation made worse by its sensitive nature. The position was important, and the woman was bright and capable. But that was beside the point. There is no way that an American woman could become a trusted insider in a patriarchal Muslim society.

Failure to Cultivate International Connections The end of the Cold War hurt our intelligence capabilities in another way. During the period of intense competition for support from third world nations between the Soviet Union and the United States, we romanced potential allies among the Arab nations. We also developed close intelligence ties with several of them. We offered financial aid to their governments and helped to train their soldiers and intelligence officers. When the Cold War ended, most of these programs stopped. No longer regarding these countries as potential chips in a two-handed game of diplomacy, we began to consider them relatively backward, poor, and unimportant. As a result, our relations with the Arab world suffered—and so did the flow of intelligence we received from Arab sources.

Foreign Intelligence: What Do We Need to Do?

American intelligence today is split into foreign intelligence, driven by the CIA, and domestic intelligence, driven by local, state, and national police agencies, most notably the FBI. Both our foreign and domestic intelligence agencies failed the nation on September 11.

In order to retool our foreign intelligence program, we need to take four major steps: refocus our technical intelligence on terrorist groups, make greater use of open-source intelligence, improve our use of human intelligence, and develop better cooperation with foreign intelligence agencies. Let's consider each of these points in some detail.

Refocusing Technical Intelligence As we've seen, technical intelligence can be an effective tool against terrorism, and we ought to keep using it aggressively. It's what we Americans do best, after all, and it gives us a tremendous advantage over adversaries who lack the technical know-how and enormous resources we enjoy.

The real issue isn't whether we *should* use our high-tech gizmos, it's *how* we use them. We must refocus our technical efforts away from purely military-oriented intelligence, such as counting the number of battleships in the Persian Gulf, and toward the new threats, such as eavesdropping on the conversations of small extremist groups planning to attack the United States or its allies. In fact, the best solution is to combine our technical intelligence with our human intelligence. This will give us a fuller picture of what our enemies are plotting.

The CIA must run our foreign technical information-gathering efforts. The Department of Defense (DoD) obviously has a need for such information, but that must not overwhelm our primary concern, which at the moment is Islamic fundamentalists targeting American civilians. Therefore, DoD ought to take a backseat to the CIA in this area.

Mining the Wealth of Open Sources America does rely too heavily on gathering clandestine military intelligence through high-tech means, rather than gathering basic, useful information and analyzing it in a methodical way. This low-tech layering of fact upon fact should be taught as Intelligence Gathering 101; instead, it is often derided as lowbrow drudge work. This is a huge mistake.

The truly astonishing amount of material available about virtually any subject is known as open-source material, because it is accessible to anyone who knows how and where to find it—including our enemies. It includes newspapers, magazines, books, TV and radio broadcasts, government reports and documents, speeches and sermons, posters and handbills, and the flood of electronic information on the Internet. A significant part of Kroll's work is accessing open-source information, analyzing it, and helping business leaders make decisions based on that information. Of course, we also try to ferret out secret or controlled information, but we are usually able to do that only because we have first sifted through the mounds of publicly available material.

With the advent of globalization and the World Wide Web, access to open-source information has greatly expanded, revolutionizing intelligence gathering. If you want to learn about Michael Cherkasky, for example, all you need to do is start up your computer and go online. With a few keystrokes, you can find out where I live, my telephone number, the name of my wife, the story of my career, what I look like, whom and what I support, whom I have sued and who has sued me, and so on.

Today it doesn't take spies or satellites to learn the weaknesses in America's critical infrastructure, or how to build a simple fertilizer bomb, a chemical or biological weapon, or even a nuclear device. This information is available in open-source documents. So is information about U.S. laws and customs. A terrorist with a computer can read up on both the general principles behind our laws and the specifics of each law—such as the current U.S. restrictions on assassination, on the CIA's use of informants, and on domestic intelligence gathering. Of course, we can learn just as much about our enemies from open-source information as they can learn about us.

Today, America's challenge is to learn as much as possible about Islamic terrorist groups. We need experts in the language, history, culture, politics, and religion of Islam and the Arab world—not just the small group of radicalized fundamentalists. In order to understand the fringe groups, we must first understand the larger culture from which they spring.

This kind of information is no state secret; it's right in front of our noses. But for various reasons we have chosen not to pay much attention to it. It's not cutting-edge or sexy to do the basic, methodical research that has always been crucial to any kind of investigative work. Nor is human intelligence the kind of big-budget technical project that an outside contractor can profit from and that members of Congress will fight to support in their districts. Finally, intelligence analysis has not received its due as a career path. High-level executives within the CIA are generally drawn from the ranks of field operatives or inside-the-Beltway bureaucrats—never analysts. This neglect of the fundamentals of intelligence gathering has left us with enormous gaps in our understanding of our enemies.

American intelligence agencies must refocus on the basics of their business. First, they must gather every piece of open-source information about a suspected enemy—culling TV shows, videotapes, books, newspapers, pamphlets, sound recordings, the Internet, radio, legal documents, business records, and so on. Then our agencies must carefully analyze what they have learned, combine this with the clandestine information we've gathered through spies and technical means, and finally process the whole data set. Only in this way will we gain a clear picture of who our enemies are, what they intend to do, when, and where.

To make the demanding job of information analysis worthwhile, we must treat our analytical experts as valuable talent, not as the second-rank bureaucratic grunts they are considered today. We must allow them to participate in decisions over how the information is used, and we must provide them with financial rewards sufficient to attract professionals of the highest caliber.

Creating and Cultivating Informants Robert Morgenthau, the crusading district attorney of New York, my former boss, and the nation's preeminent prosecutor of the last forty years, likes to say, "I would give up fifty cops for one good informant." That statement, made in the context of investigating white-collar criminals, holds just as true for counterterrorism. To supplement our awesome technical intelligence gathering, we badly need informants and friendly agents inside hostile groups.

Terrorist organizations have sent an unknown number of agents and sleeper cells (small groups of agents who anonymously blend into host communities until ordered to strike) into the United States and other target countries. They are sophisticated and disciplined, operating within a compartmentalized structure that prevents data leaks. The al-Qaeda cell that bombed the U.S. embassy in Kenya on August 7, 1998, did not know about the parallel cell that bombed the U.S. embassy in Tanzania only minutes later. Only the high-level al-Qaeda leaders who coordinated the attacks knew about both. In order to disrupt these operations, we would have needed to have an operative at a very high coordinating level inside al-Qaeda, or agents in each African cell. We had neither.

The lesson? You can never have too many informants.

We clearly need to develop a large network of agents inside terrorist organizations and the countries that protect them. Only insiders will be able to give us a truthful and detailed understanding of the structure and plans of a terrorist organization. Furthermore, insider operatives are far more cost-effective than billion-dollar spy gadgets.

It is not easy to create such assets. Nonetheless, they are indispensable for getting a clear picture of our enemy. We need to aggressively develop programs to produce more such informants. This is a critical security issue today, one that, as you'll see, demands we balance our need for information against our need to maintain moral and ethical standards. But based on my own experience, I believe an aggressive policy can be put in place without substantial damage to our core American values.

Informants are of two basic types. The *plant* is a person loyal to the United States planted inside an enemy group to gather intelligence. The *recruited informant* is a person who is already inside or on the periphery of a target organization and is willing to trade secrets for remuneration.

In my years at the DA's office, I worked with several New York police officers who became plant informants inside the Mafia and drug-running gangs. It was exciting and enormously fruitful but nerve-racking work. We asked these brave men and women to assume a new life and identity in order to fit in with the culture of the target organization. This is not easy to do, of course. First, plants have to be the right kind of person—someone of the appropriate ethnicity, age, sex, language skill, and cultural sensibility to fit into the target group seamlessly. Second, plants have to be willing to put their lives on hold for months or years and enter an environment where a single misstep could lead to death. Third, plants must appear to participate in the criminal/terrorist enterprise in a way that makes them useful and gains them the trust of the organization. Fourth, the organization must have gaps in its internal security that a plant can exploit.

Remarkably, we were able to find people who were qualified to penetrate the Mafia and willing to take the risk. The most difficult hurdle to overcome was when the plant was asked to perform a criminal act—sometimes an act of violence—in order to win the trust of the mob. As law enforcement officers, our agents couldn't commit crimes. Instead, they had to try to trick the mob. For example, an informant might make a fake drug sale to prove he or she wasn't a police officer.

Another big hurdle was the Mafia's famous *omertà*, or code of silence, and its strict internal security measures. Some Mafia families required a neighborhood or family connection before accepting a new member, and then the recruit had to be vouched for by a "made" (accepted) member of the family. Despite these high hurdles, the FBI and NYPD managed to deeply penetrate the mob on a number of occasions, which led to a widely publicized series of arrests and the steady, ongoing erosion of the Mafia's power in America. All of the successful plant infiltrations were complex, long-term projects.

Can we plant informants in terrorist organizations as we did with the Mafia? Because they operate in a strange culture on the other side of the world, terrorist organizations are even more difficult to penetrate than the mob. Today we have relatively few personnel with the pedigree, cultural skills, and motivation to attempt the task. Also, terrorist groups are extremely violent, and our agents may not be able to perform the acts of murder and mayhem required to gain the credibility and trust they'd need. Finally, such a job requires a great deal of patience and perseverance, as terrorist groups require that its members build substantial relationships before entrusting them with meaningful information.

On the other hand, recruits from all over the world—including the "American Taliban," John Walker Lindh, and other westerners— were able to join al-Qaeda simply by showing up at the training camps in Pakistan or Afghanistan. Were any of them actually CIA agents? If not, they should have been. Despite the obvious difficulties of gaining access to terrorists' inner sanctums, it is not impossible. American intelligence must make this a priority over the next five years.

"Turning" a person who is already inside, or known to a target organization, is our best hope for quickly penetrating terrorist groups. The work usually begins by trying to identify disaffected members of the enemy camp who may be convinced to cooperate. Cultivating them is a slow, painstaking process that calls for profound psychological insight and plenty of nerve. I lost one informant inside the mob-run painters' union; Jimmy Bishop agreed to cooperate with us and ended up with nine bullets in his body.

The motivations of turncoat informers vary. In some of the cases I worked with, they were motivated by anger against the mob and a desire to get revenge for personal slights or attacks they'd suffered. In some cases, we pressured people to cooperate by threatening them with prison or by leveraging the influence of their relatives. In still other cases, money was key: The government may pay tens or even hundreds of thousands of dollars for the services of informants. This applies to the war on terror. The informant who turned in Ramzi Yousef from Pakistan was paid $200,000.

The advantages of turncoat sources are obvious: They have already been accepted by the organization and are more or less trusted. But this approach has several obvious pitfalls, as we learned the hard way in the spy-versus-spy games of the Cold War. Recruited informants are notoriously unreliable and have often done bad things.

This is not a business for the faint of heart; it is dirty but necessary, something that the United States has no choice but to engage in. Those who view the world through rose-tinted glasses and cannot bear the unhappy facts of life should look away.

In the 1990s American intelligence thought that they had recruited informants inside al-Qaeda. But they turned out to be scammers or, worse, double agents trying to pass us disinformation or to find out how much we knew.

One of the most intriguing of these sources was Ali Mohamed, a sophisticated, intense, and manipulative man. Born in Alexandria, Egypt, in 1952, he served in the Egyptian army for thirteen years, during which time he earned a bachelor's degree in psychology and worked briefly with the CIA—all while secretly being a member of Egyptian *Jihad*. In 1985 he moved to America, married an American medical technician, acquired a U.S. passport, and enlisted in the U.S. Army's elite Special Forces, based at Fort Bragg, North Carolina. Fluent in Arabic, English, French, and Hebrew, he became a paratrooper, won a badge for shooting, was in excellent physical shape, and lectured on the Middle East and the Soviet forces in Afghanistan. In the meantime, he pursued a doctorate in Islamic studies and in 1988 used his leave time to make a clandestine trip to Afghanistan to fight the Russians alongside Osama bin Laden's troops.

According to Peter Bergen's book *Holy War, Inc.*, Mohamed's superior in the U.S. Army, Lieutenant Colonel Robert Anderson, found the Egyptian's strong Islamist views (he despised Israel and called Anwar Sadat "a traitor") and questionable travel (Mohamed brought back from Afghanistan the belt of a Russian soldier whom he said he had killed) so odd that he wrote intelligence reports about them. But no official U.S. action was taken, and now the reports have "disappeared." Anderson told Bergen that the only way Mohamed could have gained entry to the United States and a posting at Fort Bragg was if someone in the American government had facilitated it. While the CIA will only acknowledge working with Mohamed briefly in Egypt, it has been reported that he had indeed benefited from a visa-waiver program for intelligence assets.

Given an honorable discharge from the U.S. Army in 1989, Mohamed ostensibly went into the leather import-export business. He spent much of the next few years traveling to the Middle East on al-Qaeda's behalf—where he trained fighters and helped to move bin Laden to Sudan in 1991—and teaching courses on military tactics to Islamic militants connected to the al-Khifa Refugee Center in Brooklyn, New York. Al-Khifa was the *mujahidin* recruiting center where El Sayyid Nosair—Rabbi Kahane's assassin and one of Mohamed's students—and Ramzi Yousef, the 1993 World Trade Center bomber, spent time.

In the 1990s Mohamed moved his wife to Sacramento,

California, and took a job at a music, video, and computer whole-saler—while amassing a collection of documents on assassination, surveillance, explosives, and planning terrorist attacks, presumably for al-Qaeda. At the same time, he made repeated attempts to get a sensitive job at the FBI or DoD. In interviews with the agencies, he admitted to having trained bin Laden's bodyguards, mentioned that al-Qaeda planned to overthrow the Saudi government, and said he knew who had bombed the U.S. embassies in Kenya and Tanzania, although he wouldn't name names.

In September 1998 Mohamed was arrested on suspicion of being part of a terrorist plot. Rather than go to jail, he worked out a plea agreement with the U.S. government and testified about some of his al-Qaeda activities. It remains unclear what Mohamed's real motivations were or where his allegiances really lay.

A recruited informant is useful because he is already associated with the group targeted for investigation, and so the hard work of making him fit in is already done. But the flip side of this convenience is that such informants are likely to be violent, lying thugs with whom no reasonable person would want to associate. Furthermore, such an agent is by definition the kind of person whose loyalty can be bought or coerced. Working with these kinds of people is not for everyone, and the recruitment and handling of informants is not played by the same rules that govern our everyday lives. But that is okay. This work is extremely important to our intelligence efforts.

We should not continue to write blanket rules forbidding the CIA from working with particular categories of people or on particular types of activities, as we did in the 1990s. But there *does* need to be clear registration, oversight, and approval before certain specified acts, especially criminal acts, are allowed; approval of such actions should be carefully weighed against the interests of national security.

Improving Cooperation with Foreign Intelligence Services Critical information for our pursuit of the war on terrorism lies in the hands of other nations' intelligence services, and we need to make a better effort to obtain it. The Jordanians and Pakistanis definitely have informants inside the terror groups. We need to improve our working ties with their intelligence agencies to get access to what they are learning—not an easy matter, especially when you consider that in Pakistan, at least, the intelligence community includes a number of Islamic extremists.

In the last couple of years, the CIA and the FBI have been working hard, and with some success, at obtaining information from foreign law enforcement sources. For instance, we are now getting a lot of excellent information about Islamic extremists from Bulgarian intelligence, which has strong ties among Muslim groups. But the United States is still generally viewed by the foreign intelligence community as demanding and arrogant. The perception is that we ask other nations for information but don't offer to share our intelligence with them. This one-way street has limited both their sympathy for us and the effectiveness of our agencies.

Furthermore, the United States is viewed as taking unilateral policy positions on many issues of international interest. In the environmental arena, for example, we rejected the Kyoto accords on global warming; currently we are pushing to exclude American citizens from the jurisdiction of the new World Court. The result is that America has gained a reputation, deserved or not, for wanting the benefits of global citizenship without being willing to help shoulder the responsibilities that come with it. By acting as a bad neighbor, we build resentment in other nations—even in some of our staunchest allies, such as England, France, and Germany—which further dampens their enthusiasm for sharing valuable information with us.

The answer to these problems is clear: America needs to be willing to share more of its intelligence with others, and to adopt a more inclusive and multilateral approach to policy making.

A New Domestic Spy Agency

One of the most important steps I advocate is the creation of a new agency, which I call the Domestic Intelligence Bureau (DIB). It would be charged with a single mission: to spy (yes, *spy*) on individuals, foreign agents, or terrorist groups inside our borders that threaten to kill our citizens, destroy our infrastructure, or gather classified information about us.

Here, I will deal with the DIB only in relation to its antiterrorism activity. Modeled roughly on MI-5, the United Kingdom's domestic intelligence agency, the DIB would be responsible for gathering and analyzing all information that pertains to domestic terrorism. The CIA would retain its responsibility for foreign intelligence gathering and would have shared access to all information related to terrorism. The proven model is the way in which Britain's MI-5 works cooperatively with MI-6, the foreign intelligence agency. The DIB must be subject to careful oversight, to ensure efficiency and prevent any abuse of power. There must be clear protocols that guide exactly what the agency can and cannot do.

I'm not talking about investigating Americans for their political beliefs. We have a tremendous sensitivity to such action in this country, and I personally have a great respect for civil liberties. But there is a difference between spying on a peaceful group that disagrees with U.S. policy and spying on a violent group that threatens to destroy the country. The line between the two can be difficult to draw, but we must be willing to draw it.

As of now, law enforcement agencies' power to investigate people in America who espouse violence against the nation is restricted by statutes, by administrative regulations, and by court decrees. The war on terror demands that we reconsider those restrictions. Groups and individuals, whether at home or abroad, who threaten our safety should be treated as prime suspects in the war against terrorism. Our past unwillingness to do so has been costly.

In the early 1990s the blind cleric Sheikh Omar Abdel-Rahman moved from Egypt to New Jersey, where he preached hatred for America from a Jersey City mosque. At first the United States didn't take Abdel-Rahman seriously, but that changed after the murder of Rabbi Meir Kahane in 1990 and the 1993 bombing of the World Trade Center, actions that Abdel-Rahman had exhorted his followers to take. It is common sense to take appropriate investigative actions against people like Abdel-Rahman and his violent followers. And this is precisely the kind of situation the DIB should be designed for.

I don't suggest creating a new agency lightly. It will be an expensive and time-consuming undertaking; there will be a great deal of opposition, and there will also be political pressure to keep counterterrorism under the aegis of the FBI. Indeed, after a recent visit to MI-5, Tom Ridge, the director of homeland security, flatly stated that the Bush administration will not create such an agency in the United States.

But given the urgency of the war on terrorism, I believe that the creation of a non-law-enforcement, domestic intelligence agency like the DIB is a necessity.

Why do I favor shifting the main responsibility for antiterrorist work away from the FBI? There are a number of reasons.

The Federal Bureau of Investigation is the preeminent criminal law enforcement agency in the world. Charged with investigating violations of federal law, the bureau fields over eleven thousand agents, including many trained as attorneys, accountants, scientists, field interview agents, and experienced gumshoe investigators. If I were conducting a criminal investigation, I would want the FBI to be on the case. Indeed, we hire former FBI agents at Kroll because they are consummate investigators. And Louis Freeh, the former director of the FBI, was one of the most honest, competent, and hardworking government officials I have ever met.

The FBI is very good at investigating traditional crime in a traditional way. Its core competency is to pursue large-scale investigations of serious fraud and organized crime, although the bureau also oversees terrorism and counterespionage in the United States.

Some of the FBI's antiterrorism efforts have been laudable. The bureau did an outstanding job investigating the U.S. embassy bombings in East Africa, a cross-cultural, multidisciplinary case that was successfully prosecuted under very difficult circumstances. The FBI was involved because this was a criminal investigation, and the FBI handles such cases, through its overseas offices when necessary.

Nonetheless, the bureau has serious flaws. It's a sprawling, entrenched bureaucracy with an old-school, highly competitive, by-the-book culture. This is true even after nine years of reform efforts under Freeh. I've spent much of the last eight years trying to reform large organizations that have become calcified and sometimes corrupt, from the garbage-hauling industry on Long Island and the Teamsters Union in Chicago to the Los Angeles Police Department. I've learned that bringing about cultural change in a long-established organization is extremely difficult. And although the FBI is not a corrupt organization, it's a rigid and hierarchical society that would be nearly impossible to modernize quickly.

And no organization this side of the House Appropriations Committee knows how to protect its turf better than the FBI. The bureau has been notoriously difficult for other agencies to work with. I have spoken to members of the CIA, ATF, Drug Enforcement Administration (DEA), and state and local police who agree about few things except that the FBI is the most difficult agency to work with. I know this is a broad brush stroke and that there are many excellent FBI agents, but in interagency politics the bureau is known, as one DEA agent put it, as "a bear."

I also know about the bureau's recalcitrance from firsthand experience. As a state prosecutor in the early 1990s, I occasionally worked on cases with FBI squads. Once I was approached by a member of the FBI's Brooklyn/Queens office, who asked me to get information on an organized crime case from the FBI's Newark, New Jersey, office. I was surprised. "Why don't you just ask for the information yourself?" I wondered.

The agent looked away for a minute, then quietly responded,

"It's like this, Mike. The guys in Newark have their own investigation going. And they won't share a thing with any other FBI office. I think you've got a better shot at prying something out of them than I do."

That's the culture of the bureau in a nutshell.

A second, more serious episode convinced me that the FBI had become lost in self-importance and was more interested in conserving its own power than in protecting the American public. In January 1989 a New York County grand jury indicted John Gotti, the notorious Mafia boss, for attempted murder and first-degree assault. As we built our case in the state DA's office, we grew concerned that Gotti would attempt to fix the jury, as he had done in a previous case. In legal parlance, we had probable cause to place a wiretap in the Ravenite Social Club, one of Gotti's hangouts, to determine whether that was his plan. But the FBI had already tapped the Ravenite, and we figured we should share resources.

To ensure that there were no problems with the investigation, Bob Morgenthau, first assistant DA Barbara Jones, and I all spoke to people at different levels of the FBI, including director William Sessions, the special agent in charge of the New York region, and the head of the team running the wiretap, to work out the arrangement. We agreed on a compromise: The state agreed not to wiretap the club as long as the FBI would let us know if they overheard Gotti trying to fix our case.

We never heard a thing from the FBI. Our investigations proceeded. The DA's office built a good case against Gotti. At the end of the trial, the jury deliberated for four days before returning a verdict of "not guilty." It was one of just two cases I lost as a prosecutor. I was extremely disappointed with the verdict. I just *knew* that Gotti had committed the crime.

Gotti strutted around New York for another year, smiling for the cameras while continuing his criminal activities, until the FBI's own investigation led to charges of murder, larceny, racketeering, and, yes, conspiring to fix our state jury! The feds sent Gotti to jail for life; in 2002, he died of cancer in prison.

It turned out that the FBI wiretap at the Ravenite *had* recorded Gotti planning to fix our jury, but the bureau had reneged on our deal and had refused to tell us about it. Their explanation? It was "in the best interests of law enforcement not to reveal the wiretap." Translation: It was in the best interests of the FBI to get credit for bringing down John Gotti, never mind the fact that he was allowed to victimize people for an additional year.

These stories don't mean the FBI is incapable of conducting domestic intelligence. But they do illustrate the bureau's aversion to cooperative investigative work, an essential element in the war on terror. Our enemies today are too deadly for such petty gamesmanship. America must do what is in the best interests of the country, not just the best interests of the FBI. And, as history has shown, the two are not always the same.

The FBI culture is simply not suited for the antiterror job. It is rigid, insular, slow to change, and arrogant. By contrast, the DIB must be small, fast, highly flexible, and technologically up-to-date. It *must* be able to cooperate with federal and state agencies. State authorities are a greatly underutilized resource. The FBI treats them with disdain. But they should be the eyes, ears, and arms of the DIB.

There are three other important reasons for taking the responsibility for antiterrorist intelligence away from the FBI.

First, the FBI is a strong-willed agency with a history of overstepping its mandate and being resistant to civilian control. Giving the FBI the significant additional powers required to combat terrorism inside the United States would excessively strengthen an already large and powerful agency. By separating the responsibility for domestic intelligence gathering from the bureau's traditional law enforcement role, we will create an important prophylactic against the abuse of power.

Second, criminal investigations must be kept separate from domestic intelligence because the two skill sets are very different from each other. The DIB requires analytical, academic types with a sophisticated understanding of the world and our enemies. The

DIB must not only monitor terrorists but try to anticipate what they might do next, by building behavioral models, testing them in war games, and combining their predictions with real-time information. Most FBI agents, who have been trained to react to crimes already committed and to prepare cases for prosecution, are not equipped for such proactive tasks. Furthermore, everyday criminal investigations should be kept separate and distinct from the gathering of intelligence on terrorist groups inside America.

Finally, we need an agency that is designed to work hand in hand with foreign antiterrorism experts. This is not a job for the FBI, which is suspicious of all outsiders.

How the Domestic Intelligence Bureau Would Work

The new Domestic Intelligence Bureau (DIB) that I propose should be an independent spy agency under the guidance of the Department of Homeland Security. Its mission will be strictly defined by clear protocols based on three levels of danger.

Level I For DIB to spy on a suspicious group or individual, the agency would require certification by the secretary of homeland security. The certification would have to show that the suspicious group posed a clear and present danger to America, that all other legitimate means of policing them were unlikely to be effective, and that the narrowest and least intrusive means of surveillance would be used.

The DIB would be given a Level I green light upon notice to Congress and with the ex parte review of abuse-of-discretion standards by a rotating justice of the U.S. Supreme Court. Then the DIB could conduct basic operations, such as physical surveillance and the interception of the communications of specific suspects.

Level II If the secretary of homeland security and the president certified that a "dangerous condition" existed, then DIB would be authorized to undertake a more aggressive level of intelligence gathering, including temporary preventive detention of suspects, broadened intercepts of communications, and proactive searches for specific individuals or groups. As a safeguard, Congress would be informed of this change of status, and it would be subject to review by the Supreme Court. I believe that if there is a showing and certification of a dangerous condition, we need to allow electronic surveillance of any individual or person suspected of terrorist activity or involvement. I would allow this information to be used for intelligence only, not criminal prosecution. Of course it would be reviewed by federal courts.

Level III To reach this "red alert" level, the DIB would have to show that there was a high probability of catastrophic attack. Level III could only be designated by the president with the consent of Congress and subject to review by the Supreme Court. At Level III, the president would authorize the DIB to take emergency actions— such as searches and seizures of all members of designated groups, restrictions on speech and association, restrictions on movement, and coerced confessions—that would be effective for only five days and would need to be formally renewed thereafter.

DIB Staff and Interagency Cooperation Keeping the DIB independent of the FBI would allow it to work with other agencies, increase its efficiency as it progresses from a Level I to a Level III threat, and provides for rigorous oversight.

DIB employees would be drawn from a wide set of disciplines and backgrounds (including the FBI), and they would work with the CIA and the DoD to accomplish the agency's mandate. The DIB would also form joint task forces with local and state authorities to share information, manpower, and resources.

This does not sound like America. But America needs to change to protect itself. We will take all the government actions I set out above if we are subject to another catastrophic attack. We need mechanisms in place to prevent the attack and control the damage to our liberty by providing specific rules.

Is it constitutional? I believe our Constitution is flexible when dealing with exigent circumstances. The Constitution has never been read to prevent us from adequately protecting the lives of our people. I am confident that with appropriate oversight, and employing the narrowest means possible to accomplish the objective, this program is constitutional.

Facing Tough Choices in Intelligence Gathering

One of the greatest dangers we face is terrorists already residing in the United States who, when activated, could do cataclysmic damage to our nation. The problem includes both sleeper cells of foreign terrorists that exist here and domestically bred groups, such as the eleven people arrested by the Justice Department on terrorism charges in Lackawanna (New York), Detroit, and Seattle, and the four native-born Americans arrested in Portland, Oregon, for allegedly joining al-Qaeda.

To manage this problem, we must rethink nearly all the restrictions we impose on domestic intelligence gathering. Not only must we permit spying on U.S. citizens, but we must also be prepared to consider, and in extreme circumstances permit, other measures that are generally regarded as violations of constitutional rights if not done because of exigent circumstances.

In today's climate of political ultrasensitivity, it's difficult to have a substantive discussion about this subject. Deep-seated fears of governmental intrusion quickly surface, and these fears must be openly addressed. If we avoid the subject or allow our fears to control the debate over security, we will come to regret it.

I've already made the point that another horrific terrorist attack might well drive Americans toward draconian, truly dictatorial measures, including coerced confessions, preventive detention, restrictions on free speech and personal associations, unrestricted searches and seizures, unrestricted interceptions of communications, restrictions of free movement within the United States, internments, and even summary executions.

It's a frightening list. *But the fact is that America has implemented many of these steps at particular points in our history.*

Was this because past generations were less ethical than we are? I don't think so. It's because they were faced with extraordinary, nation-defining circumstances.

Abraham Lincoln is rightly revered as "the Great Emancipator," yet during the Civil War he suspended the writ of *habeas corpus* (the fundamental protection against arbitrary imprisonment, which dates back to the Magna Carta) and ordered the arrest of citizens for criticizing the war effort. During the Red Scare of the 1920s Attorney General A. Mitchell Palmer ordered the infamous Palmer Raids on suspected communists, anarchists, and other peaceful political dissenters. In the 1940s my father's generation, the so-called "greatest generation," shut Japanese Americans away in internment camps because they feared that they would become fifth-column agents in the United States. All of these were extreme measures, taken in times of national stress.

The United States is not alone in this by any means. Many of the draconian security measures listed above are used by other nations in the West today.

Consider Great Britain, where the Prevention of Terrorism Act was implemented in 1974 to help fight the Irish Republican Army's wave of bombings and assassinations. When distilled to its essence, the act—which is still in effect—allows the use of coerced confessions, preventive detention, restrictions on speech, unrestricted searches, and limited internment. Summary executions are not allowed by the act, but killings by the Belfast constabulary have routinely been covered up without investigation, in effect condoning street executions by the police.

The British took such strong measures because they were, in effect, at war with IRA terrorists. The Israelis have enacted similar policies in their fight against the Palestinians. So have the Germans in response to groups such as the Baader-Meinhof gang, the Italians in response to the Red Brigades, the Spanish in response to the Basque ETA, and the French in response to Algerian revolutionaries.

By American standards, many of these nations' law enforcement policies intrude on fundamental liberties. Some of us have criticized the Europeans' use of harsh methods to squash dissidents. But that was before September 11, when we Americans felt insulated from the dangers of international terrorism. In today's climate, I wouldn't bet against the U.S. public demanding equally harsh steps in response to the next wave of attacks. It would be far better for the United States to move proactively now, instituting strong security measures that are calibrated to prevent terror attacks *and* protect civil liberties.

Where do we set limits? To answer that, let's consider a number of scenarios that we should be prepared to face.

First, suppose that America has been the subject of a nuclear, chemical, or biological attack by terrorists. We have suffered a hundred thousand casualties as well as widespread economic and structural damage. Presume the terrorists threaten to attack us again with a similar weapon. What actions would America be willing to take to find the second bomb and stop its explosion? I submit that we would be willing to do virtually *anything* to prevent another attack.

Now a second scenario. Presume we have proof that there *is* a nuclear bomb planted in an American city, and that we have learned that the terrorists will detonate it within forty-eight hours. What actions would we be willing to take to find that bomb? Again, I submit we'd take virtually any action imaginable.

Here's a third scenario. Presume we have proof that terrorists are attempting to smuggle nuclear, chemical, or biological weapons into the United States. What actions would we be willing to take? I submit we'd be willing to use preventive detention, unrestricted searches, interception of communications, restriction of movement, and coerced confessions—just as other Western nations have done when faced with mortal threats. I have no doubt that Americans would be overwhelmingly in favor of tipping the balance away from liberty and toward security in such circumstances.

Finally, presume we have proof that a terrorist organization is attempting to build nuclear, chemical, and/or biological weapons, and that it has shown the willingness to explode such weapons of mass destruction in the United States. What actions would U.S. citizens want to take? *I submit that this is exactly the scenario we face today.* And all four scenarios are within the realm of possibility.

If we move quickly and implement enough tough measures without eroding fundamental privacy, then we will be able to maintain our liberty/security balance. If we lean too far toward protecting individual rights, we risk finding ourselves in scenario 1 or 2. And if we tilt too quickly toward security, we could find ourselves in scenario 3.

Today, we are confronted by scenario 4, with terrorists actively trying to inflict mortal damage on the United States. What should we do?

Under current laws and regulations, there are many extreme steps that we cannot legally take. We cannot legally detain suspects without formal charges. We cannot use psychological or physical pressure when questioning suspects. *Yet I believe that these steps are necessary under certain extreme circumstances.* And I strongly advocate that all be specifically authorized by law, so long as the specific circumstances, parameters, controls, and restrictions are spelled out and rigidly enforced.

The truth is that all of these tactics, and others still more terrible, have been and will be practiced by American operatives at times when the safety of thousands of people is at stake. The question is not whether America will ever restrict the rights of individuals in an effort to prevent far worse crimes from occurring. It will. The real question is whether such extreme actions will be taken under the aegis of the legal system or whether they will happen outside the law, limited only by the passions of the moment.

If we face the last scenario, then I fear the abuses will be far worse and the fallout far more severe. That's why I am raising these painful questions now, so that we can address them rationally, in a time of relative calm, rather than leaving them to be decided in holding cells or by mobs on street corners in a time of national hysteria.

For a hint of how we might respond to the next terrorist attack, look at what is happening today. The Bush administration has already carried out secretive arrests, forced expulsions, racial profiling, and preventive detention of U.S. citizens with no prospect of a civilian trial. I don't necessarily condemn such tactics per se, but I strongly condemn the lack of process and oversight under which they have been carried out. Our government is slowly taking away our liberty under cover of night. We cannot allow this to happen. It is particularly galling that the loss of liberty is not providing us with increased security. We need to have a very clear, very tough set of laws that allow for *specific actions* under *specific conditions* with *specific oversight*. We cannot allow this or any other administration to take such extreme measures in an ad hoc manner, for that is a slippery slope that will result in the loss of both liberty and security. But today in Washington it is politically easier for people who see what is happening, and believe it is necessary, to complain about the civil liberties intrusions than to propose legislation to control and monitor those necessary intrusions.

Liberty and security are opposites. The hard truth is that increasing one invariably decreases the other. Our challenge is to reduce the proportion by which they impact one another, so that a substantial increase in security will result in a minimal and acceptable decrease in liberty. The graph on page 152 illustrates the challenge of balancing liberty and security.

The last few pages have been difficult for me to write, and they may have been difficult for you to read. But given the realities of today's world, we have no choice but to face up to the tough choices I've outlined.

Can we effectively combat terrorism without resorting to strong tactics? I'd like to think so, but experience suggests otherwise. I believe that with hard work we can balance the contradic-

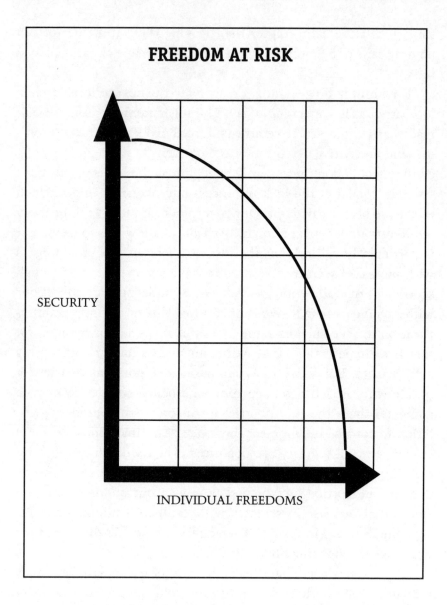

tory imperatives of freedom and security and provide effective protection in a relatively open society. Given a choice between accepting some encroachment on traditional American liberties and allowing the terrorists—mortal enemies of those liberties—a free hand to do as they please, I know which I would choose.

Chapter 7

Keeping Tabs on America

One of the most basic and important steps that we can take to mitigate risk today is to institute a national security program for screening people and goods as they move across our borders and within our nation.

The screening program I propose as part of the Proteus Plan includes three interlocking components: a national identity card, a rules-based screening system, and a cargo identification system. Such a system would be relatively easy to implement, would be relatively affordable in comparison with other kinds of security measures, and would be an effective tool against terrorism inside the United States. It would give America a flexible, durable system that uses our strengths, especially our world-class information technology, to fight the war against terrorism.

I have no doubt that ideologues on both the left and the right will be unhappy with my screening program. It's not a silver bullet that would instantly solve all of our security problems—there is no such thing, of course. But it could have prevented the catastrophes of September 11. And I'm convinced it's the most effective and efficient way to protect our citizens from terrorist attack while also protecting American freedoms.

A Right to Privacy?

Many Americans are troubled by the very idea of having their whereabouts and their actions scrutinized. They believe that the Constitution guarantees them a "right to privacy." In fact, there is no such right enumerated in the Constitution. If a right to privacy exists, it's simply by implication—part of the "penumbra" of rights—depending on whose interpretation of our legal traditions you follow. It is not uncommon for citizens to grow heated at the suggestion that our government might need to learn about their background, travels, and purchasing habits. Some even believe that new technologies such as the electronic highway toll taker E-ZPass, which do little except automate information functions that have always existed, pose a significant threat to their privacy and freedom.

Consider, for example, the position of Dick Armey, a Republican leader in the House of Representatives. In July 2002 Armey stated that "the use of biometric identifiers and Social Security numbers with these cards (national identification cards) is not consistent with a free society."

I understand these complaints, but I disagree with them. I believe the societal cost of background checking and tracking can be kept low, primarily through protective rules on the use of the information. I believe in privacy, but I also know that the value of such background information for the war on terror is potentially very high, high enough to offset the minimal cost in loss of privacy.

Furthermore, nearly all of the supposedly private information that the government would need to track about individual citizens is already available. Virtually all Americans today have reams of information about them stored in government data banks. The Internal Revenue Service (IRS), the Social Security Administration, the military, state departments of motor vehicles, local schools, and even libraries gather information about citizens.

And corporate America knows even more about you. Marketing departments have profiles of your buying habits; every time you swipe your credit card, bank card, or frequent shopper card you are providing businesses with information about what you buy, when, and where. Hence the blizzard of junk mail and hurricane of cold calls you receive at home. It's likely that the magazines you subscribe to include advertisements that are tailored to your consumer profile. The same is true of the Internet sites you visit and in some cases even the television programs you watch.

At Kroll we're well aware of the vast amount of information already available about most Americans. We run one of the nation's top five background-checking businesses. Companies hire us to look into the histories of individuals who are seeking employment with them. Even without asking for permission, we can easily lay our hands on hundreds of pieces of information about the average applicant, including criminal records, all available through open sources. And with the subject's consent, more detailed information is available, from financial and health data to school reports.

In other words, the supposed freedom from public scrutiny that some are fighting so hard to protect has already been compromised. The fight for this kind of privacy is quickly becoming anachronistic, like the now-forgotten battles over the federal income tax, social security, and even the fluoridation of drinking water. All were once viewed by some as tyrannical and anti-American, yet all are now accepted elements of our national life. Somehow our liberties have survived.

Does this capsule history show that we Americans have lost the feisty, independent spirit we once considered a national character trait? Not at all. What it shows is that the United States government can, by and large, collect information about its citizens without abusing that power. Consider, for example, the voluminous, intimate detail about Americans gathered by the IRS. For nearly a century those vast stores of information have been held in nearly perfect confidence. Yes, there have been notable exceptions—J. Edgar Hoover's illegal snooping on personal or political opponents, for example, or Richard Nixon's attempt to use the power of the audit to harass his political enemies. These kinds of abuses must be guarded against and punished severely when they occur. Yet overall the government has done a good job of restricting the use of sensitive personal information—a better job, many would argue, than private enterprise.

I'd also contend that the charge that gathering personal information gives a corporation or government agency the power to control peoples' lives is overstated. What makes totalitarian states possible is not too much access to personal information. It's the willingness to misuse that information for political power or personal gain, and the ability to do so with impunity in the absence of constitutional safeguards, a history of democratic institutions, and an independent judiciary. These three forms of protection are critical—and we in America have all three.

In any case, the question about whether our lack of privacy is a good or bad thing is largely moot. That horse has left the barn. It's highly unlikely we will be able to significantly curtail the ability of others, whether in government employ or in the private sector, to gather background information on us. So why not use that information to create roadblocks for potential terrorists? In my view, there's no compelling reason not to.

Those who are worried about our civil liberties should stop fighting a battle that is already lost. Instead, they should be fighting for legislative controls over how public information is used so that it doesn't impinge on Americans' ability to live and express themselves freely.

An Overview of the National Screening Plan

First, a brief explanation of my screening program: the U.S. ID card, rules-based screening, and national cargo ID system. This will be followed by a more detailed description of each key element in the program.

I'm proposing the creation of a national identification card used by every person inside the United States. Every citizen would be issued such a card; foreign visitors will obtain one from an American embassy before entering the country. Use of the card will be protected by a biometric screen, such as a fingerprint, retinal scan, or facial recognition system.

The ID card will be linked to a national database that will make possible rules-based screening of individuals seeking access to sensitive locations or products. With an ID card linked to a national database, we could quickly screen people in the way that the E-ZPass in your car quickly pays a toll. Those whose ID cards reflect routine activities would qualify for fast-pass treatment. They would whisk through Line A in the airport, for example, as would their baggage. Those whose cards show specific, potentially troubling patterns of behavior would be processed more slowly through Line B.

Similar rules-based screening systems might be set up at sensitive private facilities such as power plants, national shrines such as the Statue of Liberty, government offices such as the Pentagon, and other possible terrorist targets.

The third element in my plan is to identify not only who is crossing our borders and moving around our nation but also to know what that person is carrying and where. Some twenty million cargo containers enter U.S. ports every year, only 2 percent of them are inspected. The end result is we have very little idea of what is actually in those containers and where the cargo will end up.

It would be relatively straightforward to create a cargo identification system tied to an international database. The shipper would load a truck, seal it, and tag it with a bar code that explains what is in it and where it is going. The bar-coded container could pass quickly across the border and arrive on schedule. Those containers without the ID system would be carefully inspected. Obviously, firms and individuals who do a lot of cross-border shipping would have a strong incentive to participate in the ID system so as to speed their cargos past the inspectors.

The U.S. ID Card and Rules-Based Screening

Under my security plan, the Department of Homeland Security would oversee the creation of a U.S. identification system, which includes an identity card backed by an integrated database. The database will track a selection of specific *security-related* information about the cardholder. Here's a list, more or less complete, of the kinds of information that would be included in your personal record:

- Social security data

- Military record (dates of service, discharge status)

- Criminal record (convictions, outstanding warrants)

- Basic credit report data (range of annual income, credit rating)

- Residency records

- Voting information (where and when you have voted—not, of course, any indication of *how* you voted)

- Basic IRS information (whether or not you have paid taxes in a given year, your marital status, the number of children you have, where you work)

- Records of airplane travel inside and outside the United States

- Purchases of dual-use products, including guns and certain chemical or biological materials

- Substantiated investigative reports (statements by informants linking you to known terrorist groups, for example)

The information the database provides will give the United States government the basic knowledge it needs in a time of national emergency. But how would that data be used? How would national security be enhanced by the system? Here are the answers to some of the most frequently asked questions about my plan.

What Data Appear on the U.S. ID Card Itself? Like a standard driver's license, each U.S. ID card will be printed with its holder's photograph and basic information: name, address, and date of birth. The card will also have an embedded biometrics identifier, such as a person's fingerprint or retinal scan, to keep the database information associated with the card secure and to link the card with certainty to the individual carrying it.

How Will People Get a U.S. ID Card? To start with, the cards could be issued through the state driver's license bureaus. As time goes on, U.S. citizens would routinely be issued U.S. ID cards as they enter the school system, at around six years of age. All noncitizen visitors to the United States will be required to obtain a U.S. ID card from an American embassy in the country of their residence before entering the United States.

How Will the U.S. ID Card Be Read? The plastic card would slide through an electronic reader, just like a bank or credit card. The system would then compare the biometric on the card (a fingerprint or retinal scan) with that of the individual using it. If the biometric matches, the system will know to a scientific certainty that the person using the card is who he claims to be. Once the system is running smoothly, the card itself will not be needed, as people can be identified with the biometric reader.

Once an individual's identity has been established, the national database will be quickly accessed for screening purposes. If a user's biometric match cannot be established, then access to the system will be denied. The individual proffering the card will be shunted to Line B for questioning, and an alert will be recorded by the U.S. ID system.

Where Will the U.S. ID Card Be Used? Readers for the cards, with electronic links to the national database, will be placed at entrances to sensitive locations around the country. They will also be used wherever dual-purpose products are sold. A dual-use product is one that is sold for socially acceptable purposes but also can be used in lethal ways. A gun is an obvious example. Our society has decided that it is acceptable to sell a wide variety of lethal weapons to the general public. I am strongly opposed to this, but in any event the nation should monitor gun sales more tightly: Suspected terrorists should not be able to purchase guns at the corner store. Similarly, there are certain dangerous chemicals (such as cyanide) or pieces of equipment (such as those capable of manufacturing biological weapons) that are dual-use products; we may want to restrict their sale, and we should certainly know who is buying them and why.

Most people will probably encounter the U.S. ID system at airport security checkpoints. A smaller number will experience it because they work at a federal facility or a potential terrorist target site, such as a power plant, a water treatment plant, or a chemical factory. Our embassies around the world will also have access to the database.

How Will the Information in the Database Be Used? The information will be used to instantly grade the cardholder, thereby determining how he or she should be screened. The system would be a little like the widely used credit rating systems, with specific numbers of points assigned for particular background indicators. Most cardholders will be graded for fast-pass treatment. A few—no more than 2 to 3 percent—would not qualify for fast-pass treatment and would therefore be subject to more thorough scrutiny.

Under normal—that is, nonemergency—circumstances, no one should ever be prevented from doing anything legal by his or her U.S. ID rating. At worst, one might have to spend an extra fifteen minutes passing through airport security, or perhaps wait twenty-four hours before being permitted to buy a dual-use product.

Note that specific information from the database will not be available to the security personnel who check the card. All they'll see is a grade that tells the operator how to screen the cardholder.

Will My Database Records Be Available to Me? Every person will have full access to all nonclassified information in his or her database file. The only exception would be investigative data; for example, if you were being tracked by the local police as a possible terrorist, that fact would appear in a sealed portion of your file.

Will the Ratings Be Public or Secret? Only you and the security operative managing the card reader would ever need to know your personal rating. If you have questions about how your rating was determined, it should be possible to get a complete explanation—perhaps via an Internet site.

The rating system itself, along with its workings, should be transparent and publicly available. For example, the public should be able to find out how many points are assigned to particular pieces of background data—five points for a felony conviction, say, versus three points for a dishonorable discharge from the army.

How Will the Privacy of My Database Information Be Protected? Safeguards will have to be built in to prevent any abuse of the system. The IRS regulations that have worked well to shield the privacy of tax data might serve as a model. Unauthorized disclosure or use of database information would be a crime with serious penalties, and strict rules would prevent the use of the data by prosecutors, government officials, or, for that matter, IRS agents fishing for damaging information. Of course, all rules and regulations concerning the database would be subject to congressional oversight and judicial scrutiny.

Will Private Organizations Use the U.S. ID Card for Their Own Identity Programs? No, corporations could not piggyback on the national ID program. Private companies would be forbidden access to the database, except in the case of sensitive facilities such as chemical plants, and it would be a crime for any private firm to require employees or others to carry and show the U.S. ID card.

The U.S. ID System in Practice

A major virtue of the U.S. ID card is that it allows for the efficient use of our limited security resources. Let's face it: We simply will not spend the money necessary to thoroughly screen everyone who wants to board an airplane or enter a sensitive location. And even if we did, few people would willingly tolerate the delays that a true total screening would require. The U.S. ID card dramatically reduces this practical problem. It can effectively screen many people in a quick and thorough manner, and, if necessary, allow for rapid preventive action.

How would the average person be affected by the ID program? Let's consider two different U.S. ID cardholders. We'll call them Bob and Tom. The national database contains dozens of pieces of data on each of these individuals. Here are a few of the basic facts about Bob:

- Age forty-one. Born and raised in Los Angeles. Now lives in a suburb of LA.

- B.A. degree in history from the University of California at Los Angeles.

- Served three years in the U.S. Navy (1990–93); honorably discharged.

- Married with three children.

- Drives a 1995 Ford truck.

- Traveled extensively outside the United States while in the navy. Since then has visited France once.

- Pays taxes regularly. Has an extensive but poor credit history. Has worked at the same business for the last ten years.

- Has voted in each of the last five presidential elections.

- Received two speeding tickets. Has no criminal record. No special security notes.

Now compare him to Tom:

- Age thirty-seven. Born and raised in Los Angeles. Now lives in San Diego. Has lived in six different countries since 1990.

- Diploma from a local high school in northern Los Angeles.

- No military record.

- Never married.

- Does not own a car or other vehicle.

- Has traveled extensively outside the United States, including trips to sub-Saharan Africa and several Middle Eastern countries.

- Pays taxes regularly. Scanty credit record. Has worked at fourteen jobs over the past ten years, most of them menial.

- No voting record.

- Has no criminal record. In 1998 and 1999, lived at a London address mentioned by an informant as a safe house for an Islamic terror cell.

Notice that Bob and Tom's race, nationality, political views, and religion don't matter. These do not factor into the security grade or the screening process.

In many ways Bob and Tom are similar: Both are natives of Los Angeles, and they are within a few years of each other in age. But the rules-based screening system would probably grade the two men differently. Bob's point count would be low, meaning that he would be considered highly unlikely to be a terrorist or to be associated with terrorists. Not only does he have no criminal record, but the overall pattern of his life is one of stability and rootedness. He has a family, a long-standing job, and apparent ties to the community. Bob would almost certainly qualify for fast-pass treatment at any sensitive location.

Tom is a different story. He lacks the stable elements of Bob's personal history. He has traveled extensively in countries where terrorist operations are active—and did so, furthermore, with no obvious means of paying for his travel. Most alarming, an informant has placed a terror cell at an address Tom lived at just a few years ago. Based on these elements, Tom's point total would probably be too high to earn him fast-pass handling. He would have to use Line B at the airport, where agents would ask several questions about his travel plans and take an extra-careful look at the contents of his bags.

Does such grading seem unfair? Maybe a little. The system presumes a potential of guilt based on circumstantial evidence obtained from a clandestine source (the terrorist informant). But remember that no one would ever be incarcerated or otherwise punished on the basis of these database entries; at worst, Tom would be slightly inconvenienced when he flies, rents a truck, or buys a pistol. I wish it weren't so, but today's terrorist threat makes this kind of careful screening necessary today.

The U.S. ID system would facilitate a flexible, graduated response to changing risk conditions. Suppose the government had picked up intelligence indicating that a terrorist attack on a jetliner was imminent. For the next few days the national database might be instructed to screen the lists of passengers in different ways. The data might be sifted to determine whether other people associated with Tom were on the same plane, how many passengers were graded in the same way as Tom, what their common patterns of behavior might be, and so on. If the screening determined that Tom was clean of weapons yet was traveling with four companions with similar backgrounds, then authorities would alert the airliner's crew, and an armed air marshal might be assigned to the flight.

Or consider the sale of dual-use products. If Bob and Tom each attempted to buy a potentially deadly product such as nitrate fertilizer or biotech manufacturing equipment, or to rent a large truck, the U.S. ID system would respond in a measured way. Bob would raise no immediate suspicion. But Tom would be questioned about his intended use of the fertilizer, biotech equipment, or truck.

If Tom tried to rent a truck *and* to buy fertilizer near a major American city, that might indicate he is attempting to build a truck bomb. Tom might have to wait twenty-four hours to complete his purchase or rental—enough time for a local agent to visit and confirm his intentions. If the current level of terrorist alert is high enough or the intelligence about an intended attack is specific enough, Tom could be investigated further or even detained.

We Americans aren't accustomed to this kind of scrutiny. Maybe it sounds unpleasant. The changes in our daily routine might take a little getting used to. But the actual intrusion into Bob's and Tom's privacy is limited. Today we restrict who can buy guns, certain chemicals, drugs—all kinds of products. In the future, we need to be more systematic about it. And in compensation for the modest inconvenience, the nation's security is enhanced by a series of gradual, not overbearing, steps.

Challenges to the U.S. ID System

I've been speaking in public about the U.S. ID proposal for some time now. While many people like the idea, others challenge it on various grounds. Here are some of the most thoughtful criticisms I've heard, together with my responses.

First, many people wonder whether the system is technically feasible and economically practical. There's no doubt it would be a challenge to develop such a system on a national scale, but it is eminently feasible. The technology to produce the cards already exists, including that for a biometric screen. And much of the background information for the U.S. ID database is already available in public and private databases. We have credit card checking systems today that are only slightly less complicated but more extensive. And there is plenty of bandwidth available for information transmittal.

Obviously an investment would be required to build and maintain the system. The cards would have to be produced, electronic readers would have to be built and distributed, and software and customer service experts would be needed to train screeners and explain the system. But with the costs amortized over time, the system would be substantially more cost-effective than the spending the White House has already earmarked for its flawed security program.

Others are concerned about the possibility for mistakes and abuse in the system. I share that concern. Here is how I would seek to minimize it.

First, it's critical that all citizens always have easy access to all nonclassified information about themselves in the database. There should be a simple, fast method for challenging and correcting mistaken information. Inclusion of investigative data about an individual should be subject to approval by an independent office, and also subject to challenge by the affected citizen. And the rating system itself must be transparent, making it possible for everyone to find out exactly why he or she received a particular rating.

These safeguards come with a price. Making the system transparent will give a clever group of terrorists a road map for evading the system. When they know how many points are assigned to particular background facts, they can try to recruit members with desirable score totals.

This loophole in the system isn't quite as large as it might sound. It would probably be fairly hard for a cell of Islamic terrorists to recruit a group of operatives whose data profiles looked thoroughly innocent. In any case, giving this kind of "help" to terrorists is a necessary price to pay for the protections Americans will want and deserve.

Strict controls on the use of the information in the national database are also essential. Prosecutors and other government agencies, such as the IRS, must not have access to the data. Private corporations, of course, must not be able to read the information. And severe penalties must be imposed on anyone, government employee, elected official, or private citizen, who tries to misuse the data.

Finally, some people ask me whether the U.S. ID system could be circumvented by terrorists. Frankly, the answer is yes. I suspect that some highly sophisticated criminals and terrorists could probably find a way around this system. But, remember, the object of the Proteus Plan is to create layers of defense that force the bad guys to work hard. Each layer makes it more difficult for them to succeed. The more redundant and interconnected the various aspects of our national security system are, and the more people who are involved, the more likely it is that terrorists will make a mistake that betrays their intentions.

So while it is obviously preferable that our enemies don't work around the system, it is not fatal if they do. The U.S. ID card is not a static, single-layer defense, but part of a much larger security matrix.

Suppose, for example, that a terrorist cell in New Jersey is planning to build a truck bomb. To circumvent the U.S. ID system, one member of the cell could buy fertilizer while another could rent a truck. But sophisticated U.S. ID software, combined with domestic and international intelligence gathering, could identify relationships between the individuals and synthesize rumors about their plans with updates on their purchases or rentals.

This is precisely the kind of technological edge that we need to exploit but don't yet have in place. Indeed, the nineteen al-Qaeda members who hijacked the three jets on September 11—two of whom were on wanted lists at the time—would be able to freely board our commercial jetliners today. The U.S. ID system would change that.

In the United States we tend to think of a national ID card as an unusual, even radical security measure, a tool of repression. But the fact is that more than a hundred countries are using some form of national identification today, including Belgium, Denmark, and France, for everything from security to shopping to voter registration.

Denmark issues ID numbers at birth and uses them to build a national database of personal information during the lifetime of its citizens. Identification cards have been in use in Belgium since World War I. Other countries, such as Spain, Argentina, Kenya, and Germany, require their citizens to carry an identification card as a matter of course.

In 1999 Finland became the first nation to apply smart-card technology to a national ID. The Finnish card has an embedded chip that functions as a minicomputer when inserted into a card reader. When a card is matched to the cardholder, it unlocks a "digital lockbox" containing sensitive information, such as social security numbers, bank account information, and software that allows access to privileged sites. The system is still evolving, but Finnish officials believe their smart ID cards will one day provide an efficient platform for secure electronic transactions.

Today, New York City's fifty-thousand-member police department is reportedly testing high-tech ID cards. If they work, these cards will be issued to the rest of the city's two hundred thousand workers. The NYPD card is decorated with a picture of the Statue of Liberty, an ID photograph, and basic information about the bearer, such as name, shield number, tax ID number, and so on. Each card is also equipped with two microchips, one that contains vital personal information, such as blood type and emergency phone contact numbers, and a second that is equipped with a minute antenna and contains the cardholder's fingerprints and handprints. Eventually these biometrics will enable police to match the card with the person carrying it. Finally, these cards don't need to be swiped: They can be read at a distance by a proximity scanner. The NYPD hopes its new ID cards will afford users quick access, less paperwork, streamlined accounting, efficient monitoring of cops on patrol, and a host of other benefits.

National ID cards haven't always been popular or wisely used, of course. In 2002 Japan instituted a new identification system called Juki Net. Based on a national database in Tokyo, Juki Net is designed to link a set of personal information—the eleven-digit ID number already assigned to every Japanese citizen, plus name, date of birth, sex, and address—into one system. The cards are compulsory, but technical glitches and concerns about identity theft and consumer privacy led to widespread protests in Japan upon Juki Net's launch; some four million people refused to log onto the network.

South Korea's identification system, established in 1992, has been used in onerous ways. In order for South Koreans to access pornographic Web sites, for example, they must enter their national ID number. And the South Korean police have reportedly used the ID numbers to track down thirteen thousand drivers after the state health insurer revealed that they had been treated for mental illness. At least one driver lost his license, while another reportedly lost his wife.

Aside from Nazi Germany, the most notorious and despicable uses of national ID cards were in Apartheid-era South Africa and in the former Soviet Union.

Beginning in 1952, all Black South Africans over the age of sixteen were required to carry a passbook, known as a *dompas*. The *dompas* contained extensive information about an individual, including a photograph, fingerprints, address, details of employment, and whether or not the person was permitted to be in a white area. These passbooks, and the laws that governed their use, were the cornerstones of the Apartheid system and were used to regulate and control the movements of Black South Africans. At the request of any white person, Blacks were required to show their passbooks. Forgetting, losing, or having the *dompas* stolen left Blacks open to arrest and imprisonment. Over a quarter million Blacks were arrested every year for such offenses. As a result, the *dompas* became the most despised symbol of Apartheid. In 1986 the *dompas* was abolished; today South Africans of all races must carry a common identity document.

In Russia, Peter the Great first introduced identification papers, which were essentially internal passports, during the eighteenth century. Initially used to enforce military conscription and tax collection, the passports became instruments of state control under Josef Stalin. Until 1997, the Russian passports contained information about a person's residence, marital status, and military service, as well as a declaration of nationality: Jews, Germans, and others who were not ethnic Russians were identified as such on their passports. Such ethnicity-based identification helped to formalize Russian prejudice against minorities. If you were carrying "Jewish" papers, travel abroad was severely limited, as was admission to universities and many government jobs.

Today, Russians still need their passports to do everything from renting an apartment to buying a car. "For the country's most marginalized groups, including refugees, ex-convicts and the homeless, the passport system can keep them trapped—unable, for example, to get jobs or travel to another part of the country," the Associated Press wrote in 2002.

American critics still point to South Africa and the former Soviet Union as examples of how national ID systems can be used to discriminate and harass large segments of the population. Typical of this complaint are the remarks of Katie Corrigan, legislative counsel for the American Civil Liberties Union's national office in Washington, D.C., who has said: "Unlike workers in Nazi Germany, Soviet Russia, Apartheid South Africa, and Castro's Cuba, no American need fear the demand, 'Papers, please.' As a free society, we cherish the right to be individuals, to be left alone, and to start over, free from the prying eyes of the government."

While I understand such earnest complaints, and to a certain extent sympathize with them, the fact is we live in a dangerous world. It is the way a country uses the identification system, not the system itself, that is the danger. A national ID card does not *have* to be an onerous mechanism of what Corrigan calls "the prying eyes of the government." Other nations have demonstrated that such a system can be a force of good, a tool that greatly enhances security and overall efficiency. We *should* be leery of an intrusive Big Brother–like government, but we should also be leery of a simplistic, knee-jerk reaction to a system with great potential. As long as we safeguard the information in our national database, protect civil liberties, and carefully regulate how these cards are used, then I believe a national ID card will make us a stronger nation.

Screening Containers

Twenty million shipping containers enter the United States each year, yet we manage to inspect only 2 percent of them. What if one of those containers contained a dirty bomb or a chemical or biological weapon?

Catastrophe.

This is no paranoid fantasy. The United States is wide open to such an attack. Today, terrorists can probably access nuclear waste material, and they can definitely access conventional high explosives. I believe that the most dangerous terrorist groups will soon have access to a dirty bomb.

In order for a dirty bomb to be effective, it must be very large. This makes such a weapon hard to build and difficult to hide and transport. But standard shipping containers—each of which can carry many tons of material—are the ideal way to move a large dirty bomb. Containers would also be ideal for poisonous chemicals or the distribution of biological pathogens.

How do we respond to this threat?

First, our intelligence agencies must work overtime to uncover any such scheme, which would require a vast amount of organization and materiel to accomplish. Then, consistent with my layered approach to security, we need to make sure we have a system in place to stop containers loaded with weapons of mass destruction from entering our home ports. In fact, this is not as difficult as it might sound.

The United States' vibrant economy can be maintained only with the fast transshipment of massive amounts of freight across our borders. Just-in-time manufacturing has revolutionized American business and helped us to dominate global commerce for the last decade. But when traffic was slowed by increased border security after September 11, it threatened to close American factories waiting for parts manufactured abroad.

The unrestricted movement of freight is a security nightmare. The solution is a new security partnership between corporations and governments, empowered by technology.

The first step is obvious: The contents of every container coming into the United States by land, sea, or air must be inspected or certified by a reliable party. But even with the implementation of the technology for X-ray inspection that will be available shortly, there is no system that will be available soon that has sufficient throughput to allow for more than random screening at points of entry or departure.

So we need to create a reliable certification system. Here is the outline for such a plan.

A corporation sending goods across borders will be required to establish a full shipping inspection protocol, subject to approval and oversight by the Department of Homeland Security, in which approved employees who have been subjected to extensive background checks inspect, seal, and certify a container before shipment. A container's bar-coded seal would be electronically connected to a transponder, which would uplink to a satellite, then downlink to an international database. This would allow the shipper and receiver to track and monitor the integrity of the shipment as it moves around the world.

A container sealed and certified in this fashion would move across U.S. borders quickly, with occasional spot checks to ensure safety. If there were any suspicions about a container, authorities would be able to instantly pinpoint its location with the transponder and could halt it for inspection.

This security procedure would work for the majority of just-in-time shipments by large corporations. Smaller companies would either have to become certified or, if it was more economical, retain an approved firm to do their shipping. Goods that were not certified would have to be approved by American inspectors in the country of origin, then shipped in electronically sealed containers with transponders as described above. Small-package shipments would not be inspected, as the danger they represent is manageable.

This system would require a great deal of international cooperation, of course. But then, so does all effective security.

Other New Security Measures

Controlling Dual-Use Products As I've indicated, one function of the U.S. ID system would be to screen access to dual-use products. I also advocate more thorough study of the uses of such products and, in some cases, stricter controls over who gets to use them.

Corporations already gather extensive information about consumers to enhance their marketing efforts; some of this information should be made available to the national-security data bank. This will allow the government and corporations the flexibility to raise or lower their level of screening and adjust access to critical facilities as circumstances change; when needed, it would ease the use of appropriate preventive action.

In some cases, we may choose to restrict the sale of a particular item to a particular person. This is not a new concept—we already regulate who can buy or possess certain medicines, drugs, and explosives—but I suggest we expand our definition of the kinds of goods that are subject to screening.

The most obvious example of a dual-use product that needs greater regulation is, of course, guns. Many Americans like to own and shoot guns, and most of them do so in a responsible, socially acceptable way, but guns are undeniably deadly weapons, and they are sometimes intentionally used to do harm. We need to know about a potential gun owner's background, and in some cases—when the buyer has a felony conviction, for example—we need to restrict or deny that ownership. This is common sense. The companies that manufacture such dual-use products must play a role in regulating their sale.

Improved Port Security Ports are crucial hubs, encompassing transportation, trade, recreation, military transport, and education, but they are often overlooked. Given the new threat environment, we can no longer afford to ignore the vulnerability of our harbors. We must make port security a priority, akin to the security of airports, roadways, and railroads. To achieve that, we need to create national port security standards. Port security has traditionally been the responsibility of local authorities, and the result has been a wide variety of standards. We must establish a clear set of national guidelines to protect our harbors, ships, and people from terrorist attack. Some of the issues these standards should address include background checks of all port workers, screening of all travelers and their luggage, prevention of unauthorized access to sensitive areas, and the use of sensors and sniffer technology to screen ships for weapons of mass destruction.

Expanded Use of Video Surveillance Today we have extensive use of video surveillance in both public and private settings. Many wealthy private individuals employ video surveillance of their houses and grounds as a part of their security plan. Private companies use video surveillance as part of their standard operating security procedures. It is used for purposes from preventing outside break-ins at warehouses to catching shoplifters in stores, from monitoring work flow in factories to keeping track of visitors in an office building. The video surveillance camera is ubiquitous in America's private sector.

Video surveillance is also used extensively by all levels of government, both in the United States and abroad. Besides uses similar to private industry, governments use video surveillance for such diverse issues as traffic volume controls, tracking and ticketing moving violations by drivers, and maintaining surveillance of fare payment for public transit.

As useful as video surveillance has become in the last decade, with the development of facial recognition technology it promises in the near future to become a powerful tool to fight terrorism. We should take advantage of it and use recorded images as another layer of security.

As part of the Proteus Plan, I envision all people who are issued a U.S. ID card—and all individuals entering the country—having their photo taken with a digital camera, much as they do now for a driver's license. It needn't be a posed picture, and it can be taken as you wait behind the yellow line to have your passport checked or as you wait in your car. These photos would be tied together in the same database as the U.S. ID card information. Furthermore, the Proteus system would link extensive public and corporate video surveillance of those entering, say, a public monument or nuclear power plant to the national database, which would be equipped with facial recognition software. Such image-based surveillance would greatly enhance our ability to search for suspects or those wanted for questioning at times of heightened alert. It provides yet another flexible layer of protection and would not intrude on daily life except in exigencies.

Critics will jump on this suggestion as Orwellian. But the fact is that our privacy is already impacted by widespread use of video cameras. Legally, video surveillance is acceptable in areas in which there is no expectation of privacy, such as on a street, in a theater, or in a common hallway. It is not legal to monitor others on video in a private room without a court order (under most circumstances) or at private meetings at which you are not present. The Proteus Plan does not change these rules. Making video surveillance one link of a national security system will greatly increase our safety while having minimal impact on our liberty.

Can It Be Done?

One final question that I am often asked about my proposals for screening people and shipments is this: Given the political, social, and cultural history of the United States, can such a program ever be realistically implemented here?

This is perhaps the toughest question of all. It's tough because there are fairly large, vocal constituencies in the United States that will almost certainly oppose my program. They include civil libertarians of both the left and the right, advocates for minority groups who might fear that any screening process will work to their disadvantage, and the many Americans with an ingrained distrust of all large, powerful institutions, especially the federal government.

It may be that opposition from these groups will doom the Proteus Plan . . . at least until some future terrorist assault increases the public tolerance for strong, nontraditional measures to secure our safety.

Whenever the proper time comes to enact some version of my program—and I'm convinced that time *will* come, sooner or later— I hope it is done right, after vigorous public debate, a thorough educational effort, and the creation of robust safeguards against abuse. If this happens, the screening program can serve as a powerful enhancement of Americans' liberties, not a threat to them.

Individual Self-Defense— What You Can Do to Be Safer at Home, on the Street, and on the Road

America is a target-rich environment. Ironically, the freedom, mobility, and wealth that we enjoy, and which give our nation such strength, are the very things that make us vulnerable to terrorist attack.

Chances are good that the threat starts close to home. Your house is probably downwind from a petrochemical plant, a nuclear power plant, or another potential target. There may be an airport, a harbor full of container ships, or a rail hub nearby that terrorists have their eye on—indeed, captured al-Qaeda computers held detailed reports on U.S. railroads and their vulnerabilities, including photos of typical passenger and freight cars.

Even your breakfast food is a potential risk. Your orange juice is manufactured in Brazil, your coffee is from Colombia, your bacon and eggs are from the local farm, and your grapes are from Peru. It requires many people, and many steps, to bring those foodstuffs to your table, each of which is a potential weak spot.

By 2001 mad cow disease in British cattle led to 115 deaths in humans; in 1996, Guatemalan raspberries containing a parasite infected some 1,400 people; in 1993, *E. coli* bacteria in Jack in the Box hamburgers led to 708 cases of illness and four deaths; in 1989, Chilean grapes were suspected of being laced with cyanide and led

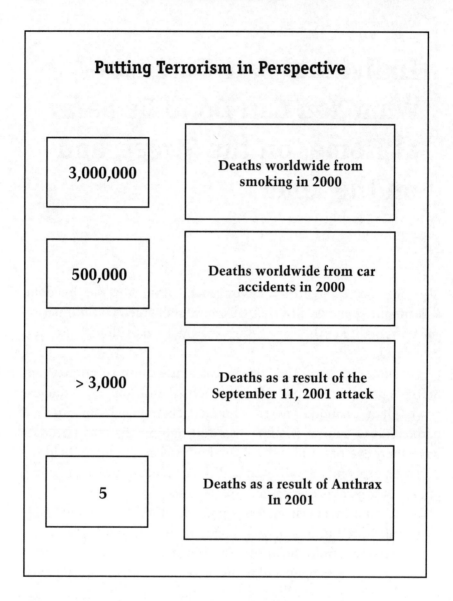

Putting Terrorism in Perspective

3,000,000	Deaths worldwide from smoking in 2000
500,000	Deaths worldwide from car accidents in 2000
> 3,000	Deaths as a result of the September 11, 2001 attack
5	Deaths as a result of Anthrax In 2001

to a widespread panic. You can imagine what might happen if a bioterrorist intentionally spread a disease.

Let's say you live in a New York suburb and commute to Manhattan for work, as I do. You probably have a predictable routine: You leave your house at the same time every morning, drive your car on the same route to the train station, park in the same parking lot, and board the same train into the city every day. Anyone watching you could predict where you'll be, and when, with a good deal of accuracy.

The train leaves from a station crowded with commuters, runs on tracks that cross bridges and pass through a tunnel under the river, and arrives at an even bigger and more crowded station at the other end. All of these machines and attendant structures are vulnerable to attack.

You arrive at your office building in midtown. While it may look like just another concrete-and-glass tower, it may have as a tenant an organization, such as an FBI office, a religious philanthropy, or a media company, that is a high-profile target. Or your office tower may be near another building with symbolic importance, such as an embassy, that is a target for attack.

Once you enter your building, another set of concerns arises. Is there a front desk with effective security in place? Is there an underground parking garage where a truck bomb could be delivered, as it was to the World Trade Center in 1993? Do maintenance workers whose backgrounds have not been thoroughly vetted have easy access to the building's HVAC systems? Where do you work— near the mailroom, where you could be affected by anthrax-tainted mail, or next to the CEO, who could be a target of attack?

I think the point is clear: Most of us are surrounded by a nearly limitless number of targets. The question is, how do we respond?

The first thing I tell people is that unless you are an especially controversial or prominent person, the chance you will be attacked by terrorists is small. You are far more likely to be the victim of a "normal" crime, such as robbery. I also remind people that no matter how many precautions they take, they will always be vulnerable to attack. Can you stop a hijacked 767 from flying into your office building? No. But, fortunately, the chances of that happening are slim to none. "Don't spend your time peering out the office window for a hijacked plane coming your way," I find myself saying to nervous office workers. "Such anxiety is counterproductive. Get on with your life."

Still, there *are* many things we can do to mitigate risk and enhance our security. The process begins with asking yourself how real the threat is and what a time- and cost-effective response might be. There are many things we *can* do to protect ourselves, but what are the things we *should* do?

You can, for example, ask what is the likelihood that the office building where you work will be targeted for attack. Your answer to that question will lead to some choices. If there is a high likelihood of attack, you may want to suggest to the leaders of your firm that they improve the building's security arrangements; you may want to urge that the company move to a different location; you may even want to consider changing jobs. On the other hand, if there is a low likelihood of attack, you should probably decide to accept the small risk and focus your energies on other things.

I believe that even the most highly visible target is very unlikely to be attacked. Again, my advice is: Don't smoke, buckle your seatbelt, and get on with life.

Take the typical commuter whose daily life I described above. Suppose such a person were to decide that he or she is particularly vulnerable to a terrorist attack—perhaps by virtue of being an executive with a firm that is a known target, or because of having made public statements about controversial political issues. There are a number of changes such a person might make in his or her daily life. If you are in that situation, you might choose to shop for food with special care, take varying routes to work using different means of transportation, and perhaps consider moving your home to some more remote location. All of these steps will help insulate you from attack, but of course they come at a cost, and even then they won't guarantee your safety.

Those at extreme risk may want to consider more extreme measures. Certain high-profile executives at the most successful American companies require sophisticated security systems around their homes and armored cars manned by specially trained drivers. You can buy an armored car that is built to withstand the explosion from a twelve-pound land mine. There is enough demand for such cars that a number of companies specialize in their production; they are expensive and they guzzle gas, but they are tough. In certain Latin American countries, where kidnapping is an industry, armored cars are common among the wealthy elite.

However, the vast majority of people, even wealthy, notable people, don't need these things. I personally haven't changed my life or my daily routine since September 11. I continue to live in a suburb of New York City and commute to work in Manhattan. I have not curtailed my travel—as a CEO, I am constantly flying around the country and the world for business. I do keep a flashlight nearby; I maintain an extra supply of water in my basement in case of emergency. But I don't carry a gas mask or a weapon in my briefcase, as some of my colleagues do. I simply keep my eyes and ears open, and try to use common sense. (Of course, my wife is quick to remind me that I am neither rich nor famous, and therefore have only the standard worries of the day.)

Surveillance and Countersurveillance

Terrorists aim to accomplish a number of things by an attack: to attract attention to their cause, increase their own prestige, maximize the damage to their adversaries, produce fear, and limit the damage to their own organization.

If you are worried about becoming a target of a criminal or terrorist attack, the first step to take is to assess your personal level of risk. Ask yourself the most fundamental questions: Who would attack you? Why? How? When? Where? To answer these questions, you need to learn to scrutinize yourself and your activities in the same way a potential attacker might. To ensure success, a terrorist would gather information about a target and carefully plan the approach, attack, and escape. The simplest way to do this is to use surveillance to identify patterns of behavior. The purpose of this is to determine a target's value and vulnerability and to give the terrorist the greatest chance of inflicting the maximum damage with the minimum risk. We humans are creatures of habit, but the more established our routines become, the more vulnerable we are to crime, whether a terrorist attack or a mugging. This is especially true if you live abroad or in a high-risk area. As U.S. government facilities become hardened, terrorists have learned to strike at softer targets—like resorts, as in the attacks in Bali and Kenya, or at people's homes.

On October 28, 2002, a Monday morning, Lawrence Foley, a senior administrator at the U.S. Agency for International Development (USAID), left his two-story villa in Amman, Jordan, to go to work, as usual. As he walked to his red Mercedes an unidentified person shot him three times in the chest, killing Foley instantly, as his wife looked on. The assailant disappeared.

This crime was hauntingly similar to the 2001 killing of an expatriate American businessman and his wife who lived in Kuwait City, Kuwait. They enjoyed their life abroad, and the executive was well protected at his workplace, but over the years the couple had established a comfortable private routine. Every evening they'd share dinner at home, then take a casual stroll a hundred meters down the street to an Internet café, where they'd check their e-mail. After an hour, they'd return by the same route and retire for the night.

One evening, not long after the attack on the Pentagon and World Trade Centers, a sedan pulled up behind them as they strolled toward the Internet café. A man, whom witnesses later described as "Pakistani-looking," got out of the car, walked up behind the couple with an AK-47 assault rifle, and shot the American executive in the back of the head, killing him instantly. The attacker shouted, "Allahu Akbar!" ("God is great" in Arabic), and turned to make his escape. When the victim's wife began to scream, the attacker turned back and shot her three times. Then he jumped into the sedan, and his co-conspirators whisked him away. The American woman was seriously injured but, amazingly, survived.

Both of these assassinations were carefully planned and, unfortunately, well executed. The attackers had observed the Americans' routines and determined that their moment of greatest vulnerability was either at home in the morning or during an evening stroll; in both cases, the victims were with their spouses and had let their guard down. It is not clear in either case whether the attackers were affiliated with al-Qaeda, but there is no doubt that the murders were acts of terrorism. The victims were chosen because they were symbols of the United States—the American government (in Foley's case), or American capitalism (in the latter case)—in an Arabian country. The victims' fatal mistake was to develop a predictable routine in an unpredictable environment.

To increase their chances of success, criminals usually monitor several people or locations before choosing a target. The things they are looking for include:

- Avenues of access and escape around the target

- The time of day when concentration of people is highest

- The strength and routines of security patrols

- The presence of guard dogs, alarms, or special equipment such as mirrors

- The response time and effectiveness of security and emergency services

In conducting surveillance, the bad guys have to position themselves where they can observe and record activity, which could expose them to a vigilant observer. Terrorists and criminals often disguise themselves, of course, but the disguise can be a giveaway. They must fit in with the crowd, have a reasonable cover story, and be able to give a logical answer when questioned.

If you know what to look for, suspicious behavior can stand out. The list below provides some behaviors to watch for. Any one of these actions, taken alone, need not set off alarms, but two or three of them linked together should prompt you to alert security personnel:

- People standing near a point of interest, making diagrams, maps or notes, or talking into voice recorders.

- A package or bag intentionally left in an unusual place, to provoke a reaction. Does anybody notice the bag? If so, is it handled with suspicion and care? If not, what happens to the bag?

- People asking odd or inappropriate questions about security.

- Pairs of people pretending to videotape each other, but actually recording the size and location of defensive barriers, security cameras, lights, fences, and so on.

- Reverse videotaping: a person standing with his or her back to the normal point of interest while videotaping avenues of approach and escape.

- People walking in a manner that suggests measuring a distance, or photographing buildings from unusual angles that would help them determine size, location, etc.

- Provoking a false emergency, such as a heart attack, in order to gauge the response of medical and security personnel.

- People sitting in a car during peak visiting hours at a landmark; people returning to the same car at the same time as the guards change their shift.

With these basic surveillance methods, criminals or terrorists are able to establish patterns and plan their attack.

How can you respond? One of the most effective ways to confound criminals is to break your established patterns and introduce randomness to your schedule. This helps to create uncertainty in the mind of would-be attackers, makes them work harder, and often convinces them that you are not worth pursuing.

If you truly believe you could be the subject of an attack, you can apply these basic lessons on surveillance and countersurveillance to your own life. Vary your daily routines. Take different routes to and from work. Choose parking spots at random. Keep your eyes open for people and activities that look odd, and enlist help from security professionals as needed.

How to Be Prepared for a Catastrophic Attack

Crises never happen when we are ready for them, and so we must take basic precautionary steps in order to respond to an emergency situation. While it's nice to think the government will protect us from disaster, the reality is that a terrorist assault—or a sudden storm, or an earthquake—can result in widespread death and destruction that could overwhelm the resources of the government's first responders on the scene. That means we must be prepared to take care of ourselves.

Each of us is responsible for securing our home, being vigilant outside of the home, and being prepared to respond to a crisis at any moment. If you build a good foundation of preparedness, you'll be able to respond to any kind of major disaster—whether it's a flood, train derailment, or even a terrorist's bomb.

The myth is that the federal government is responsible for disaster recovery.

The truth is that local governments are primarily responsible for preparing for disasters that might affect a community, and helping residents to recover from such events. The great majority of disasters are handled successfully at the local level. State and federal resources are intended to assist the community only when the community's resources are insufficient. The lesson of this is that in the event of a disaster, you must be prepared to take responsibility for yourself, your family, and your community. This means identifying the kinds of hazards that are most likely to affect your community, learning how to respond, preparing to be self-sufficient for three days, organizing community members to assist during a disaster, and identifying facilities within your community that could be used as shelter in a disaster.

The Basics of Disaster Preparedness Once a disaster is under way, it's unlikely that you will have the time or mobility to shop or search for important supplies. Experience has shown that rescue and emergency response agencies may not be available to help every individual for the first day or two of a crisis. The answer? Be prepared. Preparation gives us a greater chance of survival in the event of a crisis and will limit the success of any attack. This means taking the time to properly educate, train, and equip yourself for a worst-case scenario.

Depending on the nature of the disaster, you may need to be self-reliant for a few hours, several days, or even longer. I generally recommend that people be prepared for a seventy-two-hour emergency period. During this time, you may be responsible for some or all of your own food, clothing, and other emergency supplies.

Below is a list of basic items to stock in a large duffle bag or backpack that should be stored in a dry place near the main door of your home. Make one disaster kit for each family member, one for the whole family to share, and one for each pet.

Disaster Supply Kit

- One gallon of water

- Nonperishable food

- Manual can opener

- First-aid kit that includes the family's prescription medications

- Battery-powered radio

- Flashlight

- Extra batteries and chargers

- Candles and waterproof matches

- Special items for infant, elderly, or disabled family members

- Extra set of car and house keys

- Cash or traveler's checks (do not pack gold)

- Blankets or sleeping bags

- Clothes and durable shoes

- Extra pair of eyeglasses

- Personal hygiene supplies

- Updated list of important phone numbers

- Important family documents, such as insurance policies, social security cards, and other family records (keep them in a waterproof container in the disaster supply kit)

To maintain the disaster supply kits, remember to:

- Replace the stored water supply every three months so that it stays fresh

- Replace food every six months

- Replace batteries once a year

- Consult your doctor or pharmacist about storage times for prescription medications

Everyone in the family should know where the disaster supply kits are stored. In the event of emergency, you should pick a place to meet up with your family members. Some choose a place in the community, while others pick a place more distant—at, say, a friend's or relative's house. Create a family evacuation and/or escape plan, and make sure everyone understands it.

At a bare minimum, each family member should know how to:

- Summon assistance by dialing 911 on the phone

- Administer CPR and basic first aid

- Use a fire extinguisher and fire escape

- The location of the family gathering point or community relocation center

Adults should know their children's school emergency plan and the emergency plan for their workplace. Children should know their school's emergency preparation plan and phone numbers to contact parents at home or work. Most emergency shelters don't accept pets (with the exception of guide dogs). To many, a pet is a member of the family, and if you evacuate your home, you should be prepared to take your pets with you. Create a portable survival kit for your animal, and determine ahead of time a safe place to take your pet.

In the event of a major calamity, you may be forced out of your home for a while. To prevent dangerous leaks, explosions, and other unnecessary damage to the home in your absence, you should know where, when, and how to shut off the electricity, gas, and water at main switches and valves, and you should have the tools to do this (usually an adjustable wrench).

How will you be kept informed? A nationwide network of television and radio stations broadcasts continuous weather information from the National Weather Service. You should find out what the emergency radio/TV channel is in your area before there is an emergency.

Certain cities have Web sites dedicated to providing updates to the public and the media in an emergency situation. In

Washington, D.C., for example, the site is www.dc.gov; in New York it is www.nyc.gov.

For "amber alerts," severe weather, and utility outage information, www.emergencyemailnetwork.com serves as an emergency e-mail system.

The Emergency Alert System (EAS) is designed to provide the president with a means to address the American people in the event of a national emergency. EAS may also transmit state and local emergency information.

Another helpful Web site for further information is maintained by the American Red Cross at www.redcross.org.

What to Do If Terrorists Strike

There has been a nearly overwhelming amount of information in the popular media about the kinds of responses we should take in an emergency, and the result has generally been confusion. I am frequently asked: "What should I do if a nuclear/radiological/chemical/biological attack occurs?" The short answer is that you do what you had *planned* to do. It is all about *preparing*—yourself, your family, your community, your corporation, and our nation— for an attack.

Here are a few ideas about what you should plan to do.

What Should I Do if There Is a Chemical Attack? Most chemicals do not produce a visible cloud, but handheld chemical sensors, like the CAM (chemical agent monitor), can quickly detect a chemical attack. The emergency response teams in most cities are already equipped with such devices and will use them to determine what type of chemical agent was used. Indeed, local safety personnel trained in HAZMAT (hazardous material) response are well suited to respond to a chemical attack. Around the site of the attack, first responders will set up hot, medium, and cold zones; decontamination areas; triage areas; patient transfer points; and so on.

If you have been affected by a chemical nerve agent such as

sarin, most EMT trucks around the country are now equipped with "auto injectors"—injection devices the size of a pen that contain the drugs atropene and 2-PAMCI, which are antidotes for nerve agent poisoning.

To avoid contamination, go inside, close all windows and doors tightly, turn off all heating, air-conditioning, and ventilation systems that draw air in from the outside, and close the fireplace flue. Seal all windows and doors with duct tape; you can further seal your house with plastic sheeting over windows and doors. Some experts advise against going to the basement because chemical agents such as VX and sarin are heavier than air and will drift down and collect there. Plan to stay indoors for seventy-two hours, by which point the winds will likely have cleared the area. Listen to safety updates and for the "all clear" call on the radio or TV.

What Should I Do if There Is a Biological Weapon Attack? Biological agents such as anthrax or smallpox take anywhere from a couple of days to two weeks to take effect, so there is time to find out if you have been exposed and get treatment. Anthrax is not contagious and can be treated with antibiotics such as the cheap and effective doxycycline. Cipro has been frequently mentioned in the press, but it is expensive and requires a doctor's prescription. Smallpox is highly contagious; an effective vaccine exists, but it is controlled by the government, which is stockpiling millions of doses around the country, and is not available to the public.

Once a biological attack has been detected, you should immediately go inside and seal up your house in the same way described above. Wash your skin with soap and water. Listen for updates on the radio or TV, and be prepared to stay inside for two or three days.

What Should I Do if Terrorists Explode a "Dirty Bomb"? A dirty bomb is not the same as a nuclear bomb. It is essentially a weapon made by packaging radioactive material such as cesium 137 and strontium 90 (used in machines for irradiating food and treating cancer) with conventional explosives such as dynamite. A dirty (or radiological) bomb kills or injures by the initial blast of conventional explosives and by the subsequent spread of radiation and contamination.

Initially it won't be obvious what kind of bomb exploded. Depending on conditions at the blast site, including winds, rain, etc., it will take authorities armed with Geiger counters a couple of hours to determine whether a bomb contained radiological material.

The first thing for victims to do is go to a hospital or find a local medical unit, where you will be checked for injuries and shock; there your body will be scanned to determine if you have been exposed to radiation. If radiation is present, the doctors will ask you to strip; they will destroy your contaminated clothing, wash you down, and ask you to drink plenty of fluids to flush the radioactive material out of your body.

Should I Stockpile Potassium Iodide Pills in Case of Nuclear Attack? A nuclear explosion or the meltdown of a reactor (as at Chernobyl) produces radioactive iodine isotopes that are dangerous because they lodge in your thyroid gland and poison you. Potassium iodide pills fill your thyroid with clean iodide, thereby blocking the dangerous isotopes. Although you can buy iodide pills over the Internet (at www.nukepills.com), and some communities, including Westchester County, New York, where I live, have distributed free iodide pills to residents who live near a nuclear power plant, experts caution that preventive doses of iodine can cause harmful side effects. The only time to ingest potassium iodide pills is as soon as you know you will be exposed to radioactive iodine isotopes. The chance of a nuclear meltdown or attack is not high but it must be prepared for.

Security at Home and on the Street

Criminals are always seeking an advantage over their victims, most of all the element of surprise. Al-Qaeda relies on surprise, and so do everyday criminals. Some of the steps you need to take to protect yourself and your family from the dangers posed by terrorists are similar to those that will deter ordinary burglars, rapists, and killers.

Generally, for instance, burglars won't approach your house directly, which allows you to see them coming, but will try to sneak down a dark alley or enter through a back window. Any cover you provide them—big shadows, bushes to hide behind, an open garage, obstructed sightlines—works to their advantage and your disadvantage.

A well-designed, multilayered home security system will deter criminals before they even attempt to intrude or attack. Perhaps counterintuitively, the system should be as visible as possible. If you inform would-be intruders through a series of visual cues that your house is well protected and that the risk of detection is high, then chances are excellent that they will talk themselves out of choosing you as a target.

Placing a series of white lights activated by motion sensors around a house is one of the most effective and affordable ways to scare off intruders. The lights send a clear message to any potential attacker that this house is well protected. Another simple step to take is to prune back the shrubbery and trees around your house. This will open up sightlines and remove places where someone could crouch and hide in the shadows, particularly at night. Both of these steps are easy and effective. They maximize attackers' exposure and reduce their element of surprise, thus making your house a much less desirable target.

A well-designed home security plan has three basic layers:

- The first layer separates your property from public space. It roughly coincides with your property line. The first layer of defense should include cosmetic clues, such as a fence, designed to slow down or deter a would-be attacker.

- The second layer covers the area from the property line up to and including the building's skin. This layer includes impediments such as lights equipped with motion-detecting sensors, doors and windows with locks, bars, and/or alarms, and low hedges that make it physically harder for attackers to gain entry to the house unnoticed by the occupants, neighbors, or passers-by.

- The third layer is inside the house. It includes internal space alarms, a safe room, and perhaps weapons (I discourage this). This internal layer of defense is designed to put an intruder who has penetrated the home at a disadvantage.

Once you leave your home, you must pay attention to your surroundings. There are almost always a series of preincident indicators, behavioral signals in the people around you that indicate that they intend to do you harm and which you should be on the lookout for.

Criminals don't simply appear out of thin air, after all, like Mr. Spock being beamed down from the starship *Enterprise*. Would-be killers or kidnappers frequently use teamwork, with scouts, decoys, hand signals, and other telling indicators. Let's say you are walking down a sidewalk and a kid sitting on a mailbox glances at you, then deliberately looks away and spins his baseball cap around on his head. He may be signaling to a confederate who is waiting around the corner that you are approaching. If you don't notice this signal, or ignore it, you may be walking into a trap. When you reach the corner, the confederate might suddenly reach out to snatch your purse or punch you in the face.

What should you do to avoid this situation?

First, you should be observing the street—who is on it and what they are doing—as you walk. Second, if you become aware of a sign of danger, such as the kid on the mailbox checking you out and signaling to his accomplice, then adjust your behavior accordingly. In this case, cross the street or take a different route. This is not a paranoid reaction; it is a prudent one.

Perhaps because I have lived in New York City and work there,

I am highly attuned to my surroundings and the subtleties of body language in those around me. I love to walk in the city, and as I move through sidewalk traffic I constantly scan the street and adjust my movements to avoid wandering pedestrians, reckless taxi drivers, or those who might assault me. Maintaining this level of awareness isn't difficult, and it's a matter of common sense.

Travel: Rules for the Road

For millions of Americans, travel for business and leisure has become commonplace. But we can't take our safety for granted any longer.

The map on page 195 shows the worldwide risk assessment Kroll experts made for our clients at the end of 2001 (risk levels remain substantially the same today).

The safety of travel, air travel in particular, remains a great concern today. The world is still in what I think of as a remedial phase as we adjust our sensibilities and security measures to the new post-9/11 reality.

In June 2002, for example, I flew on an Air France plane from Paris to London for a meeting. I was seated in business class, three seats back from the flight deck, and was shocked to see that the crew kept the cockpit doors wide open. Neither they nor the flight attendants were paying the slightest attention to what we passengers were doing just a few feet behind them. There was literally no security on that plane; I could have easily walked into the cockpit.

Some people have not understood that the world has changed profoundly and that we must adapt to it with stronger defensive measures. Others have scrambled to adapt to the increased threat but have taken the wrong measures. As I have discussed earlier, too much of what we've done in this country is a total waste of time and money. I fly once a week, on average, and can speak with some authority on this subject. It is still safe to travel both at home and abroad, only now we must do so more carefully.

All Americans who travel abroad stand out, as if they have a "Made in the USA" label on their back, and are therefore vulnera-

Terrorism Risk Rankings

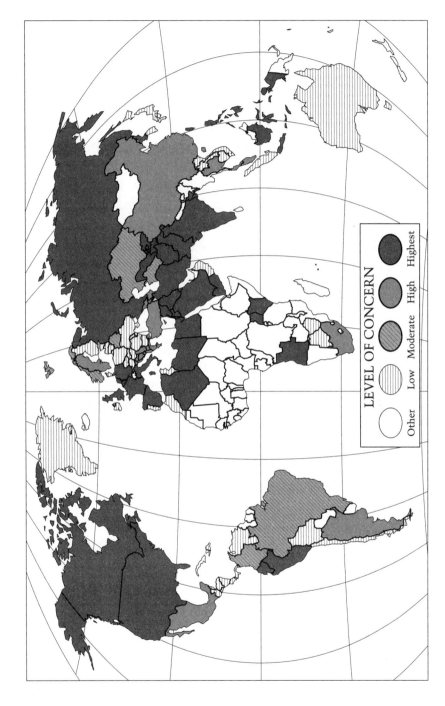

ble in a way they weren't five years ago. Today, the "ugly American" is not only an obnoxious tourist but also a target. This doesn't mean you should stop traveling; it means you should be deliberate and self-aware when you do.

Become well informed about where you're going, and behave in a reasonably careful way once you get there. This means, among other things, trying to blend in and being sensitive to cultural nuances. Even simple gestures can make a difference. In some Asian countries, for example, it is disrespectful to slap people on the back or even to shake their hand. Talking loudly is considered offensive in many cultures. Hand gestures have widely varying meanings—for example, the A-okay gesture many Americans use as a sign of approval is used in most other cultures as an obscene reference to a particular bodily orifice. These are small but telling behaviors that can make you appear to be rude and stand out. Take the time to learn the basics and practice them with sensitivity.

Before going abroad it is well worth checking the latest news and travel advisories about your destination. At one time, for instance, you could fly to Greece and expect only a wonderful, sunny, history-soaked vacation. But when the United States was conducting peacekeeping missions in the former Yugoslavia, Greece became a potentially dangerous spot for American tourists.

Even in a place as seemingly familiar as London, England, you have to be more careful now than ever before. While we share a language and many customs, the United States and the United Kingdom are very different nations. Today there is a large Muslim population in London, most of whom are peaceful and politically moderate, but some of whom definitely are not. The men accused of killing *Wall Street Journal* reporter Daniel Pearl were led by the British-born and educated Ahmed Omar Sheikh; Richard Reid, the so-called shoe bomber accused of trying to blow up an American plane, is British; and on September 11, 2002, London's Finsbury Park mosque, long considered a recruiting station for radical Islamists, celebrated the anniversary of the terrorist attacks in the

United States with a conference called "September 11: A Towering Day in History."

It would be naive to believe that just because you are on British soil you are automatically exempt from attack. Certain Muslims in London have a deep and abiding hostility toward Americans, and it is possible that one of them could prey on a clueless American tourist. Let's be clear: I am not tarring all Muslims or the city of London with the terrorist brush. But we individuals are responsible for our own safety, and we shouldn't wander into just any neighborhood because we feel like it. The same is true of Muslim neighborhoods in Germany, for example, or Algerian neighborhoods in France. Therefore, take some time before you travel to learn about current conditions in the countries and cities you will be visiting. You can do valuable predeparture homework on any number of travel-oriented Web sites, including:

- The State Department's travel advisory page: http://travel.state.gov

- The Overseas Security Advisory Council (OSAC): http://www.dsosac.org

- CIA world fact book: http://www.cia.gov/cia/publications/factbook

- ABC News country profiles: http://abcnews.go.com/sections/world/DailyNews/ geography.html

- Centers for Disease Control (CDC): http://www.cdc.gov

Another predeparture resource is to call the State Department in Washington, D.C., and speak to the regional security officer (RSO) for your destination. The RSO will generally fax you security updates based on the latest intelligence. Once you have arrived at your destination, you can also call the U.S. embassy there and ask the consular section about places or people you should be wary of in that country.

There are other security steps you should take before traveling. U.S. passports are highly valued on the international black market. In Bosnia, for example, a pilfered U.S. passport can fetch up to $5,000. To protect yourself, make several photocopies of your passport and put them in different bags. Keep the original in a safe place, such as a flat travel wallet you wear around your neck under your clothes, at all times.

Fill a small travel kit with safety essentials, such as a flashlight, locks you can affix to sliding doors and windows, a compass, and a packet of hand sanitizers (to kill bacteria and avoid illness). Some people choose to bring a pocket water purifier, a portable motion sensor, or a global satellite phone. I do not.

As you move through the airport, the increased security procedures now in place will distract you and add confusion, which creates an opportunity for people to take advantage of you. With your shoes off, your handbag being pawed through by a guard, and your laptop sitting in a pile of identical-looking laptops at the end of a conveyor belt, you are hardly in a good position to watch for a thief. Give yourself plenty of time, move deliberately through security, and mark your bags and laptop in such a way that they stand out (as with a piece of fluorescent yellow tape, for example).

Of course, on the road, as at home, you are still far more likely to be the victim of common crime—being pickpocketed, taken for a long taxi ride, or suffering a hotel room robbery—than a terrorist attack. If you wear a big gold Rolex in a Brazilian slum, you will probably be asked to hand it over. I would do so if I were you—I've heard too many stories about people being stabbed for $15 *fake* Rolexes around the world. Better yet, leave your beautiful watch at home and bring a cheap plastic one instead.

On the other hand, you have to know where to draw the line on cooperation with an attacker. If a robber demands your watch, give it up. But if the robber demands you get into a car, don't. There is no telling what could happen then, as the sad story of Daniel Pearl illustrates.

If you are knowingly traveling to a hazardous area, then you must be even more attuned to your environment. In Israel, the police have issued "Only Together Will We Stop Terror," a pamphlet to help the public identify would-be suicide bombers. In writing the pamphlet, Israeli authorities studied dozens of bombing cases and questioned over a hundred Palestinian bombers who had been intercepted before detonating their explosives. While terrorists often use disguises, such as dyeing their hair blond or wearing Israeli military uniforms, the pamphlet points out the telltale signs of people to be wary of. They include:

- A person whose clothes appear to bulge unnaturally, which may indicate that explosives are strapped to the body, or someone wearing inappropriate clothes, such as a winter coat in summer.

- A person who is nervous and sweating, talking to him- or herself, or walking quickly in a focused way

- Someone wearing a particularly heavy backpack

- Someone trying to keep away from police or military personnel

The pamphlet also warns citizens to watch out for car bombs by being aware of cars that are parked illegally, especially near a crowded market or a point of historical or religious significance; cars that appear to be heavily weighted in the back; and cars carrying forged or mismatched license plates.

I hope these travel suggestions will not deter you from ordinary business or vacation trips. The vast majority of Americans can expect to return home safely from any visit abroad. Just remember to comport yourself intelligently, with the awareness that no matter how you dress or act, you *will* stand out as an American. You should go for a tour of the local ruins, but you should *not* get roaring drunk and stumble around the streets of Bogota at 2 A.M.

Maintaining Perspective

After the calamities of September 11, many Americans were left feeling anxious—some worried about subsequent terrorist attacks, while others worried about new domestic intelligence policies that they feared would turn America into a Big Brother–like police state. Both sides have a point. But, as always, it is important to balance our fears against our ability to live our lives in a normal fashion.

Life has no guarantees. You can exercise regularly, eat well, visit every medical specialist under the sun, and still die young. Similarly, we can do everything right security-wise and still suffer a catastrophic attack like the one on September 11. The realization that there is no such thing as perfect security makes some people acutely nervous.

I have a neighbor in the suburbs, for example, who has been consumed with fear since September 11. Her husband, son, and daughter all work in Manhattan, and every day she worries that something untoward will happen to them in the city and she'll never see them again. I try to remind her, gently, to keep things in perspective.

I recently gave the same advice to the CEO of a midsized bank. He called me because he was worried about going on vacation in Western Europe. Even though he was planning to travel aboard a corporate jet and would stay in high-end hotels, he was concerned that he'd be targeted for attack. My response was: "You're not a recognizable name. You're not in a high-profile business. The corporate jet is secure. Your hotels will be well guarded. In fact, you will be just as safe, and probably a good deal safer, than the average resident or traveler in Europe. Relax and have a good time."

Then there are those who fear that we may tilt toward having too *much* security. Many worry that the tough security measures we need won't be conducive to the open, free-flowing society that keeps America so vibrant. In light of past abuses by law enforcement agencies, this is a legitimate concern, although not one that should block necessary and responsible changes.

The world has changed. We have to understand the seriousness of the threat we now face; we have to realize that we no longer live in an America of absolute openness. But we must also keep our fears of Big Brother in perspective. We have to understand that upon entering a community, any community, individuals give up a certain amount of freedom to ensure the safety of the larger society.

Chapter 9

Self-Defense for Companies

Next to the government, the most important player in making the United States more secure is our corporations. Eighty-five percent of the nation's critical infrastructure is controlled or owned by corporate America. The majority of Americans work for corporations. I believe it is in our nation's interest, as well as in the long-term interest of every company, to have adequate security. But will corporate leaders play their part? We must make sure they do. Corporations play a critical role in my Proteus security system, one they must not be allowed to duck. Indeed, Washington should legislate a minimum set of security standards for all companies doing business in America.

In February 1993, when Ramzi Yousef and his band of terrorists exploded a van packed with nitrate fertilizer in the underground parking garage of the World Trade Center, it took nearly five hours to evacuate the 110-story north tower. As a result, the building's tenants put new security measures in place. Nearly a decade later, when the hijacked planes slammed into the World Trade Center on September 11, thousands of people were evacuated from both towers in under one hour. This was an extraordinary accomplishment, largely due to the new safety and evacuation procedures put in place after the 1993 attack. Yet it still wasn't enough.

When the twin towers collapsed about an hour after being hit, we lost some 2,800 people. It was, as Mayor Giuliani memorably put it, "a loss greater than any of us could bear."

In poring over the rubble at ground zero and interviewing survivors, investigators discovered that people who had taken quick, thoughtful action in the moments of chaos right after the attack were the ones most likely to survive. And, not surprisingly, the companies that had the best crisis plans fared better than those that did not.

Sadly, many companies did not react well to the attack. There were three main problems. First, the majority of companies in the towers had poorly conceived or out-of-date crisis management plans; some had no plan at all. Second, people's roles and responsibilities in an emergency had not been clearly defined, so that after the attack there was confusion inside the burning buildings about who should do what, where, and when. Third, most companies' crisis plans consisted of a single, static response (i.e., "listen to instructions on the public address system; go down the fire escape"), with no depth or redundancy built in. When the buildings' electricity, communications system, and phones were knocked out, there was little light and no backup communication plan. Even the fire and police departments had terrible communication problems, which certainly cost lives. As admirable as the evacuation and rescue efforts were on September 11, they could have been better.

On that day, companies all over the country were caught underprepared without a meaningful crisis response plan. Many of them remain unprepared today.

In a study conducted in the summer of 2002, the consulting group KPMG discovered that while many large companies had hired risk consultants after September 11, few of them had implemented the recommended crisis plans. Of the 135 companies KPMG surveyed, all boasting more than $500 million in revenue, an astonishing 47 percent had no crisis plan at all; one-fifth of them did not rate crisis preparedness a priority. This is a tremendous mistake. Simply hoping our problems will go away will not make it so. Security is no longer a luxury or a sideshow; for any organization, having a well-conceived security plan is now part of the cost of doing business. The globalization of the economy has created unprecedented opportunities for business, but it has also opened the door for unprecedented security threats against businesspeople and their organizations. The events of September 11, 2001, weren't the first terror-style attacks in the United States, after all, nor were they the first to target businesses and their employees. Consider the assassinations of corporate executives carried out by Ted Kaczynski, the Unabomber, or the hundreds of employees who died in Timothy McVeigh's bombing of the Murrah Building in Oklahoma City. Even small businesses or rural towns can be affected, as in 1984, when the Rajneeshees, a band of New Age spiritualists, tried to poison the residents of The Dalles, Oregon, in order to usurp their land; the effort failed. Now Islamic fundamentalists have openly stated that American companies have been targeted for attack. In this climate, businesses must perform a risk assessment of their properties and employees and then must implement a comprehensive security plan on an aggressive timetable.

Simply put, good security is good corporate governance. Providing a safe work environment is now part of a company's fiduciary and moral obligation to its employees, its investors, and its customers. Indeed, corporations control most of the nation's infrastructure and benefit from that control; therefore, they have a responsibility to manage that infrastructure in such a way as to help protect both themselves and the extended community. This means protecting lives and corporate assets as well as contributing to the physical and psychological safety of the community. I believe that this responsibility is so important that it should be mandated by law, and the financial burden should be shared with the federal government.

Security and Business: The Delicate Balance

What I have found in working with many of the Fortune 500 companies is that the best-run businesses react intelligently and with foresight to security threats, while the worst-run refuse to address the problems until it's too late. Unexpected crises can strike a company at any time, anywhere—from the aisle of a local supermarket to a street on the opposite side of the globe to the ether of cyberspace. The way in which a company reacts to the crisis sets a tone and can determine whether or not the company will survive. Yet, deciding what constitutes a proper response is never an easy thing to gauge.

In a quest for efficiency, one of Kroll's large clients—I'll call it Direct Selling, Inc.—spent nearly thirty years trying to consolidate its many disparate and far-flung direct marketing operations in one central hub. Finally, in the summer of 2001, the company achieved its goal when it consolidated its critical operations in a brand-new, very expensive, custom-built facility. Peter, the company's CEO, was beaming with pride over his new building. He considered it the crowning achievement of his long and successful career. But just three months after his company had moved into the new building, news that an envelope filled with anthrax spores had been discovered in a Florida office building changed everything—literally overnight.

The business of Direct Selling, Inc., relies heavily on the mail, and the company's gleaming new building was filled with state-of-the-art mail printing, sorting, and stamping machines. It was a beautiful facility. But Peter and his executive team quickly realized that if a single anthrax-tainted envelope were to enter the facility, it might shut down the company. In a quest for efficiency, Peter had unwittingly put all of his company's eggs in one basket, making the entire firm vulnerable to the whims of an anonymous madman.

To his credit, Peter immediately understood that he had no choice but to painstakingly backtrack on his years of work and millions of dollars spent. Today, Direct Selling, Inc., has sold its custom-built facility and has once again dispersed its businesses in order to segment the risk. Now, if one facility receives a tainted letter, the others will be able to continue operating, and the company will survive. Peter confided that this was one of the most difficult decisions he'd ever made. While I'm sure that is true, I am also sure he made the right and responsible decision for the company's future—which, after all, is his job.

While it is important to be aware of potential dangers, it is also important for a business not to overreact to potential threats. Devoting too much time and money to beefing up security is inefficient and wasteful, and it will damage the corporation's ability to compete. Like everything else in this area, balance is required.

Another firm unnerved by the possibility of anthrax infiltrating its mail system—I'll call this company PackageSafe—boasted one of the best security programs in the nation, with an excellent mail-screening system in an isolated building staffed by former military police. In the weeks after the first anthrax scare of 2001, however, PackageSafe was ready to virtually stop work and revamp every security procedure it had. We convinced them that such a panicky response would prove ruinous. The fact remains that most businesses, like most individuals, are far more likely to be victims of ordinary crimes, especially theft, workplace violence, and fraud, than of a terrorist attack.

As we have seen with depressing regularity, a company's worst enemy can sometimes be its own employees—as when the top brass of companies such as Enron, Tyco, WorldCom, and ImClone allegedly perpetrated enormous financial frauds. In each of those cases, the greed at the top plunged the company into crisis and led to the destruction of shareholder value, if not the company itself. Given the end results, such scandals represent a threat to corporations that is second only to a terrorist's bomb.

The Cost of Security

Many executives have a perception that security is expensive, cumbersome, and unproductive. It is not a *profit-generating* step, they say, it is a *loss-reducing* one, and it slows down the flow of commerce. They may be right, viewed in a certain way, but by ignoring security they are putting the viability of their company, the lives of their employees, and the physical and economic security of the nation at risk.

Everyone would agree, I think, that no company can afford to have zero security. The question is, how much security does a company need and how much can it afford? How much is practical and cost-effective?

I am the CEO of a multinational corporation, and I deal with these kinds of questions every day, both in my own company and for my clients. Every move a business leader makes should be subject to a cost-benefit analysis. As competition grows increasingly fierce, corporate chiefs are being squeezed to run lean-and-mean operations. At the same time, the rewards of a slight uptick in a stock's price can be extraordinary, and, human nature being what it is, some CEOs have risked jail time in order to goose their stock a little. In this environment, the natural tendency is to ignore security or pay it lip service, to do the minimum and hope for the best.

The calculus works like this: If you're a CEO building a new $200 million headquarters, then it's not a big deal to add another $1 million to the budget for security. But if your company is based in an old building, then a $2 million retrofit for security can be daunting. (A retrofit generally costs double what new construction does.) The temptation is to ignore it. And so a flawed CEO's internal monologue on security might be: "The chances of our being attacked by a terrorist or big-time criminal are very slim. September 11 was a one-time event. It's never happened before, so why should it happen again? And even if it does, it won't happen to me. Retraining my employees, reengineering my building, and reinventing the way I run my operation is a huge, expensive, time-consuming headache. And the expense may cause me to miss my earnings-per-share estimate, which could cause my own net worth to plummet as my options tumble out of the money. So . . . forget it. I'll put a few guards in the lobby, remind our IT guys to keep an eye out for hackers, and call it a day."

This head-in-the-sand approach may give a company a short-term advantage, but the long-term consequences could be devastating. What is amazing to me is that while most companies are careful to avoid any hint of financial, legal, or public relations entanglements that might negatively affect their brand, they ignore the fundamental issue of security.

In the late 1990s, a Texas-based petroleum company sent four senior executives to Karachi, Pakistan, with no security detail and no training about terrorists. The group quickly slipped into a comfortable routine. They were kidnapped and murdered. The personal cost was devastating to their family, friends, and colleagues. The business fallout was enormous. And today the company has gone out of business.

What is the cost to a company if a Timothy McVeigh or a Ramzi Yousef detonates a truck bomb in its underground parking garage and destroys its headquarters?

These concerns must also be part of the cost-benefit analysis of security. They are all very real threats, and you can hardly schedule them to occur when you are prepared. What you can do is to *anticipate* them and make contingency plans to respond and minimize the damage.

Complicating matters is the fact that security can't be viewed as a silo cost center—a stand-alone operation within the corporate structure. Security is now a fundamental aspect of every decision that a company makes, from where to site a new building and how to construct it to whom to hire and what new international markets to enter. Security must be fully integrated into the company's systems, and its costs must be integrated into a company's overall budget.

Another security cost to bear in mind is the human one, and here we enter the realm of management theory. I often ask clients: "What is your business's most important assets: its founding idea?

its brand? its real estate?" Everyone has a different answer. Mine is that the *people* you employ are the biggest and most important asset; they are everything to you.

Investing in meaningful security measures sends the people who constitute a business several strong messages: *We are in this together. We care about you. The company is making a real effort to protect you.* If employees take these messages to heart, then their anxieties will fade and they will be willing to work all the harder.

Corporate Security: How to Achieve It

Effective security in the office, as in the home, is always built in layers. While it's easy to rip up a single piece of paper, tearing through an entire newspaper or phone book is much more difficult.

The three basic layers of effective corporate security are:

- Planning and preparedness

- Improvement of physical security and safety procedures

- Proactive gathering of intelligence and effective use of information

There are several basic steps that every company can take to build up these layers and thereby enhance its self-defense.

Threat Assessment Every company is unique, and so there's no cookie-cutter approach to assessing potential threats. There are, however, generic techniques to help executives gauge their vulnerabilities. Kroll asks clients to step back from the day-to-day hubbub and ask themselves basic questions about their company's strengths and weaknesses. Here are some of the factors we ask clients to take into consideration when assessing their own "risk equation":

- *Company profile.* If your company is an American icon—like Microsoft, Ford, or Starbucks—then it will be highly visible and associated with U.S. capitalism, and should be considered a potential terrorist target. Thus, French farmers displeased with the way American fast food was affecting their traditional way of life destroyed a McDonald's restaurant in the town of Millau, near Toulouse. Likewise, protestors opposed to American oil companies' drilling in the Amazon rain forest have blown up pipelines. If you have a low-tech, low-profile business—a clothing retailer, say—then your company profile risk is probably minimal.

- *Location*. Businesses located in major metropolitan hubs such as New York, Chicago, or Los Angeles are more obvious targets than those located in the suburbs or in rural areas. If you own a flower shop that happens to be next door to an Israeli embassy or in an office building that houses a branch of the FBI, then your risk is considerable, even though the threat has nothing to do with you or your business. The risk faced by individuals within the company will, of course, also vary by location. If you are a secretary who happens to sit near the CEO's office, your risk is exponentially higher than that of people who work in the company cafeteria. On the other hand, the mail room workers are more vulnerable to anthrax or letter bombs.

- *Type of industry*. A multinational media company based in Los Angeles is far more likely to be the target of a terrorist attack than, say, a home center in an Iowa mall. Each business has its own set of security concerns and must assess its threat accordingly. The mall retailer should be concerned about theft and workplace violence, but the media company—which purveys liberal American cultural values around the world—should be concerned about assassination, bombing, or a biological attack. American financial, energy, military, computer, and fashion industries also project our national identity around the world and therefore have a high risk profile.

- *Company-specific characteristics.* A particular company may have some historical, economic, cultural, or other characteristic that might attract the attention of a terrorist. Most of the victims of Unabomber Ted Kazcynski were scientists and executives with technology firms, because Kazcynski had become convinced that modern technology would eventually doom humanity. But one victim was an executive with the advertising firm of Young & Rubicam. Why? Because this executive had happened to participate in a television talk show on which the *Exxon Valdez* Alaska oil spill was debated. In assessing your risk profile, don't overlook peripheral or even coincidental connections like these; you can never be sure what may attract the attention of a single-minded attacker.

- *Criticality of operations.* In order to make a grand statement, those planning to attack a business usually prefer to target highly visible symbols of the company. So a headquarters building that houses the company's leadership and many of the corporation's key functions is more likely to be attacked.

- *Number of employees at facility.* Attackers often want to do the most amount of damage with a single blow, and so they aim for densely populated areas or facilities. The more people a company has at a given facility, the higher its value as a target.

- *Specific information.* Most important in assessing risk is whether there is any specific information that the corporation or its industry is a target, for whatever reason. Government agencies must share that kind of information with corporate America.

Security and Safety Assessment The second step in determining
your company's degree of risk is studying the physical setup of your
facilities. Scrutinize your office buildings, factories, warehouses,
and retail outlets the way a potential terrorist might, looking for
vulnerabilities and weaknesses. Here are some of the specific
points to consider.

- *Physical security.* The siting of a building, along with its ar-
  chitecture and engineering, provides the foundations for an
  effective and cost-efficient system. The design of access and
  egress points is particularly important; vulnerable choke-
  points and underground parking garages are unsafe, for example. The placement of closed-circuit TV cameras, the
  location of delivery areas, and the overall appearance of public areas are important design elements. Clutter provides
  hiding places and likely places for improvised explosive devices—such as a suitcase bomb. Other physical elements to
  bear in mind include security console design, electronic door
  hardware, security lighting and power requirements, and life-
  safety interfaces such as public address systems.

- *Personal security.* Employees are a company's most valuable,
  and vulnerable, asset. Steps must be taken to ensure that the
  right people can enter and exit a building quickly, while
  those who are suspicious are kept out. It is not practical for
  guards to physically check every person who enters and
  leaves a building. But an electronic identity card with a biometric component (such as a fingerprint) is an example of a
  simple screening method.

- *Information security.* Today, most of a company's intellec-
  tual property is stored in its database; it is essential to protect these "crown jewels" from hackers, saboteurs, and
  rivals.

- *Parking and approach control.* Anyone who approaches the building, whether in a car or by foot, should be screened before gaining admittance. Buildings with in-house or underground parking garages are vulnerable to the kind of car bomb attack that killed six people at the World Trade Center in 1993.

- *Access control.* Is the process of getting in and out of your office building secure and well controlled? Are the guards in the lobby efficient, or does their screening lead to long lines of frustrated people? In deciding who is allowed to enter your space, you need to focus your efforts on the small percentage of people who pose a potential threat, and expedite the passage of others. If too many employees are needlessly inconvenienced, political pressure will build to jettison the security apparatus altogether, and the attempt to improve safety will have backfired.

- *Life and fire safety.* In the event of a crisis, you must have adequate equipment, escape routes, communications systems, and protocols in place. The procedures must be up-to-date, known by everyone, and readily available for review at a moment's notice. It does no good to have an elaborate, well-designed escape plan gathering dust on someone's bookshelf, where no one will be able to find it in an emergency.

- *Lighting.* Do you have emergency lighting with its own independent power source to aid in escape during a fire, earthquake, or bombing? Do you have a flashlight in your desk or car?

- *Business-interruption planning and information security.* If an anthrax-laden letter enters your building or the mail stream of your business, will it shut down your entire operation? If a hacker attempts to steal credit card numbers off your database, do you have adequate safeguards in place? What kinds of information can a disgruntled employee access? What about a recently fired employee? Or an employee at one of the firms that acts as a supplier to your own?

Employee Readiness Assessment Preparing your employees for a disaster is not a one-time event. The people who work at your company represent a constantly changing stream of individuals; most firms experience at least 20 percent turnover in any given year. Therefore, it's not enough to ensure that the people on your staff at any given point in time are well intentioned, well trained, and capable of handling security issues, for within a few months that assurance will have become dated. Thus employee readiness must be assessed periodically and repeatedly. Here are some of the key factors to evaluate.

- *Employee and vendor background screening.* Today more than ever, it's important for companies to know whom they have hired and what their history is. Some positions carry obvious risks and therefore are likely to be carefully scrutinized—a corporate security official, for example, or the person who runs your information technology department. But other positions that may seem insignificant can be just as crucial. For example, it's easy for a cleaning person to access a company's HVAC system, especially after hours, when the hallways are deserted. A member of an alleged al-Qaeda sleeper cell was arrested recently while working as a dishwasher at an airline food-service company—an almost ideal cover for a terrorist planning to put a bomb on a jetliner. Careful screening before hiring can eliminate most troublemakers.

- *Security systems and protocols.* Security guards should not just sit behind a desk—they should conduct foot and vehicle patrols at irregular times and be willing to challenge people in a firm but friendly way. Occasionally they should introduce guard dogs or equipment such as under-car mirrors. They should carefully calculate the response time from their base to any location in or around the building, and be able to strengthen or relax the security in proportion to any given threat.

- *Mail and travel protocols.* These need to be thought out and implemented. Does every assistant know what to do when an odd-looking package arrives on his or her desk? Does every executive who travels on business for your firm know what to do in case an international emergency arises while he or she is in a foreign capital?

- *Crisis training.* It is essential to train employees how to use fire and escape equipment and to explain what they are expected to do in the event of a crisis. Again, this training is not a one-time event; it is an ongoing process. Yes, people will grumble, "Another drill? Didn't we do this three months ago?" Be happy when you hear these complaints; they're far better than the complaints you'd hear *after* an emergency if the crisis training had been neglected.

In the short term, risk assessment conducted according to the program I've briefly laid out above should help your company identify current threats and vulnerabilities, prioritize risks, and develop solutions that are easy to implement. In the long term, risk assessment can help your business develop a comprehensive crisis plan, upgrade its existing security systems, and make valuable modifications to its methods or facilities.

Once a company has assessed these three elements, it is time to take the next step: locate areas of vulnerability, make improvements, and formulate crisis plans and procedures.

Steps to Harden a Facility A building is not simply a pile of bricks and mortar. It is a complex system that depends on many people, materials, and parts to function properly. Similarly, a building's security system is made up of more than a guard and a lock on the door; it, too, is a complex system of many interconnected parts, or at least it should be.

Architects have traditionally addressed the issue of building security in a limited way. They include basic fire-safety and life-protective features in their designs, of course, but they have treated these things as add-ons, not as priorities that should be integrated with one another and into the overall design from the start. Holistic security requires the coordination of many people and functions into a cohesive system.

The design of a secure facility requires, among other things, the integration of architectural and engineering elements, careful siting, landscape design, building operations, and the unique requirements of the tenants. Whether a company is designing a new project or upgrading an existing one, it is important that it build a team that can coordinate these disciplines. This will reduce costs and delays, increase efficiency, and integrate passive solutions with new technology to arrive at an unobtrusivē and effective security program.

On September 12, 2001, the phones at security companies across the world began to ring off the hook. "Our employees are scared to go back into our office building," clients said. "What steps can we take to calm them and beef up security?" In the case of a few new clients, the answer was: "Be willing to make sacrifices now to build a safer future." But in most cases we'd reply: "Even though the world has been changed by the terrorist attack, the basic requirements for a safe building have not. Let's assess the security you have in place and make upgrades as needed."

Often the changes we suggest are subtle and practical, because the easiest and most obvious things work the best. One of our clients owns one of the most distinguished buildings on the West Coast. It had an effective internal security system in place, but after September 11 the building manager realized he had an external problem: The lobby had big plate-glass windows looking out onto the street. It would be easy for a terrorist to drive a car packed with explosives across the sidewalk, smash through the plate-glass windows, and go right into the building's lobby.

Within ten days, we had arranged for a chain of concrete "Jersey barriers" to be placed along the sidewalk in front of the building, to protect the lobby. It was a highly visible and effective solution, albeit a short-term one, and it was affordable—the barriers were erected overnight at a cost of something like $20,000. Nervous tenants were relieved, although everyone agreed that the Jersey barriers could be aesthetically improved upon. Eventually, a more permanent solution was found: stout, nice-looking marble planters. Once the planters were in place, they afforded excellent protection and integrated so well with the building's design that they looked as if they had always been there.

To protect against attacks, consider enhancing:

- Fences and heavy barriers

- Lighting

- Controlled access points (biometric ID)

- Restricted parking (no under-building garage)

- Shatterproof glass

- Solid wood or sheet-metal doors

- Theft-proof high-end equipment, such as computers with fiber-optic cables attached to a building-wide alarm system

- Video cameras with time stamp

- Well-trained security force

As in the case described earlier, concrete Jersey barriers can be used to prevent or delay an intruder from using vehicles to breach a border or gain access to the interior of a building. Also, white lights can be used to fully illuminate the base of a building, to scare off intruders and expose them to the occupants of the building. And surveillance cameras located both inside and outside the facility can help security personnel evaluate a threat and plan a response; a time stamp allows for retroactive review of the tape, to help in the investigation of, say, a computer theft.

The Bottom Line The price of making a building secure can be steep and must be balanced against its benefit. As I've noted, the design and construction of an up-to-date security system in a retro-fitted building costs nearly twice as much as one in a brand-new building. But even those designing new buildings sometimes need convincing that security is worth investing in.

In the early nineties, Kroll designed a new corporate campus for a large oil company in Texas. Sited on seventy-eight acres, the campus was surrounded by a rugged wooded lot that was nearly impossible to penetrate. In an effort to restrict access, our team had designed a single entry point: a road that crossed a bridge over a deep ravine. The original bridge design had been narrow, with one lane for incoming traffic and another for outgoing traffic. But in working through a security assessment, we suggested making the bridge wider, with four lanes, two incoming, two outgoing, and a gatehouse in the middle, with mechanical gates, for enhanced protection. Our team was told the new bridge would cost too much. The campus had cost over $100 million to build, but the company's executives didn't want to spend an extra $100,000 for a wider bridge and gatehouse, even though they agreed it would be safer.

This conversation took place in February 1993. The following week Ramzi Yousef detonated a car bomb under the World Trade Center. The oil company immediately called us back and agreed to build the wider bridge and guardhouse.

The Human Factor The biggest variable in securing a building is, of course, the human beings that are in and around it.

The best security comes from people keeping their eyes and ears open and working together. There *is* strength to be found in numbers. If an employee spots something out of place or notices a strange person wandering in an area he or she is not supposed to be in, then the employee should challenge the person or call security and ask them to follow up. Again, it is far more likely that a company will be the victim of theft or workplace violence than a terrorist attack.

On the other hand, humans are unpredictable. It is part of our fallible nature to occasionally be lazy, arrogant, or anarchistic. In other words, people don't always follow rules, even if those rules have been established to maximize their safety. Here is a typical real-world example: In a building where access is controlled by a revolving door designed to let only one person through at a time, followed by an electronic identity card reader, the management explicitly says: "One person in a revolving-door quadrant at a time. Do *not* share your card." But it's almost inevitable that two or three rushed people cram into a quadrant together and then try to jam their way through the card reader. The result is that their violation of protocol sets off the alarms, and everyone behind them is delayed because the guards have to intervene.

Without people's participation, even the best security measures in the world won't work.

Computerized Terrorism Approximately 75 percent of the information in the world is stored in computers today. Ninety-seven percent of new information created in the United States is stored on computers. E-mail has become a potent new communications tool. Global networks integrate the multinational economy. For better and for worse, the global village is wired.

Terrorists who abhor the West's ultramodern technology often use that technology as a weapon against it. An al-Qaeda operative, for example, can use a satellite-based phone to access the Internet and download information—instructions for a poison gas attack in a Chicago subway station, say—that is then compressed and encrypted and slipped into an innocuous digital photograph, such as a beautiful NASA portrait of planet Earth. The digital disguise hides the dangerous material. This Trojan-horse-like file can then be e-mailed anywhere in the world. Even if the National Security

Agency manages to intercept the file, it is extremely difficult to find, decompress, and decrypt the hidden message.

Another tactic that terrorist organizations use is to combine high-tech equipment with ancient, low-tech tools. A terrorist in the Afghan desert might download sensitive material onto a laptop, print it out in a dusty local shop, and then send it to his confreres in Peshawar via donkey over a rugged moutain pass. This kind of communication is common and very difficult to trace or stop.

But computers can also help to solve crimes and protect innocent people. Not long ago, a corporation that owns hotels around the world received an e-mail at its headquarters that read, in part: *There is a bomb in one of your hotels. Unless you deposit $100,000 in a numbered bank account within 24 hours, I will detonate the bomb. This will destroy your hotel, kill thousands of people, and ruin your business.*

This kind of technology-enabled terrorism has blossomed in recent years. As society's reliance on information technology has deepened, terrorists and other criminals have grown increasingly brazen and sophisticated about using computers, e-mail, and electronic networks for illegal ends. Law enforcement agencies around the world—which are often underfunded and less sophisticated than the criminals they are chasing—have struggled to keep up with a growing number of hackers, cyber thieves, and terrorists. Sometimes the victims turn to private security firms for technical assistance.

In the case of the hotel bomb, the corporation's head of security forwarded the threatening e-mail to Alan Brill, a Kroll senior managing director who heads our computer crime group. The first thing that Brill noticed was that the threatening e-mail had originated from a Hotmail account. (Hotmail is a free e-mail service that anyone with computer access can use from any part of the world.) The perpetrator evidently believed that using Hotmail would preserve his anonymity. But by analyzing the information in the e-mail's header, Brill was able to deduce that the sender had been in a particular region of the world when he sent the message: Scandinavia.

With further scrutiny, Brill was able to determine that the message had originated from a specific country in Scandinavia, and then from a specific company in that country, and even from a specific office within that company. Brill called an old friend at the U.S. Department of Justice, who had a friend in that nation's Ministry of Justice, who put the local police on the case. With Brill's coaching, the Scandinavian police were eventually able to pinpoint which computer in that office had generated the threat. And then came a scene right out of Hollywood: the race against the clock to find the user of that computer before the bomb went off. The hotel chain was frantic with worry that it would soon face a major catastrophe at one of its many hotels around the world. Which one had the bomb? Would they be able to stop it from exploding? If not, how serious would the damage be?

The Scandinavian police tracked the perpetrator to an apartment in a medium-sized city and went in heavy, with bomb-sniffing dogs and a heavily armed SWAT team shouting, "Where's the bomb?" The man inside meekly surrendered, confessing: "There is no bomb . . . I just wanted the money." The entire drama, from the receipt of the hoaxer's threatening e-mail to his capture, took only a few hours. Through a mixture of skill and good fortune, the good guys won that time. But there is good reason to worry about your company's exposure to a similar attack.

Hackers and the Terror Connection The most infamous computer-based criminals are hackers—the sometimes mischievous, sometimes malicious computer aficionados who have learned how to break through electronic barriers and gain access to e-mail, home pages, and even sensitive government networks.

Shockingly, there may be a connection between computer hacking and terrorism. According to a survey conducted by the FBI and the Computer Security Institute, in the year following the September 11 attacks, some 90 percent of big corporations and government agencies uncovered security breaches in their computer networks. The security firm Riptech reports that cyber attacks jumped some 64 percent in the same time period, especially from terrorist-friendly states such as Iran and Pakistan.

It has been reported that October 2002 was the worst month for digital attacks on record, with an estimated 16,559 attacks carried out on systems and Web sites. Pro-Islamic hacker groups such as USG (Unix Security Guards), FBH (Federal Bureau of Hackers), and the BuGz have defaced Web sites with messages supporting Palestinians and opposing a war on Iraq: "USA I think that you are all about to become war criminals. UK you are a slave to USA."

More worrisome, the rise in pro-Islamic hacking coincided with an unprecedented denial-of-service attack on nine of the thirteen root DNS servers that form the spine of the Internet. While Washington downplayed the likelihood of cyber terrorism, computer experts said the concerted attack highlighted the vulnerability of the Web's infrastructure. Reuters reported that computer detectives have traced Internet users in Saudi Arabia, Kuwait, Pakistan, and Indonesia who are sleuthing out information about our nuclear power plants, communications, power transmission, and water storage facilities.

Yet while it's clear that awareness of computer security has risen dramatically, it is not clear that companies are actually taking the steps necessary to protect themselves. In a survey by Computer Economics, 77 percent of 233 corporations polled said they had reinforced their defenses against hackers, viruses, worms, and other attacks. But speaking to the *Wall Street Journal*, Alex von Someren, the CEO of U.K.-based Internet security firm nCipher PLC, complained, "Companies are paying lip service to security, but very few are speaking up with their wallets."

Small companies are especially vulnerable. While almost all large corporations have extensive network security software in place, *USA Today* reports that the nation's 5.6 million small companies, those with under $1 million in annual revenue, which employ half of all U.S. workers, face a substantial risk of cyber attack. Small firms lack the money and sophistication to have robust information technology security in place, and they don't often consider themselves likely targets for attack.

Many hackers are "script kiddies" who, in search of thrills and bragging rights, electronically break into servers and destroy home pages, find holes in corporations' networks, or try to sabotage operating systems. But increasing numbers have a more serious agenda. Some are politically motivated, as in the case of the Web war that erupted in 2001 after China forced a U.S. Navy plane to land and Chinese and American hackers defaced each other's sites. Lately a new breed of "hacktivists" have combined street protests with Web site attacks to protest the policies of the World Bank, the International Monetary Fund, and the World Trade Organization.

Fighting Back Technology experts have been developing tools to combat computer crime. Several security firms have developed hardware and software that allow for the replication, backup, and recovery of "lost" data. "Instead of blood and firearms, we dig around in computer data and storage," says Kroll security expert Alan Brill. "We have the ability to resurrect 'vampire' data—data that was assumed to be dead and buried. The recovery of lost material can literally save a company, and if necessary we can present it in court in a way that is as evidentially accurate as any other forensic science."

In the last few years, security companies have also created software that allows the monitoring of financial transactions and e-mail traffic, and the protection of corporate information. During the Gulf War the Department of Defense used this kind of technology to create huge databases of "people of interest"—everyone from government leaders to suspected terrorists—and to electronically track assets that Saddam Hussein had transferred out of Iraq and hidden in offshore accounts and dummy corporations.

Thwarting the Cyber Terrorists

Software/Hardware Security operates on the assumption that you must defend everything with equal vigilance—all routes into your home, office, or computer. But an attacker only needs to find one weak link in your armor to break in and cause problems. In the case of computer security, this could mean a loophole in the office network, or a weakness in the security software of your home computer.

Hackers can, for instance, launch a denial-of-service attack against another computer or Web site, which will clog or knock down the target's service. One way to accomplish this is to surreptitiously plant a "zombie" program in several computers; on command, the hacker will trigger all of the computers rigged with a zombie to start sending a stream of messages to the target computer, at, say, Amazon.com or the White House, in an attempt to overwhelm the network and shut it down.

Even with basic security software in place, a computer that uses a cable modem or a high-speed DSL (digital subscriber line) connection is vulnerable to attack, because your address is visible to cyber sharks cruising the Internet and your computer is always plugged into a network. The simplest and most affordable response is to:

- Ensure that you have security software installed on your computer and that it is updated on a regular basis.

- Purchase, or download for free, a firewall that hides your computer on the Internet and protects it against intrusions by hackers.

- Buy a router, a relatively inexpensive electronic device that puts an additional layer of security between your computer and those cruising the Internet looking for a vulnerable system to exploit. For laptops, consider getting a wireless router, which will give you an encrypted wireless connection to the Internet.

Passwords and Identity Theft If a hacker gains access to a computer or Web site, he or she can download sensitive personal data, such as addresses, phone numbers, and social security or credit card numbers, which are often sold to others. And so it is mystifying to me that people still choose easy-to-figure-out passwords to protect their accounts; among the most common are "secret" and, yes, "password." Beyond that, password-breaking software is now able to crack even difficult codes.

In 2000, the U.S. Federal Trade Commission reported approximately 500,000 victims of identity theft. In 2001, that number rose to approximately 700,000, making it today's fastest growing white-collar crime. And in November 2002, the largest identity theft ring in U.S. history—a Nigerian group based in New York that electronically swiped the identities of 30,000 people and used the information to steal thousands of dollars from bank and credit accounts—was broken up by federal agents. Identity thieves have often been disgruntled, or greedy, company insiders who were never subjected to rigorous background checks.

Fortunately, there are many steps companies can take to prevent identity theft:

- Screen everyone with access to personal information, including all temporary and part-time employees

- Keep hard copy personnel information in locked files

- Develop an encryption system for computer-based information and evaluate its effectiveness regularly

- Use shredders to dispose of confidential information

- Develop and enforce procedures for transmitting personal information (via fax, e-mail, etc.)

- Adopt a written protection policy and publish it in your company's literature and on your Web site

- Add a photo element to business cards, ID cards, and name badges

Laptop Basics For many of us, the laptop computer is our virtual office when we're on the road. As such, laptops are extremely vulnerable to theft, accident, or sabotage. Here are a few laptop dos and don'ts:

- *In the office:* It is easy for a messenger walking by your desk to slip a laptop into his bag and stroll away unnoticed. Always secure the laptop to your desk with a fiber-optic cable linked to a building-wide alarm system and backed up with security cameras. Or, at the very least, lock it inside your desk, or secure it to the desk with a cable lock that attaches to the hole provided for that purpose in the side of the laptop.

- *In a hotel:* Lock your laptop in the hotel safe, or use the cable-lock system described above. Do not assume that because your hotel room door and windows are locked that your equipment is safe.

- *In the airport:* Security regulations now often require you to take your computer out of its case and run it through the X-ray machine. The result has been that people sometimes leave their laptops behind as they rush off to catch a flight, or they grab someone else's computer, or someone swipes the computer. By marking your laptop with something unique—fluorescent yellow tape, which is ugly but effective—you will know that you are grabbing the right computer, and other people will know they are grabbing the wrong one.

- *Anywhere:* Increasingly popular are key-chain memory devices, also known as flash memory devices—portable data storage devices that are about the size of your finger, can be carried on your key ring, and plug into your computer's USB port. Useful for storing confidential data that you don't want to leave on your hard drive, these remarkable little sticks weigh only an ounce or two, contain from 32 to 512 megabytes of memory (enough for several PowerPoint presentations), and cost as little as $30. The latest, the Thumbdrive, is the size of your thumb and has a biometric lock: It reveals its data when triggered by your fingerprint rather than a password.

- *Laptop bags*: A fancy leather carrying case, or a bag embroidered with a prestigious corporate logo, is guaranteed to draw attention to itself and will tempt fate. A thief will assume that a fancy bag contains an expensive computer, and maybe other valuable goodies, and will go out of his or her way to relieve you of it. Better to use an understated bag that wandering eyes will hardly notice.

Old Computers and Disks Even if you erase all of the information on your computer, the fact is that it remains accessible. And that can be a big headache.

When a large accounting firm upgraded its computer system, it reformatted the hard drives of its old machines and auctioned them off. A techie bought the drives, de-reformatted them, and uncovered the raw audit notes for a number of important clients. He offered to sell the drives back to the accounting firm for a $25,000 "consulting fee." The district attorney's office deemed this extortion, and the techie plea-bargained. But it was an embarrassing mistake for the accounting firm.

So what is the answer?

You can now buy data-wipe software from security firms that literally wipes the data off your drive; not even the best computer technicians can retrieve it. As for information stored on compact disks, the best way to render that irretrievable is to destroy the disk. Some people put the CD in a microwave oven for five seconds, which produces fireworks. By simply breaking the disk, you risk taking a plastic splinter in the eye; better to use a "disk destroyer," a machine that pits a CD's metallic layer in two seconds.

Security and Corporate Citizenship

In the last year, over half of the corporations that hired Kroll to do risk assessments have not implemented our security recommendations. This includes companies that control critical pieces of America's infrastructure, as well as universities, hospitals, and other important businesses. Why? Some companies made reasonable decisions based on the security they had in place or the low threat they faced. But most of these decisions were based purely on a profit-and-loss calculation. These organizations, both for-profit and not-for-profit, believed they could not afford additional security because of the faltering economy.

But America cannot afford to allow corporations to decide, for their own self-interested reasons, how secure our nation should be. We don't let businesses employ children, set the minimum wage, determine the size of their political contributions, or monitor their own environmental impact, after all. These kinds of issues have been deemed too important to the society as a whole to be left to corporations to regulate. Rather than let a company decide how safe its factory should be, we have put into place the federal Occupational Safety and Health Administration (OSHA) to oversee workplace safety. This makes eminent sense, and the same must be done for security.

The federal government must set security standards for corporations on behalf of the nation. This is an area of responsibility that is often overlooked, but I feel it is so crucial that it demands legislation. Because the private sector controls much of the nation's critical infrastructure and benefits from that control, companies have an obligation to help defray the cost of securing it.

The next time terrorists strike they will almost certainly choose a different kind of target and means of attack than they have in the past. The United States and Western Europe are filled with potential targets. Our extensive and interconnected infrastructures are packed with densely populated cities, extensive manufacturing and fabrication plants (including chemical, biological, and nuclear facilities), transportation hubs with staggering amounts of traffic, and miles of pipeline, electrical wires, and fiber-optic cable. We frequently have large gatherings of people in stadiums, malls, or convention halls. The terrorists have literally millions of targets to choose from that we need to protect.

Can we defend ourselves at a reasonable cost, both in money and in convenience? Yes. But isolated, fragmented security plans don't work, and they waste resources. Instead, each target must have an individual security plan that is part of a much larger system of defense—a system that would necessarily be a private-public collaboration. Just as a neighborhood watch system is more effective than a lock on the door of your house, so would a collaborative corporate-national security system be more efficient than any stand-alone protection.

Consider, for example, the Alaskan oil pipeline. It stretches some eight hundred miles across the tundra and is built above the ground, vulnerable to weather, earthquakes, accidents, and sabotage. The economic and environmental impact of a bomb blowing a hole in the pipeline is incalculable, yet the government and companies that operate it have done little to protect it. And it's clear why this is so: The challenge is immense.

We could harden the pipeline's security by burying it and encasing it in cement. But it would remain vulnerable to explosives. So we'd have to add fencing, for approach protection. But fences are penetrable. So we'd need to monitor the fence with cameras, motion detectors, and guards. But this static defense would not be enough to stop a determined al-Qaeda operative willing to martyr himself in an attack on the oil supply of "the Great Satan." It takes no genius to blow a hole in the fence, park a four-wheel-drive vehicle loaded with dynamite over the buried pipeline, and detonate it. In an instant, the terrorist would have defeated hundreds of millions of dollars' worth of security.

It's clear, then, that simply hardening facilities such as the Alaska pipeline is inadequate. There are too many targets and too many ways to defeat a static defense. The only answer is to harden security at critical facilities and establish a wide-ranging, information-based, collaborative system of protection—like my proposed Proteus Plan. While such a system would certainly be expensive, it is a long-term investment that will benefit both the corporation and the community.

We need to take this issue seriously and craft legislation to mandate it. This legislation would group industries based on certain characteristics, such as criticality of operation, potential lethality of an attack, economic importance of a business, and association with the image of America. Individual corporate characteristics need to be factored in, too, such as a company's location and size. (There are obviously many other characteristics that need to be considered.) A range of security measures should be prescribed for each industry group, and then each corporation should be required to adapt those security steps on a reasonable timetable. The implementation of these federal security requirements should be policed by state and local agencies, which should be given real powers of enforcement. If a corporation is not willing to protect its people and facilities, then it should face stiff fines and/or have its business license revoked.

While such legislation would require a tremendous psychological and cultural shift, the alternative is to risk terrorist strikes against our critical facilities, which could result in an American Bhopal or Chernobyl, or worse.

Corporations must also be responsible for the ways their goods and services may be misused by terrorists. Companies should be required to screen buyers of certain dual-use products that they manufacture and sell—that is, goods that have a primary, socially acceptable use as well as a secondary, potentially dangerous use.

My proposed Proteus Plan will require U.S. corporations to become both proactive and static partners in the nation's security system. Companies will proactively screen purchasers of dual-use products, provide information about them to the national ID database, and help the government to restrict sales of potentially deadly commodities. Companies will also provide static protection, hardening their security measures and preparing to respond to an attack.

Helping to defend America's security should be considered a basic element of corporate citizenship in the twenty-first century.

Chapter 10

A Safer Tomorrow

In the pages of this book, we've seen how profoundly our national intelligence and security apparatus failed us in the past. And we've seen how far our current plans and programs fall short of what ought to be done to provide greater security in the present.

What about the future? What new threats will we face five, ten, fifteen, or twenty years from now? And how should we prepare ourselves to meet them?

Terrorism and Security in the Year 2015

Of course, no one can predict the future with certainty. But after years of sparring with the many forces of worldwide terrorism, we have a reasonably good basic understanding of their methods and goals. We can see, too, the frightening consistency and determination of their efforts to weaken and ultimately destroy the edifice of Western-style capitalism and democracy. Theirs is a wrath fed by centuries of exploitation and humiliation, real and perceived. The terrorists won't be easily dissuaded from their malevolent course. Thus it's possible to make educated guesses about what sort of threats we will face in the future, always with the proviso that our enemies are smart, ruthless, and eager to remain two steps ahead of us by continually outwitting and surprising our best strategic minds.

Here, then, are my forecasts for the next several years of our ongoing war with terror.

A Continuing Threat of Terrorism Terrorists of many stripes will pose an ongoing and increasing threat around the world for the foreseeable future. This is a long-term problem with no quick fixes. Islamic terrorist organizations will continue to attack moderate Muslim leaders and Western—especially American—interests at home and abroad. And state-sponsored terrorist warfare will become more prevalent.

The downside of globalization will become increasingly apparent. As the ability of nations to control their physical borders and the flow of information to and from their citizens diminishes, small groups of extremists that learn to skillfully manipulate the new forms of global power will begin to wield a disproportionately large influence on the world. Large, wealthy industrialized nations, for example, will probably be blackmailed by small, underdeveloped third world countries threatening the use of weapons of mass destruction to gain concessions. Radical environmental groups opposed to the effects of globalization and the perceived ills of multinational corporations will likely turn to terrorism to make their points. So will other extremists, such as antiabortion activists, various militia groups, and Branch Davidian–like religious cults.

It becomes easier every day to obtain the expertise and materials needed to build weapons of mass destruction. Every week, it seems, we hear of an attempt somewhere in the world to kill a large number of innocent civilians. Sadly, I only see this problem growing worse.

International Cooperation In the event of further tragic attacks, I hope and believe that the civilized world will react not with rigid oppression but with thoughtful, measured cooperation. However, this will be hard to do if we face another attack as destructive as September 11, or worse.

Although many haven't noticed, the era of the superpower acting unilaterally effectively ended on September 11. While the United States is still, by all measurements, the world's leading military, economic, and cultural power, we cannot act alone and only for our own interests. All the countries of the world must learn to cooperate and to share resources, information, technology, and security. There is safety in unity, and, increasingly, only in unity.

Security 2015 I hope that by 2015 a cornerstone security system will have been established within the United States—a system that includes the steps I have recommended in these pages under the rubric of the Proteus Plan. Such a system would allow broad human liberty in a low-threat environment but shift to permit greater government intrusiveness and control when the nation faces a clear and present danger. The core elements of the system are the U.S. ID card, the national database behind it, and the government/corporate system to certify and seal the contents of all cargo containers before they enter the United States.

The Proteus Plan is a system we can live with. It may be a system we cannot live without.

By 2015, my proposed Domestic Intelligence Bureau (DIB) or some equivalent thereof will be the consolidating agency for all information about terrorism. By then, it should have built a reputation for excellent information gathering and analysis, as well as for rigid compliance with civilian oversight. I hope the DIB will have used the intrusive powers granted under Level II or Level III conditions only rarely.

As for protective security, our buildings, public facilities, and key infrastructure elements should be hardened long before 2015. In fact, the hardening of facilities against attack should simply be part of everyday architectural and engineering practice. The ugly cement Jersey barriers that we see in front of buildings today, for example, should have been replaced by aesthetically harmonious and durable permanent barriers.

By 2015, electronic detectors for bioterror weapons should be in place in areas of high traffic density, such as convention halls, indoor stadiums, or theaters. Corporations should have raised their hard security practices up to code as established by DHS. Corporate identification cards will be optional, except when the corporation controls any part of our nation's key infrastructure; in those cases, a corporate ID system must be in place by 2015. In other, very sensitive cases, such as at nuclear power plants, the U.S. ID screening program will be used.

The sale of potentially dangerous dual-use products will be strictly controlled through the U.S. ID system. A photo surveillance system will have been established, using the database controlled by the DHS. During times of heightened danger, it will be able to tie in to corporate systems to help identify suspected terrorists.

What If . . . ?

What if we continue down our current path? What if political expediency and the power of entrenched interests dominate the decision-making process in Washington, rather than the demands of serious security planning? If that happens, what will the United States look like ten or fifteen years from now?

I have no crystal ball, but I believe that if we do not tackle our security problems in an organized, systematic manner, we will suffer a serious loss of our liberties. This is what I see in America's future if we don't act soon. . . .

It's a beautiful spring day in the San Francisco Bay Area in 2012. For the past decade, attacks on the Western-style democracies by extremists have continued, both here in the United States and in foreign lands on every continent. Within the last three years, car bombers have taken over five hundred lives inside the United States. Last year, Islamic terrorists seized a Miami temple during Rosh Hashanah services, taking three hundred people hostage. When local police launched a commando-style raid to free the hostages, all fifteen terrorists were killed—but so were seventy of the hostages.

Today, the United States is in a red alert status. Foreign intelligence has given us overwhelming evidence of a terrorist plot to bring a dirty bomb into the United States. But we do not know where or when the attack will occur. Because no one knows what we can do to protect ourselves, American society is largely paralyzed. Millions of people are getting up, brushing their teeth, eating breakfast . . . and then staying home, with the blinds drawn and the television on.

At each bridge crossing in the Bay Area, every vehicle is being stopped and searched. As a result, local news reporters are warning of one- to two-hour delays, further discouraging people from traveling. In downtown San Francisco, shops, restaurants, and theaters are almost empty. The world champion Chicago Cubs are in town to play the Giants, but only fifteen hundred fans showed up for last night's game. And there are rumors that the baseball players' association is planning to advise their members to quit playing altogether until the security risk is lessened.

At 2:38 in the afternoon the dreaded news finally breaks. ABC television interrupts an episode of *All My Children* with a report from Los Angeles: A chartered jet has crashed in the downtown area, detonating a dirty nuclear device. Hundreds are killed immediately. Hundreds of thousands are exposed to radiation, which will sicken many of them over time. Area hospitals are overwhelmed. Roads headed north, south, and east out of the city are flooded with refugees. There are reports of rioting and looting throughout the area. The governor has called out the National Guard, and federal troops are reportedly on their way.

By 5:30 the president is before the television cameras, flanked by the FBI director and the secretary of homeland security. The president is wearing the same look of suppressed wrath and unyielding determination that President Bush used to wear back in the early days of the war on terror. His comments sound familiar, too. Tapping a fist on the podium with the presidential seal, he vows, "We will root out the terrorists. We will hunt them to the ground and bring them to justice." Millions of Americans pray it will happen—this time.

Fast-forward three and a half years . . .

It is a beautiful fall day in the Bay Area in 2015. The Department of Homeland Security has the United States in stand-down mode. There is no information about any imminent terrorist attack. Life in America is what passes for normal these days.

You get up, brush your teeth, eat breakfast, and start your drive to work. To get from your home in Sausalito to your office near Market Street, you'll be taking the Golden Gate Bridge, so you leave an extra hour for the morning commute. As usual, the lines are long. Every car is stopped, every driver is asked his or her business in the city, every third trunk is popped for a visual inspection by the machine-gun-toting soldiers on duty. Pictures of the drivers are taken, and cars are randomly screened for explosives by automated sniffers. Inconvenient? Sure. But you don't really feel like complaining.

At least you're not a foreigner or a Muslim. They don't even try to cross the bridge anymore. For the past three and half years they haven't been allowed on the bridge or in any other restricted area.

You have tickets for tonight's ball game. Better leave work early. The game starts at seven-thirty, but you'll need to show up by five if you want to catch the first pitch. Parking within one hundred and fifty yards of the stadium has long been shut down, and searches and photo scanning will slow you down at the gates. Again, no Muslims or foreigners will be allowed. That bothers you a little. You remember Mafuz, the engineer from Egypt who worked with you until his deportation last year. Mafuz was a Giants fan; you even went to a couple of games together. That wouldn't be possible today. It seems a little unfair. But damn it, your college-age daughter and two of her friends will be meeting you at the game, and you don't want to take any more chances.

A Possible Tomorrow

But there is an alternative. There's another future possible, provided we are willing to pay the price today for the freedoms we want to keep tomorrow.

It's a beautiful fall day in the Bay Area in 2015. Unfortunately, all is not well. The morning news is reporting that the Domestic Intelligence Bureau has issued a Level II alert. Information gleaned from informants inside a U.S.-based al-Qaeda cell, satellite surveillance, wiretaps, and foreign sources has led the DIB to suspect that a terrorist attack is imminent. Law enforcement agencies prepare for emergency action.

You feel a bit of anxiety in the pit of your stomach when you hear the news. Fortunately, this is not the norm in 2015. On most days, the United States is in Level I, stand-down status. You wake up, brush your teeth, eat breakfast, and drive across the Golden Gate Bridge to work. Your car is videotaped as it crosses the bridge, but you know this is only a security precaution and hardly think about it. Instead, you check out the spectacular view of the city and the bay. It's an unusually clear morning. In the skies overhead appear the vapor trails of jumbo jets heading across the Pacific Ocean. Below you appears the wake of a container ship passing under the bridge. Neither one triggers an anxious thought. You know that the planes, the ship, and their cargoes are secure. Rather than a terrorist attack, you're thinking about enjoying that evening's ball game.

But occasionally there is reason for worry.

For the past twenty years, America, Israel, and most of the Western European nations have endured a steady, low-level siege by Islamic terror groups. Some of the attacks have been horrifyingly brazen and destructive, like the bombing of a U.S. airfield in Saudi Arabia that killed seventy American servicemen last year. But because the United States has implemented a strong security system, focusing its resources on stopping terrorists *before* they strike, most of the attacks have occurred abroad. Several potentially disastrous attacks inside the United States have been thwarted. But the possibility of disaster always lurks.

Today's Level II alert sets many gears in motion. Additional electronic surveillance of terror suspects is authorized, and random stops of certain suspects or members of carefully defined groups have been approved. Because there is no intelligence indicating that the terrorists intend to use nuclear, biological, or chemical weapons, no further encroachment on civil liberties has been authorized.

Meanwhile, the technical and analytical resources of the DIB, CIA, NSA, and DoD are working together under the leadership of the secretary of homeland security to pinpoint useful intelligence on the impending attack. The CIA shares information on terrorist activities with other nations; in return, America urgently requests any relevant intelligence that other secret services might have. Such information sharing is conducted on a careful and selective basis.

Corporations that operate critical infrastructure, such as power or chemical plants, have restricted access on an as-needed basis and are using the U.S. ID card to screen all visitors. State and local police officers have met with their respective DIB task forces and are sharing in full intelligence briefings. Suspected terrorists are being kept under surveillance and questioned. Emergency response teams are put on alert, and equipment and medicines are distributed nationwide in preparation for a grim possibility—an attack that results in massive casualties and destruction.

In stores, dual-use products are being sold under Level II restrictions, which limits some purchases, such as nitrate-based fertilizers, or rentals, such as trucks, and increases the waiting time for others, such as guns.

Out at the airport, delays are few, as every passenger and piece of baggage is automatically screened. When passengers reach the security checkpoint, they swipe their U.S. ID card and are biometrically scanned; their background information is checked against the national data bank. Because of today's alert, more people than usual fail to qualify for fast-pass treatment—something like 5 percent rather than the usual 2 to 3 percent. Those who fail are taken aside, photographed, and thoroughly questioned. Their bags are searched for guns, explosives, and weapons like knives (although nail clippers and the like are allowed on board). In the cockpits, pilots are armed and secured behind locked and armored doors. In the cabins, well-trained sky marshals dressed in plain clothes are hidden among the passengers.

In San Francisco Bay, meanwhile, container ships with pre-screened and sealed containers continue to move in and out of the harbor. With a Level II security alert in place, all ships carrying cargo or containers that have not been certified according to America's new security protocols are denied entry; they must wait at a secure outer anchorage for inspection. In addition, Coast Guard cutters are moving about the harbor, randomly stopping boats of all sizes for quick inspections. There is international cooperation to maintain the flow and security of shipping.

On your drive to work this morning, the line of traffic at the Golden Gate Bridge is a little longer than usual. Every van and truck trying to enter the city is channeled into special truck lanes. The drivers' U.S. ID cards and biometrics are verified against the national database. The trucks' transponders are also checked to verify that their cargo has been inspected and sealed. Those whom the U.S. ID database raises questions about, only one or two drivers out of a hundred, are moved into a special waiting area for further questioning and inspection.

Your car moves slowly through the E-ZPass lane as photographs of every driver are taken and cars are randomly screened for explosives by automated sniffers. Today you are thinking about terrorism and the inconvenience it causes, but you don't really feel like complaining. After all, this is the first Level II alert in over two months. Not bad, you reflect. But better get to the ballpark early tonight. Random searches and photo scanning will be in effect at the gates, and no close-in parking will be available. You reach your office building. Today you're required to stop outside the underground parking lot and insert your corporate identification into a portable reader, which ties into a corporate database that identifies you biometrically. The gate rises and you're allowed to enter the lot. When you arrive at your desk, your computer's screen saver reminds you of your company's emergency plan. It asks whether you've checked your first-response emergency kit lately. The kit contains a flashlight, water, dried food, a breathing mask, a knife/screwdriver, and a flashing beacon. You check your kit, fill the canteen with fresh water, and go about your day.

As you drive toward the stadium late that afternoon, you hear the news on your radio: At nine-thirty this morning, an emergency response team, operating on intelligence provided by the DIB and other agencies, intercepted an al-Qaeda agent driving a truck full of nitrate fertilizer toward the Bay Bridge. The terrorist was arrested and the bomb defused. A search is on for his co-conspirators. The secretary of homeland defense has announced that the Level II alert is over.

This is how I hope to see the world of security at work in 2015.

The Choice Is Ours

To me, both of these visions of life in 2015 are plausible. They represent different destinations based on the path we choose today and in the months ahead.

In both of these futures, some of the freedoms we now take for granted have been compromised. The demands of security have created some inconveniences that people will have to accept. But in the dystopian vision of a world where the hard decisions about security have been evaded or ignored, the damage to liberty is far greater, without providing the safety we so desperately crave.

By contrast, if we follow the path of sanity and prudence, investing today in systems that will create a flexible, reasonable, measured degree of security based on fair and open rules rather than arbitrary and draconian restrictions, we'll be able to enjoy both a large measure of our traditional freedoms and a far greater measure of safety than we now experience.

The choice is ours. Which path will we follow?

Acknowledgments

Although this book contains a lifetime's worth of experience, it was written in a little over three months. This was a tremendous challenge, and a terrific collaborative experience. Many people deserve thanks for their help along the way.

Foremost is our editorial advisor, Karl Weber, whose hard work, deft touch, and good humor were indispensable. We thank the book's co-agents, Judith Ehrlich and Karen Gantz Zahler, for bringing us together. At Ballantine, we thank Tracy Brown and Nancy Miller for urging us on with constructive criticism.

We are indebted to many people at Kroll. Linda Ingerman and Meg Reiss were stellar researchers. And for their time and expertise we'd like to thank the following: Jules Kroll, Norb Garrett, Jeff Schlanger, James Francis, Alan Brill, Steven Kuhr, Gary Schiff, Dominic Simpson, Kelly McCann and Crucible Security, and the ever-capable Diane Delaney.

We'd also like to thank the many men and women in the law enforcement and intelligence communities who offered their help and encouragement. In particular, we thank Patrick Dugan, of the New York County District Attorney's office, and Los Angeles City councilman Jack Weiss.

The views expressed in these pages are ours, and should not be attributed to Kroll, Inc.

Michael Cherkasky
Alex Prud'homme

Notes

Introduction

Page x: "We are living in an age when the enemies of God . . . lamented in July 2002." From "Al-Qaida Spokesman Makes New Threats," by Salah Nasrawi, Associated Press, July 10, 2002.

Page xvii: "Among its provisions . . . mistake." The White House's fingerprinting program was announced by Attorney General John Ashcroft on June 5, 2002. Reported by many journalists, including Carolyn Lochhead, *San Francisco Chronicle*, June 6, 2002.

Chapter 1: Twenty Years of Terror

Pages 3–4: "One day John was telling Chris Isham . . . He was right." From a *Frontline* documentary, "The Man Who Knew," by Michael Kirk, aired by PBS on October 3, 2002. Transcript at www.pbs.org/wgbh/pages/frontline/shows/knew/john/timeline.html

Pages 5–8: "October 6, 1981 . . ." Most of the material about Norb Garrett witnessing the assassination of Anwar Sadat is taken from Prud'homme's interviews with Garrett, August 9 and August 21, 2002.

Page 9: "Fast forward now to November 5, 1990 . . ." Background information on the Kahane killing from Cherkasky's recollection and numerous press accounts, including, "Militant Rabbi Kahane Slain by N.Y. Gunman Assassination," by John J. Goldman, *Los Angeles Times*, November 6, 1990, and "Kahane Killer Apparently Acted Alone, Police Say," by Jonathan W. Oatis, Reuters, November 6, 1990.

Pages 14–18: "Within minutes of the explosion . . ." Much of the detail in this section, linking the investigation of Ramzi Yousef back to the case of El Sayyid Nosair, comes from Cherkasky's personal experience, supplemented by the authors' interview of an investigator for the New York District Attorney.

Page 17:   "The obligation of Allah . . . Jihad for the sake of Allah." Sheikh Abdel
              Rahman quote from *Jihad in America*, executive producer Steven
              Emerson, aired by PBS on November 21, 1994.

Page 19:   "As Mark Bowden reported . . . Soviets in Afghanistan." From Mark
              Bowden, *Black Hawk Down*, Signet, New York, 2001, p. 133.

Page 19:   "Muslims did not believe . . . American occupation troops." Osama
              bin Laden speaking to CNN, from Peter L. Bergen, *Holy War, Inc.*, The
              Free Press, New York, 2001, p. 22.

Page 20:   "A gloating bin Laden told the al-Jazeera . . . cowardice of the U.S.
              troops." Osama bin Laden interview with al-Jazeera television,
              June 10, 1999. Transcript at www.terrorism.com/terrorism/binLaden
              Transcript.shtml

Page 20:   "As he was flown back to New York . . . money and explosives,' Yousef
              replied." From "A Day of Terror," by James Risen and David Johnston,
              New York Times, September 12, 2001.

Page 22:   "In May 1998, bin Laden told ABC News . . . all targets,' he said."
              From John Miller interview of Osama bin Laden on ABC News, May
              28, 1998. Transcript at abcnews.go.com/sections/wold/Dailynews/
              miller_binladen_980609.html

Page 23:   "The Kenyan embassy was attacked . . . 'what we Muslims have
              tasted.' " From a two-hour al-Qaeda videotape that has been widely cir-
              culated on the Internet. The quote attributed to bin Laden here is
              taken from Bergen, *Holy War, Inc.*, p. 27.

Pages 23–   "On December 14, 1999 . . . Los Angeles International Airport dur-
    24:       ing the holiday rush." From "Security Concerns Bring Focus on Trans-
              lating Body Language," by Ann Davis, Joseph Pereira and William M.
              Bulkeley, *Wall Street Journal*, August 15, 2002.

Page 25:   "It established a commission . . . integrated governmental structures."
              From "Road Map for National Security: Imperative for Change," by
              Gary Hart and Warren B. Rudman. The Phase III Report of the U.S.
              Commission on National Security/21st Century. January 31, 2001, fi-
              nal draft, p. viii.

Page 27:   "Our martyrs are ready . . . attacks against America." From "Bin Laden
              Alive, Taped Message Asserts; More Al Qaeda Attacks Threatened;
              Member Is Said to Have Bombed Tunisian Synagogue," by Howard
              Schneider, *Washington Post*, June 24, 2002.

Page 28:   "The Chechens executed . . . 128 of the hostages." From news reports,
              including, "Putin Unleashes His fury Against Chechen Guerillas," by
              Elaine Sciolino, *New York Times*, November 12, 2002.

Page 31:   "The U.S. intelligence community . . . at yellow (elevated) for now."
              Excerpted from an E-mail circulated by the National Infrastructure
              Protection Center (NIPC), "Potential Al-Qai'ida Threat to Economic
              Targets in the United States and Abroad," Infrastructure Sector
              Notification, October 23, 2002. Contact nipcwatch@infragard.org for
              more information.

Chapter 2: Understanding Our Enemies

Page 33: "The time of humiliation . . . in their heartland." From "New Tape Suggests al Qaeda's Role," by Hugh Pope, *Wall Street Journal,* April 16, 2002.

Page 34: "The threat environment . . . battles lost." Taken from the testimony of George J. Tenet, director of the Central Intelligence Agency, before the Committee on Intelligence, October 17, 2002.

Pages 34–35: "The best definition . . . 'subnational group.'" From Philip Heymann, *Terrorism and America,* MIT Press, Cambridge, Massachusetts, 1988, p. 6.

Page 37: "As Islam spread . . . less voluntarily." From Matthew S. Gordon, *Islam,* Oxford University Press, Oxford and New York, 2002, p. 9.

Page 37: "It's true that most Arabs . . . of Muslims." Ibid, pp. 14–15.

Page 38: "A prime example . . . lesser *jihad* to the greater *jihad*." Ibid, p. 68.

Page 39: "The colonial powers instituted . . ." For background in this section we consulted Bernard Lewis, *What Went Wrong?,* Oxford University Press, New York, 2002, p. 62.

Pages 39–40: "Religious movements within . . . secularization and modernization." From Timothy Demy and Gary P. Stewart, *In the Name of God: Understanding the Mindset of Terrorism,* Harvest House, Eugene, Oregon, p. 81.

Page 41: "Disillusionment with the West . . . Muslim politics." From John L. Esposito, *Unholy War: Terror in the Name of Islam,* Oxford University Press, Oxford and New York, 2002, p. 84.

Page 41: "Today, as journalist Thomas Friedman . . . 'living in a world of delusion.'" Background and quote from Kemal Salibi in Thomas L. Friedman, *From Beirut to Jerusalem,* Anchor, New York, 1995, p. 103.

Page 42: "And on the evening of September 11, 2001, six thousand . . . America." From "Lights, Cameras, Revolution" reported by Bob Simon, *Sixty Minutes II,* aired October 23, 2002.

Page 43: "In 1982, Assad . . . in Hama." Friedman, *From Beirut to Jerusalem,* pp. 76–105.

Pages 43–44: "According to Patrick Seale's . . . consequences of rebellion." Patrick Seale's biography *Asad: The Struggle for the Middle East* (University of California Press, 1988), as cited in Friedman, *From Beirut to Jerusalem,* p. 79.

Page 47: "In his book . . . unacceptable." Quote from Charles Kimball, *When Religion Becomes Evil,* Harper San Francisco, 2002, p. 44.

Page 48: "In the spring of 2001 . . . personally." Esposito, *Unholy War,* p. 154.

Page 48: "The West hated us . . . the community of Muhammad." Kamel Daoudi's letter was excerpted in "Portrait of the Arab as a Young Radical," by Elaine Sciolino, *New York Times,* September 22, 2002.

Page 50: "When Iraq invaded Kuwait . . . easily." Esposito, *Unholy War,* p. 12.

Page 50: "In November 1989, for instance, he publicly praised . . . assassination in Pakistan." From Rohan Gunaratna, *Inside al Qaeda,* Columbia University Press, New York, 2002, p. 23.

Pages 51–52: "Al-Qaeda is more than just a terrorist group . . . operations from exposure." Many of the details about al-Qaeda in the next four paragraphs come from Gunaratna, *Inside al Qaeda.* The quote is from p. 1.

Page 52:   "Through strategic alliances . . . operations from exposure." From Mark Baker, "World: 11 September Does al-Qaeda Represent a Different Type of Terrorism?" (Part 2), Radio Free Europe, Radio Liberty. Transcript at www.rferl.org/nca/features/2002/09/02092002142833. asap

Page 53:   "Steven Emerson, a specialist . . . in Pittsburgh." From Steven Emerson: "Get Ready for Twenty World Trade Center Bombings," in *Middle East Quarterly,* June 1997, p. 78.

Page 54:   "We know that Osama bin Laden has devoted . . . to aid his cause." The value of Osama bin Laden's fortune is difficult to assess. The authors have been told it ranges anywhere from $30 million to $250 million. Terrorism expert Rohan Gunaratna estimates that bin Laden inherited some $25 to $30 million, which he invested profitably. See *Inside al Qaeda,* p. 19. In an April 13, 1999, *Frontline* interview, conducted by *New York Times* reporters and shown on PBS, the journalist Lowell Bergman asked: "He's not worth $250 million?" To which Pakistani journalist Said K. Aburish replied: "I do not believe so. I believe the most that Osama bin Laden took out of Saudi Arabia is probably somewhere between $30 and $40 million. But he is happy for people to think that he took $250 million out. Or $500 million out. Because then he does not have to answer the question of, 'Where does the money to support his operations come from?' . . . He gives the impression that he's paying for it himself. In fact, I believe that money comes from inside Saudi Arabia, from other people who belong to merchant families. And perhaps from members of the royal family itself."

Page 55:   "Harvard Professor Joseph S. Nye . . . pluralistic democracy." Definition of "soft power" from Joseph S. Nye Jr., *The Paradox of American Power,* Oxford University Press, Oxford and New York, 2002, pp. 8–12.

Chapter 3: The Threats We Face

Page 63:   "During the last two years . . . bombers." From "Dread and Dreams Travel by Bus in Israel," by James Bennet, *New York Times,* October 27, 2002.

Pages 64–65:   "While there has been much debate about securing our airports . . . weapons in the near future." From conversations with security officials, and articles such as, "Key Senators Sound Warning on Missiles," by William C. Mann, Associated Press, December 2, 2002, and "The Air Industry's Worst Nightmare," by Paul J. Caffera, on Salon (November 22, 2002), archive.salon.com/news/feature/2002/11/22/missiles/index_np.html.

Page 65:   "Every day large fleets of trucks travel . . . for hours at a time." From "Possibility of Using Trucks for Terror Remains Concern," by Andrew C. Revkin, *New York Times,* October 20, 2002.

Pages 65–
66: "Shortly after September 11, a cargo ship bound for Toronto . . . Thailand, and Egypt." From "Canada, Italy Work on Stowaway Case," by Joel Baglole and Christopher J. Chipello, *Wall Street Journal,* October 29, 2001.

Page 66: "As Stephen E. Flynn . . . 'global transport lifelines.'" From "America the Vulnerable" by Stephen E. Flynn, *Foreign Affairs,* vol. 81, no. 1, (2002) p. 70.

Page 66: "In the past, terrorists have reportedly used . . . and Asia." From "Challenging Terrorism at Sea," by Vijay Sakhuja, article no. 679, January 19, 2002, Institute of Peace and Conflict Studies, www.ipcs.org/issues/newarticles/679-ter-sakhuja.html.

Page 66: "For example, maritime . . . shores." Robert Bevelacqua's warnings are quoted in "Security Questions/Potential for Terrorism at Ports Called Alarming," by Thomas Frank, *Newsday,* January 15, 2002.

Page 67: "In 2002 former senators Gary Hart and Warren B. Rudman . . . in multi-state blackouts." From Gary Hart and Warren B. Rudman, "America Still Unprepared—America Still in Danger," report of an independent task force sponsored by the Council on Foreign Relations, 2002, cfr.org/pdf/Homeland_TF.pdf.

Page 67: "Not built to withstand the force . . . commercial jet." From "Safeguarding the Nation's Energy", a brief by Matthew Brown for the National Conference of State Legislatures, in the series "Protecting Democracy: States Respond to Terrorism," www.ncsl.org/programs/press/2002/issues/energy.htm.

Pages 67–
68: "The oil and gas pipelines . . . stop the leak." From "Hardening the Targets," by Mark Murray, et al., in *National Journal,* August 10, 2002.

Page 69: "In a 1998 speech . . . 'biological or chemical weapons.'" From a speech by Secretary of Defense William Cohen at the National Press Club, March 17, 1998.

Pages 69–
73: "Chemical agents . . . Biological agents . . ." Much of the background here about chemical and biological weapons comes from Prud'homme's interviews with Steven Kuhr, Managing Director of Kroll's Emergency Management Group, September 24, 2002, and October 11, 2002.

Page 71: "Compare, for example, the biological agent anthrax with the nerve gas sarin." This information is widely available, in, for example, a presentation on the American Medical Association's Web site (ama-assn.org/meetings/public/annual99/edu/eitzesave1.ppt, slide 13).

Pages 74–
77: "Nuclear weapons . . ." Some of the basic background information in this section is based on material in "Terrorism: Questions & Answers," a Web site run by the Council on Foreign Relations and the Markle Foundation, www.terrorismanswers.com.

Pages 76–
77: "Several Soviet suitcase bombs . . . support these claims." From "Radiation Bomb: Crude but Deadly Device Is Most Feared Nuke," by Jim Krane, Associated Press, November 10, 2001.

Page 77: "A twenty-five-page document was discovered . . . design for a nuclear weapon." From a CNN report, "Al Qaeda Documents Outline Serious

Weapons Program," by Mike Boettcher and Ingrid Arnesen, aired January 25, 2002. Transcript at www.cnn.com/2002/US/01/24/ inv.al.qaeda.documents/index.html

Page 77:   "If I have indeed acquired [nuclear] weapons . . . to do so." From "Nuclear Terrorism: It's the Plutonium, Stupid," by Graham T. Allison, *Los Angeles Times*, November 18, 2001.

Chapter 4: National Security—The Missing System

Page 82:   "We have talked a lot about homeland security . . . utterly irresponsible." Taken from remarks made by Senator Robert C. Byrd, D-West Virginia, in a debate over homeland security on the senate floor: November 19, 2002. Transcript at archive.salon.com/news/feature/ 2002/11/21/byrdremarks/

Page 85:   "The best available bag-screening machines . . . will have to be inspected by hand!" For more information about today's $1 million X-ray machines, and their 25-percent failure rate, see "Tough Issues on Baggage Screening Remain," by Matthew L. Wald, *New York Times*, November 5, 2002.

Page 85:   "Every year, some four hundred ninety million people cross U.S. borders . . ." From Flynn, "America the Vulnerable," p. 70.

Page 85:   ". . . along with some twenty million cargo containers." From "The Globalization of Fear," by Dr. Maryann Cusimano Love, assistant professor of politics at the Catholic University of America, Washington, D.C., www.hnp.org/publications/hnpfocus/The%20Globalization%20 of%20Fear—A%20Reflection%20on%209-11.pdf. Containers are a rapidly growing security problem. According to the Office of National Drug Control Policy, about 16 million cargo containers arrived in the United States in 1999; by the following year, that number had increased exponentially to 52 million containers. From the Office of National Drug Control Policy's National Drug Control Strategy 2000 and the National Drug Control Strategy 2001, www.ncjrs.org/ondcp-pubs/publications/policy/ndcs00/chap3_4.html and www.ncjrs.org/ ondcppubs/publications/policy/ndcs01/chap3_5.html

Pages 86–89:   "Port and maritime security . . ." Many of the facts in this section are taken from Hart and Rudman: "America Still Unprepared—America Still in Danger," pp. 17–18, cfr.org/pdf/Homeland_TF.pdf.

Pages 86–87:   "The Port of Los Angeles, for example . . . the nation's trade." Specific information about the Port of Los Angeles comes from "Proposal to the Port of Los Angeles for a Vulnerability Assessment & Feasibility Study," by Kroll, Inc., June 28, 2002.

Page 88:   "In October 1985 . . . body into the Mediterranean." Details of the Klinghoffer murder were taken from several contemporaneous press accounts, including, "Plane with Palestinian Hijackers Forced Down in Italy Where They'll Be Tried," by Jennifer Parmalee, Associated Press, October 10, 1985.

Page 88:   "The U.S. Coast Guard provides the front line of maritime . . . the

Coast Guard remains stretched thin." From "Hearing on Port Security," the Subcommittee on Coast Guard and Maritime Transportation. Witnesses: the Honorable Norman Mineta, Secretary Department of Transportation, and Admiral James M. Loy, Commandant United States Coast Guard. Transcript at www.house. gov/transportation/cgmt/12-06-01/12-06-01memo.html

Page 90: "Not surprisingly . . . the program's implementation." From "Citizen Spy Net Won't Take Flight; Security Act Forbids Highly Criticized Plan" by David Eggen, *Washington Post*, November 29, 2002. And "Bush Borrows a Page from '1984'" by David E. Brown, *Newsday*, December 9, 2002.

Pages 90– "During World War II . . . prisoners of war." The fact that 110,000
91: Japanese-Americans were interned during the war comes from "For Whom the Liberty Bell Tolls," *The Economist*, August 31, 2002, p. 19.

Pages 91– "For several years, nationals of Iraq, Libya, and Syria . . . ties to terrorist
92: organizations." From various press accounts, including, "US to Finger-print Selected Foreign Travelers," by Thomas Ginsberg, *Philadelphia Inquirer*, September 11, 2002, www.philly.com/mld/inquirer/news/nation/4046727.htm.

Page 92: "The effect will be to encourage . . . heavy-handed bully." The Council on American-Islamic relations (CAIR) estimates that there are 1.2 billion Muslims in the world, www.cair-net.org/asp/aboutislam.asp.

Page 92: ". . . by discriminating against . . . terrorist cause." From Heymann, *Terrorism and America*, p. 100.

Page 95: "during the summer of 2001, FBI agents in Minnesota . . . for a warrant." From "Secret U.S. Court Handed New Power to Fight Terror," by Scott Shane, *Baltimore Sun*, October 29, 2001.

Page 96: "We are at war with al-Qaeda . . . against them." From "CIA Is Reported to Kill a Leader of Qaeda in Yemen," by James Risen with Judith Miller, *New York Times*, November 5, 2002.

Pages 97– "On August 20, 1998, President Clinton . . . for damages." Details
98: about the al-Shifa attack were taken from a confidential report prepared by Kroll Associates UK Ltd., January 18, 1999.

Page 97: "(about twenty militants . . . Kashmiri terrorists.)" From Bergen, *Holy War, Inc.*, pp. 208–9.

Page 99: "President Bush had no qualms . . . 'hunt them down.'" From "US Hellfire Wipes out Gang of Osama Thugs," by Niles Lathem and Kate Sheehy, *New York Post*, November 5, 2002.

Chapter 5: A Security System That Works

Page 112: "But the attacks of September 11 . . . an estimated $95 billion." From "Report: Sept. 11 Cost NYC Some $95 Billion," Reuters, September 4, 2002.

Page 114: "For over forty years . . . spread terror." The first recorded hijacking took place in Peru, in February, 1931. In 1948, four Chinese hijackers attempted to take over a Cathay Pacific plane from Macau to Hong Kong; the plane crashed into the sea. In April 1958, the "Cuban shuttle" began when a hijacked Cubana Airlines plane was flown to Mexico, starting a two-way flow of hijacked planes between Cuba and the United States and Mexico.

From "Chronology—Major Aircraft Hijackings," Reuters, September 11, 2001.

Page 116–
117:
"Since September 11, we've rushed . . . well-trained marshals." Although the exact number of air marshals is classified, it has been estimated at some six thousand members. These marshals face a daunting task: protecting roughly twenty thousand flights every day in the United States. Putting an air marshal on every flight would cost an estimated $5 billion; even putting marshals on 20 percent of all flights would cost about $1 billion. From "Aviation Security and Terrorism: A Review of the Economic Issues," by Cletus C. Coughlin, Jeffrey P. Cohen, and Sarosh R. Khan, *Federal Reserve Bank of St. Louis Review*, September 1, 2002.

The federal marshal program got off to a rocky start. In the summer of 2002, two incidents highlighted the importance of proper training for both marshals and airline passengers. On August 31, a federal air marshal trained his gun on passengers for thirty minutes on a Delta Air Lines flight from Atlanta to Philadelphia. Several passengers had ignored orders to stay in their seats after a man was detained when he was observed rummaging through luggage. A few days later, on September 12, a National Airlines flight from Las Vegas to New York was escorted by military jets to the airport after a woman who spoke limited English didn't understand an instruction to stay in her seat. The plane was diverted to Philadelphia and landed uneventfully.

From "Diverted Planes Up Tension: 1 here and 4 others blamed on mix-ups," by Michael Hinkelman, *Philadelphia Daily News*, September 14, 2002.

In the meantime, air marshals have been working long days without a break, and their morale has reportedly been poor. According to a leaked memo, some 1,250 marshals reported sick during a three-week period in the height of the summer of 2002 travel season—claiming it was the only way they could get a day off.

From "Air Marshals' Low Morale Spelled Out," by Blake Morrisson, *USA Today*, October 24, 2002.

Chapter 6: Intelligence in the Age of Terror

Pages 120–
121:
"The FBI ignored warnings . . . changed in only minor ways." There have been numerous press accounts documenting the failure of the FBI and CIA to work together and to stop the attacks of September 11, 2001. Among these articles is, "Not Much Has Changed in a System That Failed," by James Risen and David Johnston, *New York Times*, September 8, 2002.

Page 123: "In the case of Pearl Harbor ... 'competing for attention).' From "Fixing Intelligence," by Richard Betts, *Foreign Affairs*, vol. 81, no. 1, 2002.

Pages 123–124: "Another crucial factor at Pearl Harbor ... September 11, 1998." From "Pearl Harbor as Prologue," by Tim Weiner, *New York Times*, September 8, 2002.

Page 126: "Sources in Washington have told me ... is true." From Cherkasky's conversation with members of the U.S. intelligence community.

Page 128: "Our eye-in-the-sky satellites ... 10 percent of them." From Robert Steele, *On Intelligence*, OSS International Press, Oakton, 2001, p. 102.

Page 133: The al-Qaeda cell that bombed the U.S. embassy in Kenya ... knew about both." The fact that al-Qaeda's African cells worked independently has been widely reported, including in a *60 Minutes II* segment, "By the Book," which aired on February 20, 2002. In that piece, Jerrold Post, a CIA veteran and terrorism expert who testified in the bombers' trial, said: "Those working on the bombing in Tanzania did not know that a simultaneous operation was being planned in Kenya except for one individual who was in overall charge of the two operations."

Pages 136–138: "One of the most intriguing ... where his allegiances really lay." Background on Ali Mohamed from Bergen, *Holy War, Inc.*, pp. 127–33, and Gunaratna, *Inside al-Qaeda*, pp. 31, 35, 154.

Page 139: "The Jordanians and Pakistanis definitely have informants inside the terror groups." From Cherkasky's conversations with members of the U.S. intelligence community.

Page 141: "Indeed, after a recent visit to MI-5 ... the United States." From "Ridge Doubts Domestic Spy Service," by Darlene Superville, Associated Press, November 18, 2002.

Page 148: "Consider Great Britain ... street executions by the police." For further information about the Prevention of Terrorism Act, see www.theirishworld.com/Resource/PTA.html.

Chapter 7: Keeping Tabs on America

Page 154: "Consider, for example, the position of Dick Armey ... 'not consistent with a free society.' " From "Rescued by Dick Armey from Big Brother," by Nat Hentoff, *Washington Times*, July 29, 2002.

Page 168: "Denmark issues ID numbers at birth ..." From "National ID Cards: One Size Fits All," by Daniel J. Wakin, *New York Times*, October 7, 2001.

Page 168: "In 1999, Finland ... national ID." For more information on the Finnish smart card, see www.cabinet-office.gov.uk/innovation/2002/privacy/report/annex-b.htm#05

Page 168: "Today, New York City's fifty-thousand-member police department ... host of other benefits." From "City Adds High-Tech ID Cards," by Murray Weiss, *New York Post*, November 1, 2002.

Pages 168–169: "In 2002, Japan instituted ... upon Juki Net's launch." From various news accounts, including "Getting to Know All About You: Japanese

Privacy Protests Offer Lesson for US," by Ari Schwarz, *Chicago Tribune*, August 23, 2002, and "Japanese Drop Out of New National ID System," by Yuri Kageyama, Associated Press, August 11, 2002.

Page 169:   "South Korea's identification system . . . reportedly lost his wife." From, "Japanese Fear New ID System Is a Shoji Screen for Big Brother Asia," by Mark Magnier, *Los Angeles Times*, August 11, 2002.

Page 169:   "Beginning in 1952, all Black South Africans . . . a 'common identity document.' " For more information on the *dompas*, see david.snu.edu/~dwilliam.fs/f97projects/apartheid/laws.htm and africanhistory.about.com/library/bl/blsalaws.htm.

Pages 169– "In Russia, Peter the Great . . . the Associated Press wrote in
170:    2002." From "In Russia, Internal Passports Control Everything, Even Human Dignity," by Sarah Karush, Associated Press, March 24, 2002.

Page 170:   "Typical of this complaint . . . 'prying eyes of the government.' " From testimony of Legislative Counsel Katie Corrigan before the House Government Reform Subcommittee on Government Efficiency, Financial Management and Intergovernmental Relations, November 16, 2001.

Chapter 8: Individual Self-Defense—What You Can Do to Be Safer at Home, on the Street, and on the Road

Page 177:   "By 2001, Mad Cow . . . 115 deaths." From "Risk of Mad Cow Disease Is Less Than Previously Feared," an article on careworld.net, September 20, 2002, careworld.net/Articles.

Page 177:   "In 1996, Guatemalan raspberries . . ." From news accounts and "Epidemiologic Studies of *Cyclospora cayetanensis* in Guatemala," by Caryn Bern, Beatriz Hernandez, Maria Beatriz Lopez, Michael J. Arrowood, et al., *Emerging Infectious Diseases*, vol. 5, no. 6., (www.cdc.gov/ncidod/eid/vol5no6/bern.htm#5).

Page 177:   "In 1993, E. coli . . . four deaths." From "The Bug That Ate the Burger: E. Coli's Twisted Tale of Science in the Courtroom and Politics in the Lab," by Emily Green, *Los Angeles Times*, June 6, 2001.

Pages 177– "In 1989, Chilean Grapes . . ." A fact widely reported at the time,
178:    available in "Product Tampering," by Deborah Lowe, Ph.D., and Doug Ramsey and John Warner, posted April 23, 1999, on http://www.facsnet.org/tools/ref_tutor/tampering/jguide.php3.

Page 182:   "On October 28, 2002, Monday morning, Lawrence Foley . . . assailant disappeared." From numerous press accounts, including, "US Diplomat Shot Dead Outside Home in Jordan," by Suleiman al-Khalidi, Reuters, October 28, 2002.

Pages 190– "A dirty (or radiological) bomb . . . radiation and contamination."
191:    From "Dirty Bombs," in "Terrorism: Questions & Answers," the Council on Foreign Relations, terrorismanswers.com.

Pages 196– "Today there is a large Muslim population in London . . . 'A Towering
197:    Day in History.' " From "At a Mosque in London, Bin Laden Is Hailed as a Hero," by Alan Cowell, *New York Times*, September 13, 2002.

Page 199: "In Israel, the police have issued . . . mismatched license plates." Background on the Israeli anti-terror pamphlet from "Israelis Write the Book on bombers," by Uri Dan, *New York Post,* August 29, 2002.

Chapter 9: Self-Defense for Companies

Page 203: "In a study conducted in the summer . . . 'a priority.' " From "Many Businesses Lack Crisis Plans," by Jim Krane, Associated Press, September 13, 2002.

Pages 215–218: "Steps to Harden a Facility . . . The Bottom Line . . ." Much of the material on facility security is based on Prud'homme's interview of Gary Schiff, president of Kroll Security Services Group, September 20, 2002.

Pages 219–228: "Computerized Terrorism . . ." Background for this section from Prud'homme's interview of Alan E. Brill, senior managing director of Kroll, Inc., August 19, and September 12, 2002.

Pages 221–223: "According to a survey . . . likely targets for attack." From "Firms Beef Up Cybersecurity as Breaches Soar," by Jim Hopkins, *USA Today,* August 20, 2002.

Page 222: "It has been reported . . . water storage facilities." From "Pro-Islamic Hackers Gear Up for Cyber War, Experts Say," by Michael Christie, Reuters, October 29, 2002.

Page 229: ". . . the Alaskan oil pipeline. It stretches some eight hundred miles . . . and sabotage." For information on the Alaskan oil pipeline see: infoplease.com/ipd/A0699695.html.

Index